JUNIOR CYC

LESS STRESS MORE SUCCESS

Maths Revision
Ordinary Level
Book 2

Geometry and Trigonometry Strand and
Statistics and Probability Strand

Brendan Guildea & Louise Boylan

g GILL EDUCATION

Gill Education
Hume Avenue
Park West
Dublin 12
www.gilleducation.ie

Gill Education is an imprint of M.H. Gill & Co.

© Brendan Guildea and Louise Boylan 2021

978 07171 9071 3

Print origination: MPS Limited
Artwork: MPS Limited, Andriy Yankovskyy

All rights reserved. No part of this publication may be copied, reproduced or transmitted in any form or by any means without written permission of the publishers or else under the terms of any licence permitting limited copying issued by the Irish Copyright Licensing Agency.

Any links to external websites should not be construed as an endorsement by Gill Education of the content or view of the linked material. Furthermore it cannot be guaranteed that all external links will be live.

For permission to reproduce photographs, the authors and publisher gratefully acknowledge the following:
© Alamy: 235, 236; © iStock/Getty Premium: vii, 111, 147, 149, 221, 223, 224, 225, 227, 232; © Shutterstock: 140, 146, 151.

The authors and publisher have made every effort to trace all copyright holders. If, however, any have been inadvertently overlooked, we would be pleased to make the necessary arrangement at the first opportunity.

Acknowledgements

The authors would like to thank Carol Guildea, Joe Heron and Paula Keogh who helped with the proofreading, checked the answers and made valuable suggestions that are included in the final text.

CONTENTS

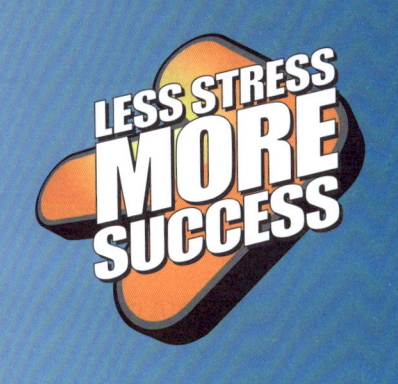

- Introduction iv
- 1. Coordinate Geometry of the Line 1
- 2. Geometry Theorems 26
- 3. Constructions 51
- 4. Transformation Geometry 63
- 5. Trigonometry I 83
- 6. Trigonometry II: Real-World Applications 101
- 7. Perimeter, Area, Nets and Volume 116
- 8. Fundamental Principles of Counting 144
- 9. Probability 153
- 10. Statistics I: Statistical Investigations 176
- 11. Statistics II: Central Tendency and Spread of Data 185
- 12. Statistics III: Representing Data 197
- 13. Classroom-Based Assessments (CBAs) 220
- Glossary of Statistical Terms 233
- Calculator Instructions 235

Please note:

The Exam questions marked by the symbol ![exam Q] in this book are selected from the following:
1. SEC Exam papers
2. Sample exam papers
3. Original and sourced exam-type questions

Introduction

aims
- ☐ To learn how to revise most effectively
- ☐ To familiarise yourself with the four elements of assessement
- ☐ To learn to allocate the correct time for each question
- ☐ To know and understand the words which appear often on the exam paper
- ☐ To familiarise yourself with the syllabus

The aim of this revision book is to help you get as high a mark as possible in your Junior Cycle Ordinary Level maths course. This book is designed to be exam focused and can be used in conjunction with **any** textbook.

Graded examples and exam questions

Throughout this book **examples and exam questions are graded by level of difficulty.**

The level of difficulty is indicated by calculator symbols, as follows:

The number of calculators shown beside a question tells how difficult the question is. One calculator indicates a question which is relatively basic. As the questions get harder, the symbol will have more calculators. Three calculators will indicate an average-level question, whereas five calculators indicate that it is a very challenging question. These questions may be beyond some students, but give them a go! **Students hoping to achieve a high grade should aim to complete all of the five-calculator questions. The calculator symbol given for each question relates to the most difficult part of that question. It is important to not be discouraged by a challenging question.** As in the Junior Cycle exam, difficult questions can sometimes begin with one or two simple parts. You should attempt as much as you can.

Preparing for your Junior Cycle maths exam

It is very important to realise that **you are your own best teacher**. Revision is when you begin to teach yourself. Thus, it is very important for you to start your revision as soon as possible. Make notes while you are revising. If you are having difficulty with a particular question, seek help from your teacher, a friend or a member of your family. As with all subjects, the best examination preparation is to work through past examination or sample papers so that you are familiar with the layout and style of questions.

INTRODUCTION

So, let's start at the beginning. If you want to do well in your Junior Cycle, then you must do two things:

- Revise effectively
- Be familiar with the exam paper and so be prepared on the day of the exam.

These may seem obvious, but it's worth taking a moment to think what these tips mean.

How to revise most effectively

If you are going to do well in the Junior Cycle, you will have to spend quite a bit of time revising. Spending a little time learning how to revise effectively will help you get more from your time and help you absorb and understand more of the material on the course. So, here are some tips to help you revise for maths.

- Find a quiet place where you can work. This place should be dedicated to study, free of potential distractions. Turn off the TV, computer and mobile phone.
- Draw up a study plan. Don't be afraid to ask your parents/teachers/guidance counsellor for help at this stage.
- Do the more challenging revision first, when you are fresh. Trying to focus on difficult problems when you are tired can be counter-productive.
- Your maths course is based on understanding, so while you can 'learn' some elements of the course, it is important that you develop an understanding of the material.
- Drill and practice are essential ingredients for success in maths.
- Try to link any new material to things you know already. This is learning through association and helps long-term retention.

> **key point**
> **Study in small chunks of time lasting 25 to 35 minutes.** Your memory and concentration will work better if you study in short frequent bursts.

> **key point**
> Don't get hung up on more difficult material. Concentrate on understanding the fundamental concepts and being able to answer all of the straightforward questions. Then, with time, you can build up to the more challenging problems.

Junior Cycle maths assessment

Your assessment in Junior Cycle mathematics consists of four elements. We will look at these four elements in detail and in the order in which you will be completing them.

Classroom-Based Assessment 1 (CBA 1) – Mathematical Investigation (during second year)

Format: A report may be presented in a wide range of formats.

Preparation: A student will, over a three-week period in second year, follow the Problem-Solving Cycle to investigate a mathematical problem.

The Problem-Solving Cycle is as follows:

1. Define a problem
2. Decompose it into manageable parts and/or simplify it using appropriate assumptions
3. Translate the problem to mathematics, if necessary
4. Engage with the problem and solve it, if possible
5. Interpret any findings in the context of the original problem

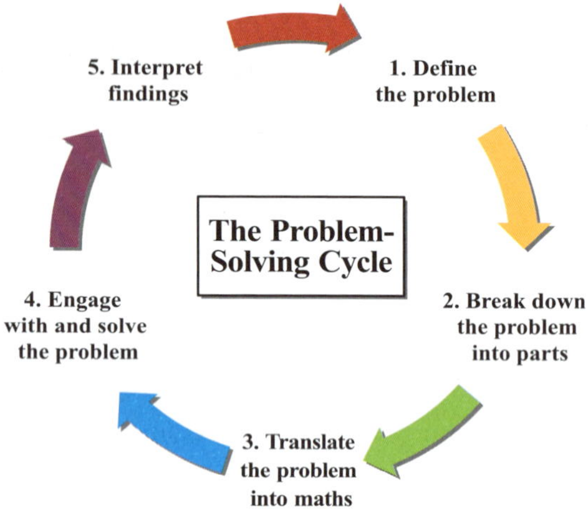

The Problem-Solving Cycle
1. Define the problem
2. Break down the problem into parts
3. Translate the problem into maths
4. Engage with and solve the problem
5. Interpret findings

Assessment: The CBA is assessed by the class teacher. A student will be awarded one of the following categories of achievement:

- Yet to meet expectations
- In line with expectations
- Above expectations
- Exceptional

Classroom-Based Assessment 2 (CBA 2) – Statistical Investigation (during third year)

Format: A report may be presented in a wide range of formats.

Preparation: A student will, over a three-week period in third year, follow the Statistical-Enquiry Cycle to investigate a mathematical problem.

The Statistical-Enquiry Cycle is as follows:

1. Formulate a question
2. Plan and collect unbiased, representative data
3. Organise and manage the data
4. Explore and analyse the data, using appropriate displays and numerical summaries
5. Answer the original question, giving reasons based on the analysis section

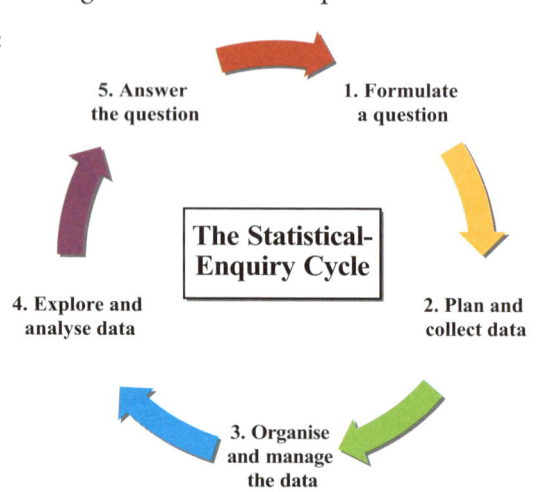

The Statistical-Enquiry Cycle
1. Formulate a question
2. Plan and collect data
3. Organise and manage the data
4. Explore and analyse data
5. Answer the question

Assessment: The CBA is assessed by the class teacher.
A student will be awarded one of the following categories of achievement:

- Yet to meet expectations
- In line with expectations
- Above expectations
- Exceptional

Assessment Task (during third year, after CBA 2)

Format: The Assessment Task is a specified written task, completed by students during class time.

Preparation: The Assessment Task is specified by the NCCA and is related to the learning outcomes on which CBA 2, the Statistical Investigation, is based.

Assessment: The Assessment Task is corrected by qualified teachers, as assigned by the SEC. The assessment task is allocated 10% of the marks used to determine the grade awarded by the SEC in Junior Cycle mathematics.

The written exam paper (end of third year)

Format: A two-hour written exam, taking place at the end of third year.

Assessment: The exam is corrected by qualified teachers, as assigned by the SEC. The written exam is allocated 90% of the marks used to determine the grade awarded by the SEC in Junior Cycle mathematics.

> **exam focus**
>
> Read the exam paper right through at the start, to determine which question is the easiest one to start with. Your mind may also be subconsciously processing some of the other problems.

> **key point**
>
> Attempt marks (partial credit) are valuable, so it is vital that you attempt all questions. Leave **NO** blanks.

Further exam tips

- There is no such thing as rough work in maths – all work is relevant. If the examiner doesn't know how you reached an answer – even a correct answer – then full marks will usually not be awarded. Thus, **show all your work**.
- It is a good idea to show each stage of a calculation when using a calculator (in case you press a wrong key). **Familiarise yourself** with your calculator. Know your **book of tables and formulae well and write down any formula that you use.**

> **key point**
>
> Your calculator and book of tables are two extremely valuable resources to have in the exam. Make sure that you are very familiar with how your calculator works and that you know how to perform all functions on it. Also familiarise yourself with the book of tables so that there is no time wasted in the exam, trying to find formulae.

- Attempt marks (partial credit) will be awarded for any step in the right direction. Therefore, **make an attempt at each part of the question**. Even if you do not get the correct answer, you can still pick up most of the marks on offer if you show how you worked it out. Also, **draw a diagram where possible**, because this can help you to see the solution.
- If you cannot finish part of a question, leave a space and come back to it later. **Never scribble out any work or use Tipp-Ex.** Put a single line through it so that the examiner can still read it. **Avoid using pencil** because the writing can be very faint and difficult to read.
- **Do not judge the length of your answer based on the size of the space provided.** Sometimes large spaces are provided for questions where only a short solution is required.
- If you run out of space in your answer booklet, **ask the supervisor for more paper**. Then clearly write the number of the exam question and the solution on the extra paper.

Glossary of common phrases used throughout your mathematics course and on the examination paper

Analyse, Investigate
Observe, study or examine something in detail, in order to establish facts and reach new conclusions.

Apply, Use
Select and use knowledge, skills or rules to put theory into practice and solve a problem.

Calculate, Find, Determine
Obtain your answers by showing all relevant work. Marks are available for showing the steps leading to your final answer or conclusion.

Classify
Group things based on common characteristics.

Comment on, Discuss, Interpret
After studying the given information or your answers, give your opinion on their significance. Use your knowledge and understanding to explain the meaning of something in context.

Compare
Give an account of the similarities and (or) differences between two (or more) items or situations, referring to both (all) of them throughout.

Construct
Draw an accurate diagram, usually labelled, using a pencil, ruler, set square, compass and protractor. Leave all constructions on your diagram.

Convert
Change from one form to another.

Estimate
State or calculate a rough value for a particular quantity.

Evaluate
Usually to work out, or find, a numerical value by putting in numbers for letters.

Explain, Show that, Prove, Verify, Justify
Demonstrate that a statement is true. This could be a given statement or to be able to show that your answer is correct.

Give your answer in the form ...
This means the examiner wants the final answer in a particular form, for example, as a fraction, in surd form, in index notation, rounded to a particular number of decimal places, etc. Watch out for this, as your will lose marks if your answer is not in the correct form.

Generalise
Generate a general statement, based on specific instance.

Generate
To produce or create.

Hence
You *must* use the answer, or result, from the previous part of the question.

Hence or otherwise
It is recommended that you use the answer, or result, from the previous part of the question, but other methods are acceptable.

Mathematise
Generate a mathematical representation (e.g. graph, equation, geometric figure) to describe a particular aspect of a phenomenon.

Plot
Indicate the position of points on a graph, usually on the x- and y-planes.

Sketch
Make a rough diagram or graph, labelled if needed.

Solve
Find the solution, or root, of an equation. The solution is the value of the variable that makes the left-hand side balance with the right-hand side.

Understand
Have detailed knowledge of, be able to use appropriately, and see the connections between parts.

Write down, State
You can write down your answer without showing any work. However, if you want you can show some workings.

Syllabus checklist for Junior Cycle Ordinary Level maths: Geometry and Trigonometry Strand and Statistics and Probability Strand

Throughout your course you will be asked to apply your knowledge and skills to solve problems in familiar and unfamiliar contexts. In problem solving, you should use some of the following strategies:

- Trial and improvement
- Draw a diagram
- Look for a pattern
- Act it out
- Draw a table
- Simplify the problem
- Use an equation
- Work backwards
- Eliminate possibilities

The syllabus stresses that in all aspects of the Junior Cycle maths course, students should be able to:

- ☐ Explore patterns and formulate conjectures
- ☐ Explain findings
- ☐ Justify conclusions
- ☐ Communicate mathematics verbally and in written form
- ☐ Apply their knowledge and skills to solve problems in familiar and unfamiliar contexts
- ☐ Analyse information presented verbally and translate it into mathematical form
- ☐ Devise, select and use appropriate mathematical models, formulae or techniques to process information and to draw relevant conclusions

Unifying Strand

Throughout the Junior Cycle maths course, students should develop the skills associated with each of the following elements:

Building blocks
Students should understand and recall the concepts that underpin each strand, and be able to carry out the resulting procedures accurately, effectively, and appropriately.

Representation
Students should be able to represent a mathematical situation in a variety of different ways and translate flexibly between them.

Connections
Students should be able to make connections within strands and between strands, as well as connections between mathematics and the real world.

Problem-solving
Students should be able to investigate patterns, formulate conjectures, and engage in tasks in which the solution is not immediately obvious, in familiar and unfamiliar contexts.

Generalisation and proof
Students should be able to move from specific instances to general mathematical statements, and to present and evaluate mathematical arguments and proofs.

Communication
Students should be able to communicate mathematics effectively in verbal and written form.

Geometry and Trigonometry Strand

Area and Volume

- ☐ Calculate, interpret, and apply units of measure and time.
- ☐ Investigate 2D shapes and 3D solids so that you can:
  - Draw and interpret scaled diagrams
  - Draw and interpret nets of rectangular solids
  - Find the perimeter and area of plane figures made from combinations of discs, triangles, and rectangles, including relevant operations involving pi
  - Find the volume of rectangular solids, cylinders, and combinations of these, including relevant operations involving pi
  - Find the surface area of rectangular solids.

Geometry

- ☐ Recall and use the concepts, axioms, theorems, corollaries and converses:
  - Axioms 1, 2, 3, 4 and 5
  - Theorems 1, 2, 3, 4, 5, 6, 9, 10, 13, 14, 15 and appropriate converses, including relevant operations involving square roots
  - Corollaries 3, 4 and appropriate converses.
- ☐ Use the terms:
  - Theorem
  - Proof
  - Axiom
  - Corollary
  - Converse
  - Implies.
- ☐ Create and evaluate proofs of geometrical propositions.
- ☐ Display understanding of the proofs of theorems 1, 2, 3, 4, 5, 6, 9, 10, 14, 15, and of corollaries 3, 4 (full formal proofs are not examinable).

Constructions

- ☐ Perform the following constructions:
  - 1. Bisector of a given angle, using only compass and straight edge
  - 2. Perpendicular bisector of a segment, using only compass and straight edge
  - 3. Line perpendicular to a given line l, passing through a given point on l
  - 4. Line parallel to given line, through given point

- 5. Division of a segment into 2, 3 equal segments, without measuring it
- 6. Line segment of given length on a given ray
- 7. Angle of given number of degrees with a given ray as one arm
- 8. Triangle, given lengths of three sides
- 9. Triangle, given SAS data
- 10. Triangle, given ASA data
- 11. Right-angled triangle, given the length of the hypotenuse and one other side
- 12. Right-angled triangle, given one side and one of the acute angles (several cases)
- 13. Rectangle, given side lengths.

Trigonometry

- Evaluate and use trigonometric ratios (sin, cos, and tan, defined in terms of right-angled triangles) and their inverses, involving angles between 0° and 90° at integer values.

Coordinate Geometry

- Investigate properties of points, lines and line segments in the coordinate plane so that you can find and interpret:
  - Distance
  - Midpoint
  - Slope
  - Point of intersection
  - Slopes of parallel lines.
- Draw graphs of line segments and interpret such graphs in context, including discussing the rate of change (slope) and the y intercept.
- Find and interpret the equation of a line in the form $y = mx + c$; $y - y_1 = m(x - x_1)$; including finding the slope, the y intercept, and other points on the line.

Transformation Geometry

- Recognise and draw the image of points and objects under:
  - Translation
  - Central symmetry
  - Axial symmetry
  - Rotation.
- Draw the axes of symmetry in shapes.

Statistics and Probability Strand
Fundamental Principle of Counting
- ☐ Generate a sample space for an experiment in a systematic way, including tree diagrams for successive events and two-way tables for independent events.
- ☐ Use the fundamental principle of counting to solve authentic problems.

Probability
- ☐ Demonstrate understanding that probability is a measure on a scale of 0–1 of how likely an event (including an everyday event) is to occur.
- ☐ Use the principle that, in the case of equally likely outcomes, the probability of an event is given by the number of outcomes of interest divided by the total number of outcomes.
- ☐ Use relative frequency as an estimate of the probability of an event, given experimental data, and recognise that increasing the number of times an experiment is repeated generally leads to progressively better estimates of its theoretical probability.

Statistics
- ☐ Generate a statistical question.
- ☐ Plan and implement a method to generate and/or source unbiased, representative data, and present this data in a frequency table.
- ☐ Classify data (categorical, numerical).
- ☐ Select, draw and interpret appropriate graphical displays of univariate data, including:
  - Pie charts
  - Bar charts
  - Line plots
  - Histograms (equal intervals)
  - Ordered stem and leaf plots.
- ☐ Select, calculate and interpret appropriate summary statistics to describe aspects of univariate data. Variability – range. And the following measure of central tendency:
  - Mean
  - Median
  - Mode.
- ☐ Evaluate the effectiveness of different graphical displays in representing data.
- ☐ Discuss misconceptions and misuses of statistics.
- ☐ Discuss the assumptions and limitations of conclusions drawn from sample data or graphical/numerical summaries of data.

1 Coordinate Geometry of the Line

aims
- ☐ To know where to find the coordinate geometry formulae in the booklet of formulae and tables
- ☐ To learn how to apply these formulae to procedural and in-context examination questions
- ☐ To gain the ability, with practise, to recall and select the appropriate technique required by the exam questions

Coordinating the plane and plotting points

Coordinates are used to describe the **position** of a point on a plane (flat surface).

Two lines are drawn at right angles to each other.

The horizontal line is called the *x*-axis.

The vertical line is called the *y*-axis.

The two axes meet at a point called the **origin**.

The plane is called the **Cartesian** (kar-tee-zi-an) plane.

Every point on the plane has two coordinates, an *x*-**coordinate** and a *y*-**coordinate**.

The coordinates are enclosed in brackets.

The *x*-coordinate is always written first, then a comma, followed by the *y*-coordinate.

On the diagram, the coordinates of the point *A* are (3, 2).

This is usually written as *A*(3, 2).

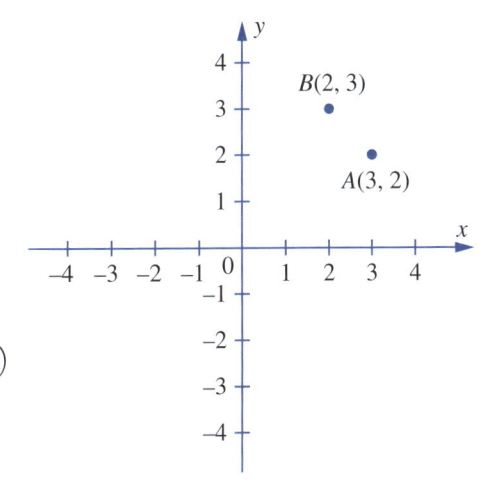

key point

In a couple (x, y) the order is important. The first number, x, is always **across**, **left** or **right**, and the second number, y, is always **up** or **down**.

The graph above shows the point *A*(3, 2) is different to the point *B*(2, 3).

Example

Write down the coordinates of the points P, Q, R, S and T

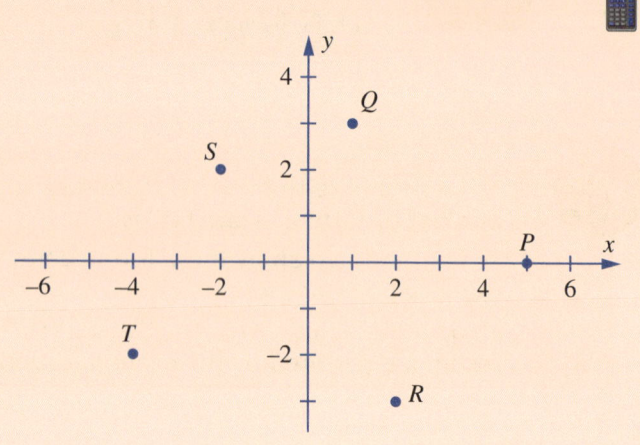

Solution

$P = (5, 0)$ $Q = (1, 3)$ $R = (2, -3)$ $S = (-2, 2)$ $T = (-4, -2)$

---

exam Q

An archaeologist has discovered various items at a site. The site is laid out in a grid and the position of each item is shown on the grid. The items found are a brooch (B), a plate (P), a ring (R), a statue (S) and a tile (T).

(a) Write down the coordinates of the position of each item.

$B = (\ 2\ ,\ 7\ )$
$P = (\quad,\quad)$
$R = (\quad,\quad)$
$S = (\quad,\quad)$
$T = (\quad,\quad)$

(b) Each square of the grid represents 1 m². Find the total area of the grid.

(c) Which of the items is nearest to the tile (T)?

(d) Find the distance between the brooch (B) and the statue (S).

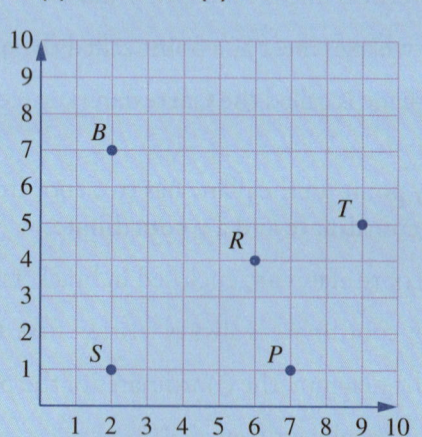

Solution

(a) $P = (7, 1)$ $R = (6, 4)$ $S = (2, 1)$ $T = (9, 5)$

(b) Count the grids: 10 up by 10 across
    $= 10 \times 10 = 100$ m²

(c) By observation the ring (R) is nearest to the tile (T).

(d) $B(2, 7)$ to $S(2, 1) = 6$ m

> **key point**
> Count each box as one unit.

COORDINATE GEOMETRY OF THE LINE

Midpoint of a line segment

If (x_1, y_1) and (x_2, y_2) are two points, their midpoint is given by the formula:

$$\text{Midpoint} = \left(\frac{x_1 + x_2}{2}, \frac{y_1 + y_2}{2}\right)$$

(See booklet of formulae and tables, page 18)

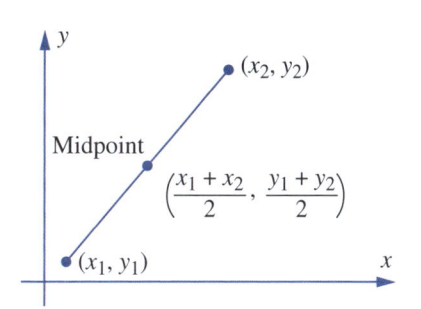

> **key point**
>
> When using coordinate geometry formulae, always allocate one point to be (x_1, y_1) and the other to be (x_2, y_2) before you use the formula.

Example

Noah is positioned at $(8, 5)$ and a bus stop is positiond at $(-10, 11)$. There is a traffic light exactly half way between Noah and the bus stop. Find the coordinates of the traffic light.

Solution

Midpoint (halfway) formula $= \left(\dfrac{x_1 + x_2}{2}, \dfrac{y_1 + y_2}{2}\right)$

Let $(x_1, y_1) = (8, 5)$ and $(x_2, y_2) = (-10, 11)$

Coordinates of the traffic light $= \left(\dfrac{8 - 10}{2}, \dfrac{5 + 11}{2}\right) = \left(\dfrac{-2}{2}, \dfrac{16}{2}\right) = (-1, 8)$

exam Q

P, Q and R are the midpoints of the sides of the triangle ABC.

(i) Find the coordinates of P, Q and R.

(ii) The number of parallelograms in the diagram is

(a) 0 ☐
(b) 1 ☐
(c) 2 ☐
(d) 3 ☐

Tick the correct answer.

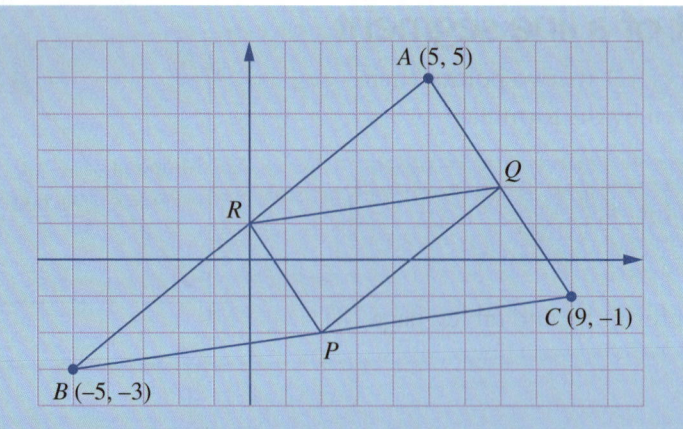

Solution

(i) Use the midpoint formula $\left(\dfrac{x_1 + x_2}{2}, \dfrac{y_1 + y_2}{2}\right)$ three times.

Midpoint of [AB]	**Midpoint of [AC]**	**Midpoint of [BC]**
$(x_1, y_1) = (5, 5)$	$(x_1, y_1) = (5, 5)$	$(x_1, y_1) = (-5, -3)$
$(x_2, y_2) = (-5, -3)$	$(x_2, y_2) = (9, -1)$	$(x_2, y_2) = (9, -1)$
$R = \left(\dfrac{5-5}{2}, \dfrac{5-3}{2}\right)$	$Q = \left(\dfrac{5+9}{2}, \dfrac{5-1}{2}\right)$	$P = \left(\dfrac{-5+9}{2}, \dfrac{-3-1}{2}\right)$
$R = \left(\dfrac{0}{2}, \dfrac{2}{2}\right)$	$Q = \left(\dfrac{14}{2}, \dfrac{4}{2}\right)$	$P = \left(\dfrac{4}{2}, \dfrac{-4}{2}\right)$
$R = (0, 1)$	$Q = (7, 2)$	$P = (2, -2)$

(ii) (d) 3 ☑ The shaded triangle in the diagram forms half of three different parallelograms.

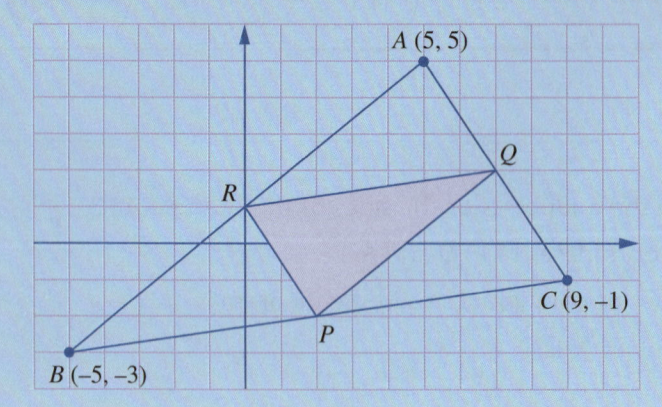

COORDINATE GEOMETRY OF THE LINE

Translations

In mathematics, movement in a straight line is called a **translation**.

Under a translation, every point is moved the same distance in the same direction. A translation is one of several types of transformations on our course. See Chapter 4 for more on transformations.

Example

Describe the translation that maps the points:
(i) G to H
(ii) R to D

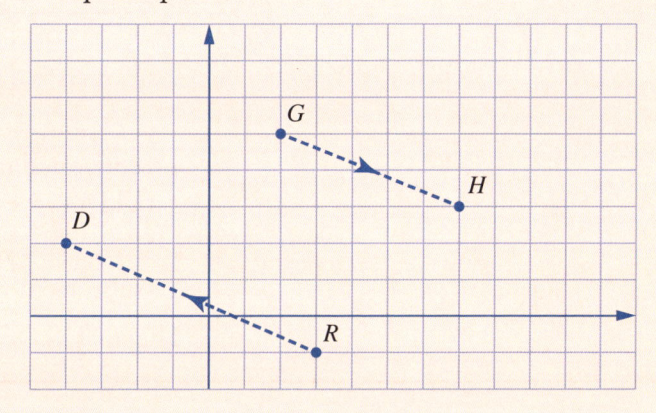

Solution

(i) $G \rightarrow H$ is described by 5 units to the right and 2 units down.

This translation can be written as $\begin{pmatrix} 5 \\ -2 \end{pmatrix}$.

(ii) $R \rightarrow D$ is described by 7 units to the left and 3 units up.

This translation can be written as $\begin{pmatrix} -7 \\ 3 \end{pmatrix}$.

Example

$A(-1, 1)$ and $B(4, -2)$ are two points.
Find the image of the point $(-1, 3)$ under the translation $\vec{AB}$

Solution

Under the translation $\vec{AB}$: $(-1, 1) \rightarrow (4, -2)$

Rule: Add 5 to x, subtract 3 from y, this can be written as $\begin{pmatrix} 5 \\ -3 \end{pmatrix}$.

Method 1	Method 2
Mathematical Method	**Graphical Method**
(Apply the rule directly)	Plot the point $(-1, 3)$ and split the move into two parts:
$(-1, 3) \rightarrow (-1 + 5, 3 - 3) = (4, 0)$	
We say the image of $(-1, 3)$ is $(4, 0)$.	

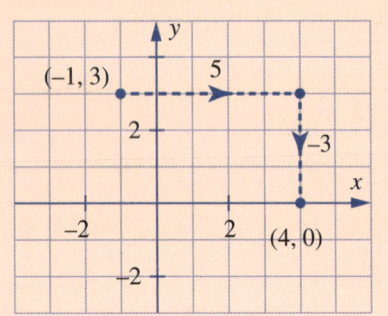

Method 2 details:
- Horizontal move: 5 units to the right (add 5 to x)
- Vertical move: 3 units down (subtract 3 from y)

The image of $(-1, 3)$ is $(4, 0)$.

In some questions, we will be given the midpoint and one end point of a line segment and be asked to find the other end point.

To find the other end point use the following method:

1. Draw a rough diagram.
2. Find the translation that maps (moves) the given end point to the midpoint.
3. Apply the same translation to the midpoint to find the other end point.

Example

If $K(5, -3)$ is the midpoint of $[PQ]$ and $P = (4, 1)$, find the coordinates of Q.

Solution

1. Rough diagram

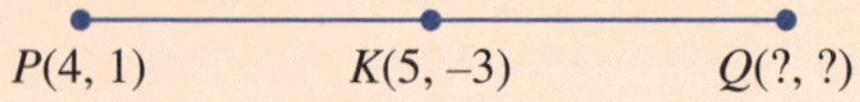

$P(4, 1)$ $K(5, -3)$ $Q(?, ?)$

2. Translation from P to K, $\vec{PK}$.

Rule: add 1 to x, subtract 4 from y. This can be written as $\begin{pmatrix} 1 \\ -4 \end{pmatrix}$.

3. Apply this translation to K:
$K(5,-3) \rightarrow (5+1, -3-4) = (6,-7)$

∴ The coordinates of Q are $(6, -7)$.

Distance between two points

The given diagram shows the points $A(x_1, y_1)$ and $B(x_2, y_2)$.
$|BC| = y_2 - y_1$ and $|AC| = x_2 - x_1$

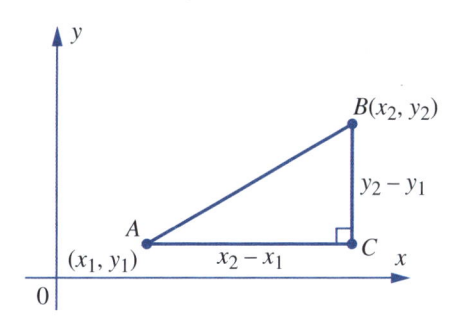

Using the theorem of Pythagoras:
$|AB|^2 = |AC|^2 + |BC|^2$
$|AB|^2 = (x_2 - x_1)^2 + (y_2 - y_1)^2$
∴ $|AB| = \sqrt{(x_2 - x_1)^2 + (y_2 - y_1)^2}$

The distance between $A(x_1, y_1)$ and $B(x_2, y_2)$ is $|AB| = \sqrt{(x_2 - x_1)^2 + (y_2 - y_1)^2}$ (see booklet of formulae and tables, page 18).

Example

Carol is positioned at the point $(3, 2)$ and Siobhan is positioned at the point $(5, -4)$. Find the distance between them.

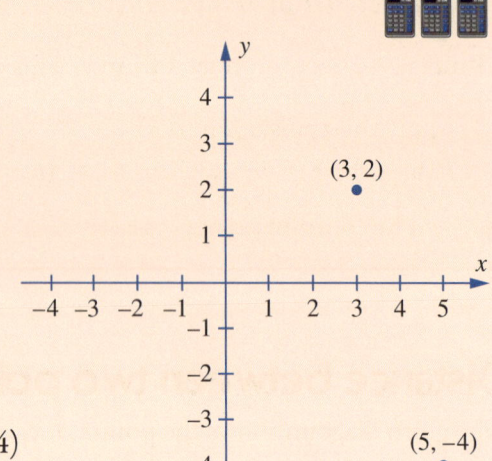

Solution

Let $(x_1, y_1) = (3, 2)$ and $(x_2, y_2) = (5, -4)$

Distance between Carol and Siobhan:

$= \sqrt{(x_2 - x_1)^2 + (y_2 - y_1)^2}$

$= \sqrt{(5 - 3)^2 + (-4 - 2)^2}$

$= \sqrt{(2)^2 + (-6)^2}$

$= \sqrt{4 + 36}$

$= \sqrt{40}$

$= 2\sqrt{10}$ (using a calculator)

key point: At this stage, all numbers are always positive.

exam Q

$ABCD$ is a rectangle with $A(3, 1)$ and $B(-3, 9)$. Given $|BC| = \dfrac{1}{5}|AB|$, calculate the area of $ABCD$.

Solution

Let $(x_1, y_1) = (3, 1)$ and $(x_2, y_2) = (-3, 9)$

$|AB| = \sqrt{(x_2 - x_1)^2 + (y_2 - y_1)^2}$

$= \sqrt{(-3 - 3)^2 + (9 - 1)^2}$

$= \sqrt{(-6)^2 + (8)^2} = \sqrt{36 + 64} = \sqrt{100} = 10$

$|BC| = \dfrac{1}{5}|AB| = \dfrac{1}{5}(10) = 2$

Area rectangle $ABCD$ = (length)(width) = $(10)(2) = 20$ square units

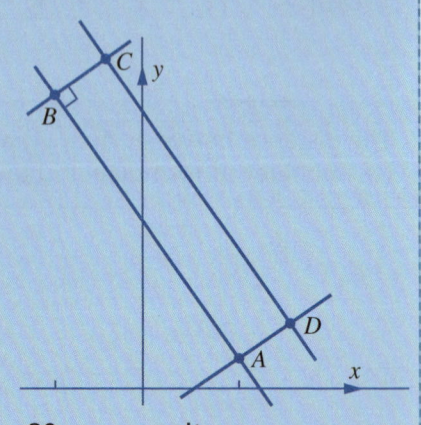

COORDINATE GEOMETRY OF THE LINE

(a) Write down the coordinates of the point A and the point B on the diagram.

(b) Use the distance formula to find $|AB|$.

(c) Write down the distance from O to A and the distance from O to B.

(d) Use the theorem of Pythagoras to find the length of the hypotenuse of the triangle OAB.

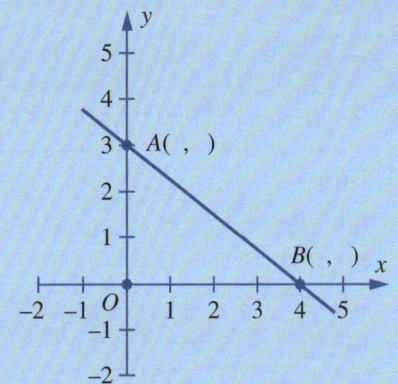

Solution

(a) $A = (0, 3)$

$B = (4, 0)$

(b) Let $(x_1, y_1) = (0, 3)$ and $(x_2, y_2) = (4, 0)$

$|AB| = \sqrt{(x_2 - x_1)^2 + (y_2 - y_1)^2}$

$= \sqrt{(4 - 0)^2 = (0 - 3)^2}$

$= \sqrt{(4)^2 + (-3)^2}$

$= \sqrt{16 + 9}$

$= \sqrt{25}$

$= 5$

(c) $|OA| = 3$

$|OB| = 4$

(d) The theorem of Pythagoras

$(\text{Hyp})^2 = (\text{Opp})^2 + (\text{Adj})^2$

$|AB|^2 = (3)^2 + (4)^2$

$|AB|^2 = 9 + 16 = 25$

$|AB| = 5$

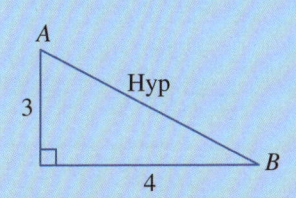

key point

Answer to part (b) = Answer to part (d).

Given the points on the diagram:

B	C	E	F
(2, 0)	(−4, −4)	(−6, 0)	(4, −4)

(i) Find:
  (a) $|BE|$
  (b) $|CF|$
  (c) $|EC|$
  (d) $|BF|$

(ii) Hence, prove the triangle BCE is congruent to the triangle BCF.

Solution

(i) By observation from the diagram we can say:
  (a) $|BE| = 8$
and (b) $|CF| = 8$

> **key point**
> For parts (a) and (b) count the width of each box as one unit.

We use $\sqrt{(x_2 - x_1)^2 + (y_2 - y_1)^2}$ for both $|EC|$ and $|BF|$.

(c) $|EC|$
$(x_1, y_1) = (-6, 0)$
$(x_2, y_2) = (-4, -4)$
$|EC| = \sqrt{(-4 - (-6))^2 + (-4 - 0)^2}$
$ = \sqrt{(-4 + 6)^2 + (-4)^2}$
$ = \sqrt{(2)^2 + 16}$
$ = \sqrt{4 + 16}$
$ = \sqrt{20}$

(d) $|BF|$
$(x_1, y_1) = (2, 0)$
$(x_2, y_2) = (4, -4)$
$|BF| = \sqrt{(4 - 2)^2 + (-4 - 0)^2}$
$ = \sqrt{(2)^2 + (-4)^2}$
$ = \sqrt{4 + 16}$
$ = \sqrt{20}$

> **key point**
> $|EC| = |BF|$ and $|BE| = |CF|$. These two pieces of information will be very useful in answering part (ii) of this question.

COORDINATE GEOMETRY OF THE LINE

(ii) Consider $\triangle BCE$ and $\triangle BCF$

$|BC| = |BC|$ same

$|EC| = |BF| = \sqrt{20}$

$|EB| = |CF| = 8$

Hence (by SSS), $\triangle BCE$ is congruent (identical) to $\triangle BCF$.

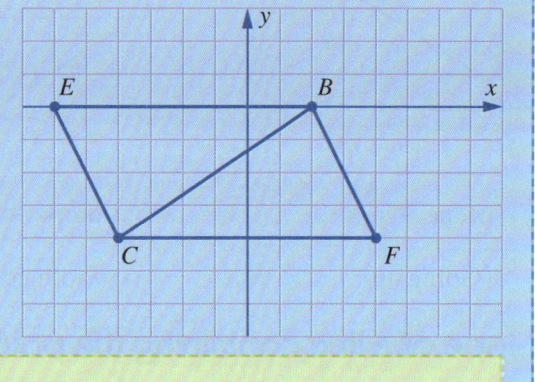

key point

The four cases for congruent triangles are covered in Chapter 2, Geometry.

exam focus

- Part **(ii)** above is an excellent example of an exam question linking two different topics on our course. In this case, we see coordinate geometry of the line linked with geometry theorems.
- In a recent exam, a similar question on congruence was asked, but it was worth very few marks. For not answering this part, candidates lost 1 mark out of a total of 27 marks awarded for the question.

Remember: Do not become disheartened, continue to do your best for every part of every question and you will do well.

Slope of a line

All mathematical graphs are read from **left to right**.
The measure of the steepness of a line is called the **slope**.
The vertical distance, up or down, is called the **rise**.
The horizontal distance across is called the **run**.
The slope of a line is defined as:

$$\text{Slope} = \frac{\text{Rise}}{\text{Run}}$$

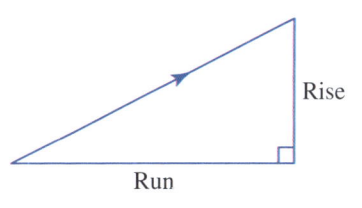

key point

The rise can also be negative and in this case it is often called the **'fall'**. If the rise is zero, then the slope is also zero.

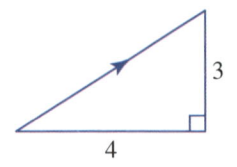

12 LESS STRESS MORE SUCCESS

Slope = $\dfrac{3}{4}$

(Going up)

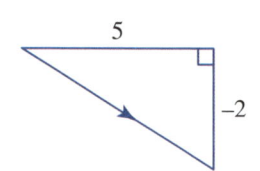

Slope = $\dfrac{-2}{5}$

(Going down)

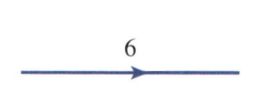

Slope = $\dfrac{0}{6} = 0$

(Horizontal)

Slope of a line containing the points (x_1, y_1) and (x_2, y_2):

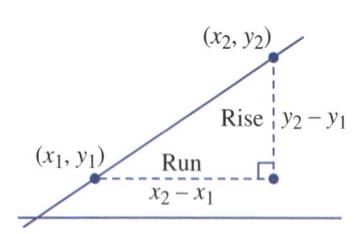

If a line contains two points (x_1, y_1) and (x_2, y_2) then the slope is given by the formula:

$$m = \dfrac{y_2 - y_1}{x_2 - x_1}$$

(see page 18 in the booklet of formulae and tables)

exam Q

In a certain country, the slope of a hill is defined as $\dfrac{\text{Rise}}{\text{Run}}$.

Which hill is the steepest? Which hill is the least steep? Justify your answers.

(i) 18%   (ii) 1 in 10   (iii) 2:7   (iv) 1 in 20

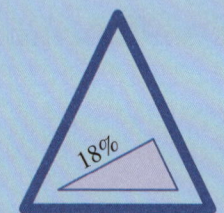

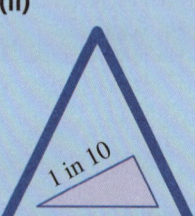

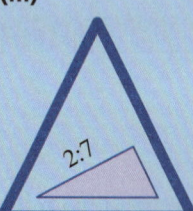

Solution

(i) $18\% = \dfrac{18}{100} = 0.18$

(ii) 1 in 10 = $\dfrac{1}{10} = 0.1$

(iii) $\dfrac{2}{7} = 0.2857$

(iv) $\dfrac{1}{20} = 0.05$

key point

Converting to decimals is the easiest way to compare the slopes.

By observing the above four calculations we conclude:

Hill number **(iii)** has the greatest slope and so it is the steepest.

Hill number **(iv)** has the smallest slope and so it is the least steep.

The work above is my justification.

COORDINATE GEOMETRY OF THE LINE

Example

Which of the lines g, h, k, l in the diagram has:

(i) A slope of zero?

(ii) A positive slope?

Justify your answers.

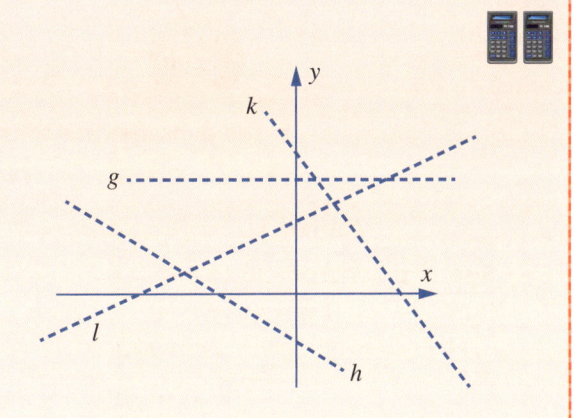

Solution

(i) By observation, line g makes no angle with the x-axis (it is horizontal)
$\Rightarrow g$ has a slope of zero.

(ii) Reading the diagram from left to right, we observe line l is going up
$\Rightarrow l$ has a positive slope.

exam focus

Some exam solutions may be short and wordy.

---

exam Q

An accountant plots the value of a computer over a three-year period on the given graph. Find the average rate of change.

Interpret your answer in the context of the question.

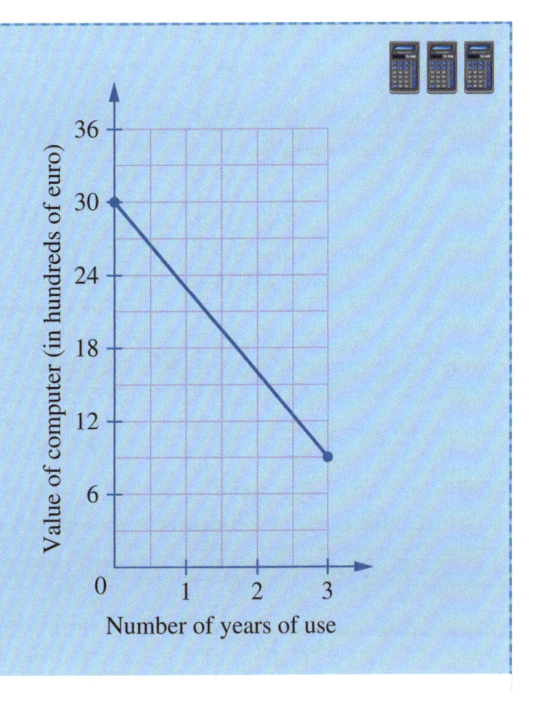

Solution

key point

The average rate of change = m = the slope of the line

Method 1

$$m = \frac{\text{Rise}}{\text{Run}} = \frac{\text{down from 30 to 9}}{3 \text{ years}}$$

$$= \frac{-21}{3} = -7$$

Method 2

$(x_1, y_1) = (0, 30)$ and $(x_2, y_2) = (3, 9)$

$$m = \frac{y_2 - y_1}{x_2 - x_1} = \frac{9 - 30}{3 - 0} = \frac{-21}{3} = -7$$

In the context of this question, a slope of $-7(=-€700)$ indicates the rate of change in the value of the computer each year.

exam focus

Either method will gain full marks in this case.

---

exam Q

The graph below shows the total number of times Peter checked his phone from 8 a.m. to 6 p.m. on a given day. For example, by 6 p.m. Peter had checked his phone a total of 65 times.

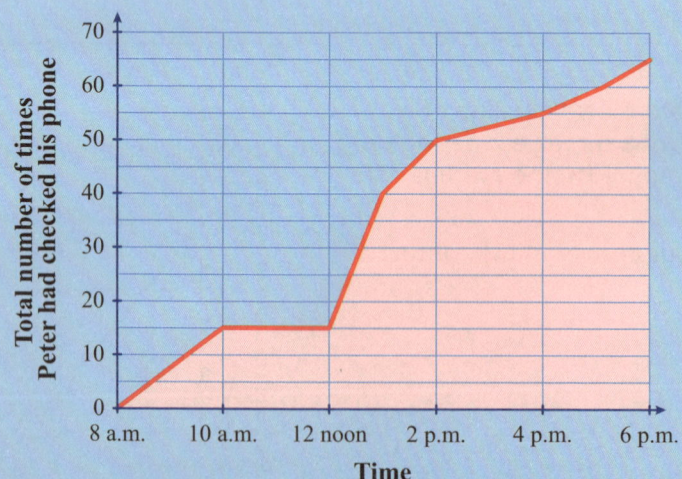

(a) Use the graph to answer each of the following questions. In each case, tick (✓) the correct box only.

(i) By 2 p.m., the total number of times Peter had checked his phone was:

15 ☐   40 ☐   50 ☐   55 ☐

(ii) Peter did not check his phone at all from:

    10 – 12 noon   12 – 2 p.m.   2 – 4 p.m.   4 – 6 p.m.

    ☐   ☐   ☐   ☐

(iii) Peter checked his phone most often from:

    10 – 12 noon   12 – 2 p.m.   2 – 4 p.m.   4 – 6 p.m.

    ☐   ☐   ☐   ☐

(b) From 8 a.m. to 6 p.m. on that day, Peter checked his phone on average 6·5 times each hour. He uses this to estimate N, the total number of times he had checked his phone, as: $N = 6·5 \times H$
where H is the number of hours after 8 a.m. on that day.

(i) Use this formula to find the value of N when H is 8.

(ii) Peter uses his formula to estimate that he will have checked his phone 156 times by 8 a.m. the following day (when $H = 24$). Do you think that this is a reasonable estimate?

Solution

(a) (i) From the graph (orange arrow), we can see that at 2 p.m., Peter has checked his phone 50 times.

    15   40   50   55

    ☐   ☐   ✓   ☐

(ii) The part of the graph where Peter didn't check his phone is represented by a horizontal line (coloured in blue).
This happened between 10 a.m. and 12 noon.

    10 – 12 noon   12 – 2 p.m.   2 – 4 p.m.   4 – 6 p.m.

    ✓   ☐   ☐   ☐

(iii) The part of the graph where Peter checked his phone most often is represented by the steepest section (coloured in green).
This happened between 12 noon and 2 p.m.

    10 – 12 noon   12 – 2 p.m.   2 – 4 p.m.   4 – 6 p.m.

    ☐   ✓   ☐   ☐

(b) (i) Let $H = 8$:

$$N = 6·5 \times H$$
$$N = 6·5 \times 8$$
$$N = 52$$

exam focus

Being able to substitute values in for variables is a vital skill for you to have. You will use this skill quite often as you work through the exam paper.

(ii) This formula is based on Peter's day-time usage between 8 a.m. and 6 p.m. (10 hours duration). It is unlikely that his usage will be the same for the other 14 hours of the 24-hour period. For example, Peter will not be checking his phone while he is asleep.
So, the estimate of 156 times is probably a bit too high and we can conclude that it is not a reasonable estimate.

Parallel lines

To prove whether or not two lines are parallel, do the following:

1. Find the slope of each line.
2. (a) If the slopes are the same, the lines are parallel.
   (b) If the slopes are different, the lines are **not** parallel.

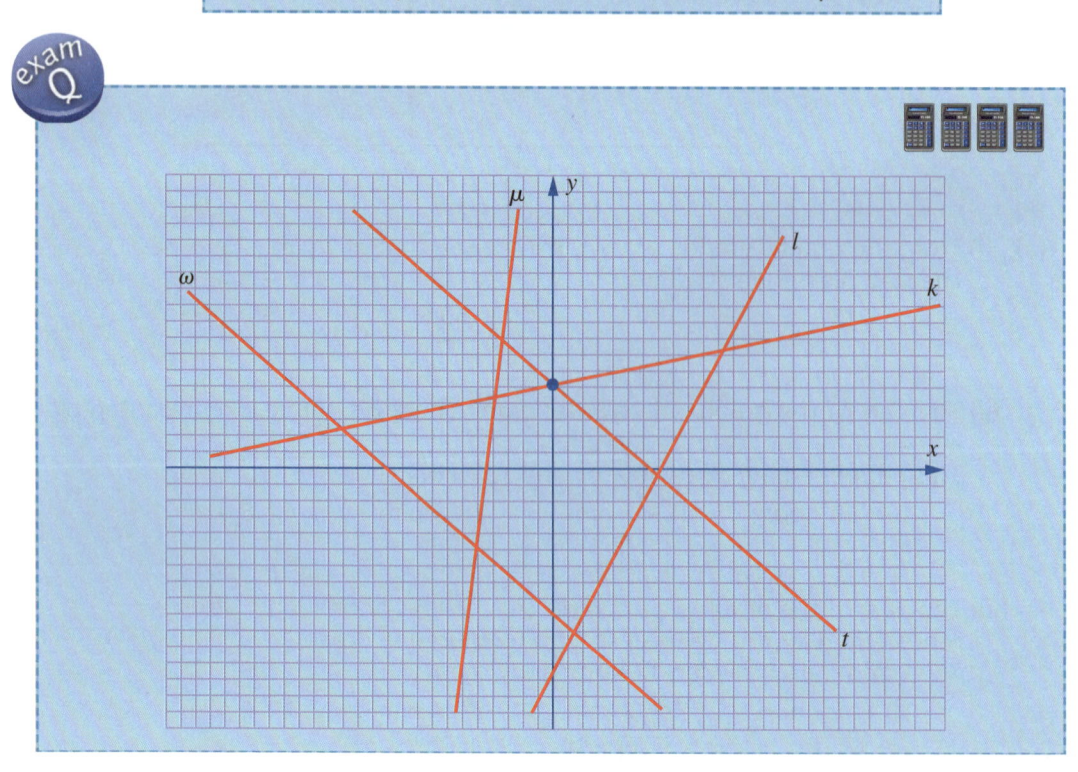

exam Q

COORDINATE GEOMETRY OF THE LINE

Five lines μ, ω, t, l and k in the coordinate plane are shown in the diagram above. The slopes of the five lines are given in the table.
Complete the table, matching the lines to their slopes.

Slope	Line
$\frac{1}{6}$	
$\frac{5}{3}$	
$-\frac{9}{10}$	
13	
$-\frac{9}{10}$	

key point

Two lines have slope $-\frac{9}{10}$. This means two lines are parallel.
$\therefore$ t has slope $-\frac{9}{10}$ and ω has slope $-\frac{9}{10}$.

Solution

l, k and μ all have positive slopes (because they are all rising).
By observation, μ has the steepest positive slope.
$\therefore$ μ has slope 13.
Also by observation, k has the least steep positive slope.
$\therefore$ k has slope $\frac{1}{6}$.
Since the only remaining line is l and the only remaining slope is $\frac{5}{3}$ $\Rightarrow$ l has slope $\frac{5}{3}$.

Slope	Line
$\frac{1}{6}$	k
$\frac{5}{3}$	
$-\frac{9}{10}$	t
13	μ
$-\frac{9}{10}$	ω

The equation of a line

The formula: $y - y_1 = m(x - x_1)$ (see booklet of formulae and tables, page 18)
gives the equation of a line when we have:
- A point on the line (x_1, y_1)
- The slope of the line, m.

Example

Find the equation of the line through the point $(5, -1)$ whose slope is $\dfrac{2}{3}$.

Solution

$y - y_1 = m(x - x_1)$

$(x_1, y_1) = (5, -1)$ and $m = \dfrac{2}{3}$

$\therefore \quad y - (-1) = \dfrac{2}{3}(x - 5)$

$y + 1 = \dfrac{2}{3}(x - 5)$

$3(y + 1) = 2(x - 5)$ (multiply both sides by 3 to remove the fraction)

$3y + 3 = 2x - 10$

$3y = 2x - 10 - 3$

$3y = 2x - 13$

---

exam Q

P is the point $(-1, 7)$ and Q is the point $(1, -3)$. Find the equation of the line PQ.

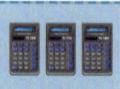

key point: The slope is missing. We first find the slope and then use **either** point to find the equation.

Solution

$\left. \begin{array}{l} P(-1, 7) = (x_1, y_1) \\ Q(1, -3) = (x_2, y_2) \end{array} \right\}$ Slope $= m = \dfrac{y_2 - y_1}{x_2 - x_1} = \dfrac{-3 - 7}{1 - (-1)} = \dfrac{-10}{1 + 1} = \dfrac{-10}{2} = -5$

Equation of PQ with slope $= m = -5$ and $Q = (1, -3) = (x_1, y_1)$

$y - y_1 = m(x - x_1)$

$y - (-3) = -5(x - 1)$

$y + 3 = -5x + 5$

$y = -5x + 5 - 3$

$y = -5x + 2$

COORDINATE GEOMETRY OF THE LINE

The slope of a line when given its equation

To find the slope of a line when given its equation, do the following:

> Get *y* on its own, and the number in front of *x* is the slope.

Note: The number in front of *x* is called the **coefficient** of *x*.
The number on its own is called the *y* **intercept**.
In short: write the line in the form $y = mx + c$.

$$y = \underset{\downarrow}{mx} + \underset{\downarrow}{c} \quad \text{(see booklet of formulae and tables, page 18)}$$

$$y = (\text{slope})x + (\text{where the line cuts the } y\text{-axis})$$

Example
Write down the slope, *m*, of each of the following lines.

(i) $y = 4x - 3$ (ii) $y = 8 - 2x$ (iii) $y = x + 5$
(iv) $2y = 7x - 10$ (v) $y - 6x = 0$ (vi) $3y + 2x + 12 = 0$

Solution
Using $y = mx + c$ in each case:

(i) $y = 4x - 3 \Rightarrow m = 4$

(ii) $y = 8 - 2x \Rightarrow m = -2$ (be careful to include the minus)

(iii) $y = x + 5 \Rightarrow m = 1$ (not zero)

(iv) $2y = 7x - 10$ (divide each term by 2 to get)

$$y = \frac{7}{2}x - 5 \Rightarrow m = \frac{7}{2}$$

(v) $y - 6x = 0$

$$y = 6x \Rightarrow m = 6$$

(vi) $3y + 2x + 12 = 0$

$$3y = -2x - 12 \quad \text{(divide each term by 3 to get)}$$

$$y = \frac{-2}{3}x - 4 \Rightarrow m = -\frac{2}{3}$$

exam Q

k is the line $2x - y + 5 = 0$.

Find the equation of the line that is parallel to k and passes through the point $(-1, 4)$.

Solution

Find the slope of the line k:
$$2x - y + 5 = 0$$

Slope $= -\dfrac{\text{Number in front of } x}{\text{Number in front of } y}$

Slope $= -\dfrac{2}{-1}$

Slope $= 2$

Since k is parallel to the required line, the slope of the required line is $+2$.

Find the equation of the line with slope, $m = 2$ and passes through the point $(-1, 4) = (x_1, y_1)$:
$$y - y_1 = m(x - x_1)$$
$$y - 4 = 2(x - (-1))$$
$$y - 4 = 2(x + 1)$$
$$y - 4 = 2x + 2$$
$$0 = 2x - y + 2 + 4$$
$$0 = 2x - y + 6$$

To verify that a point belongs to a line

To verify that a point belongs to a line, substitute the coordinates of the point into the equation of the line. If the coordinates satisfy the equation, then the point is on the line. Otherwise, the point is not on the line.

Example

Investigate if the points $(-2, 9)$ and $(-5, 3)$ are on the line $5x - 3y + 34 = 0$.

Solution

$(-2, 9)$ $\quad 5x - 3y + 34 = 0$
Substitute $x = -2$ and $y = 9$
$$5(-2) - 3(9) + 34$$
$$= -10 - 27 + 34$$
$$= -37 + 34$$
$$= -3 \neq 0$$
Does not satisfy the equation
$\therefore (-2, 9)$ is not on the line.

$(-5, 3)$ $\quad 5x - 3y + 34 = 0$
Substitute $x = -5$ and $y = 3$
$$5(-5) - 3(3) + 34$$
$$= -25 - 9 + 34$$
$$= -34 + 34$$
$$= 0$$
Satisfies the equation
$\therefore (-5, 3)$ is on the line.

COORDINATE GEOMETRY OF THE LINE

Example

(i) The point $(k, -2)$ is on the line $4x + 3y - 14 = 0$. Find the value of k.
(ii) The point $(1, 2)$ is on the line $3x + ty - 11 = 0$. Find the value of t.

Solution

(i) $4x + 3y - 14 = 0$
Substitute $x = k$ and $y = -2$
$4(k) + 3(-2) - 14 = 0$
$4k - 6 - 14 = 0$
$4k - 20 = 0$
$4k = 20$
$k = 5$

(ii) $3x + ty - 11 = 0$
Substitute $x = 1$ and $y = 2$
$3(1) + t(2) - 11 = 0$
$3 + 2t - 11 = 0$
$2t - 8 = 0$
$2t = 8$
$t = 4$

Graphing lines

To draw a line, we need only two points. The easiest points to find are where lines cut the x- and y-axes. This is known as the **intercept method**.

> **key point**
> On the x-axis, $y = 0$. On the y-axis, $x = 0$.

To draw a line, do the following:

> 1. Let $y = 0$ and find x.
> 2. Let $x = 0$ and find y.
> 3. Plot these two points.
> 4. Draw the line through these points.

If the constant in the equation of a line is zero, e.g. $3x - 5y = 0$, or $4x = 3y$, then the line will pass through the origin, $(0, 0)$. In this case the **intercept method** will not work.

To draw a line that contains the origin, $(0, 0)$, do the following:

> 1. Choose a suitable value for x and find the corresponding value for y (or vice versa).
> 2. Plot this point.
> 3. A line drawn through this point and the origin is the required line.

key point

One method that usually works is to let x equal the number in front of y and then find the corresponding value for y (or vice versa).

Example

Graph the line $3x + 4y = 0$.

Solution

1. Let $x = 4$ (number in front of y).

$$3x + 4y = 0$$
$$\downarrow$$
$$3(4) + 4y = 0$$
$$12 + 4y = 0$$
$$4y = -12$$
$$y = -3$$

2. Plot the point $(4, -3)$.
3. Draw the line through the points $(4, -3)$ and $(0, 0)$.

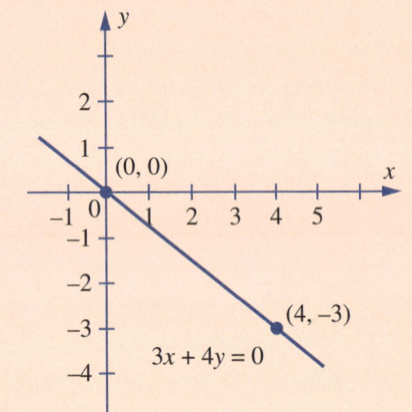

Lines parallel to the axes

$x = 2$ is a line parallel to the y-axis through 2 on the x-axis.
$y = -1$ is a line parallel to the x-axis through -1 on the y-axis.

key point

$y = 0$ is the equation of the x-axis.
$x = 0$ is the equation of the y-axis.

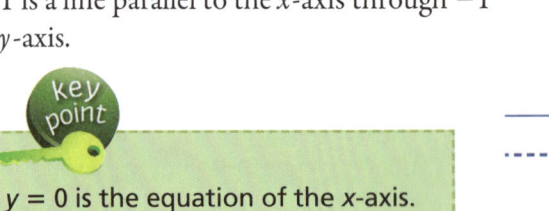

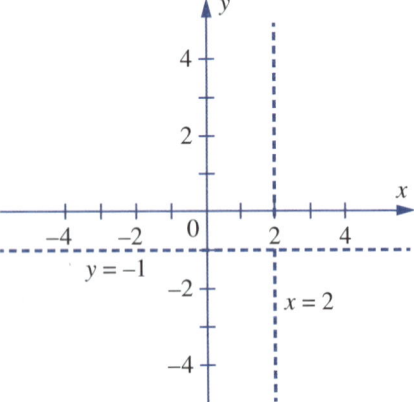

exam focus

All horizontal lines (parallel to x-axis) have an angle of inclination of 0°, which shows their slopes are zero.

All vertical lines (parallel to y-axis) have an angle of inclination of 90°, which shows their slopes are infinitely steep.

COORDINATE GEOMETRY OF THE LINE

exam Q

p is the line $5x - 6y + 30 = 0$.

p cuts the x-axis at A and the y-axis at B.

(i) Find the coordinates of A and B.

(ii) Draw the graph of p.

(iii) Find the area of the triangle OAB, where O is the origin.

Solution

(i) On the x-axis, $y = 0$.

On the y-axis, $x = 0$.

$$5x - 6y = -30$$

$y = 0$	$x = 0$
$5x - 0 = -30$	$0 - 6y = -30$
$x = -6$	$6y = 30$
$(-6, 0)$	$y = 5$
	$(0, 5)$

(ii) Graph showing line p passing through $A(-6, 0)$ and $B(0, 5)$.

The coordinates are $A(-6, 0)$ and $B(0, 5)$.

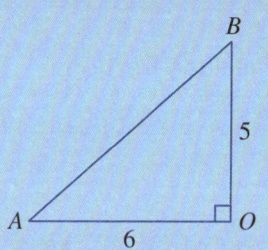

(iii) Right triangle with vertices A, B, O; base 6 (from A to O), height 5 (from O to B).

Area of triangle OAB

$= \dfrac{1}{2}$ (base) (perpendicular height)

$= \dfrac{1}{2}(6)(5)$

$= 15$

exam Q

k is the line $2x - 5y + 15 = 0$.

(i) Find the slope of k.

(ii) k cuts the x-axis at the point Q. Find the coordinates of the point Q.

Solution

(i) $2x - 5y + 15 = 0$

$-5y = -2x - 15$

$5y = 2x + 15$ (multiply each term by -1)

$$y = \frac{2}{5}x + \frac{15}{5}$$

∴ The slope of the line $k = \frac{2}{5}$. (using $y = mx + c$)

(ii) On the x-axis $y = 0$, hence, we put $y = 0$ into

$2x - 5y + 15 = 0$

$2x - 5(0) + 15 = 0$

$2x - 0 + 15 = 0$

$2x + 15 = 0$

$2x = -15$

$x = -\frac{15}{2}$

When $y = 0$, $x = -\frac{15}{2}$.

The line k cuts the x-axis at the point $Q\left(-\frac{15}{2}, 0\right)$.

exam focus

Sometimes the answers to challenging questions may include fractions.

exam Q

$l: x + 2y = 4$ and $k: x + y = 3$ are the equations of two lines shown on the diagram.

(i) From the graph, write down the point of intersection of l and k.

(ii) Solve algebraically the simultaneous equations

$x + 2y = 4$

$x + y = 3$

and verify your answer to part (i).

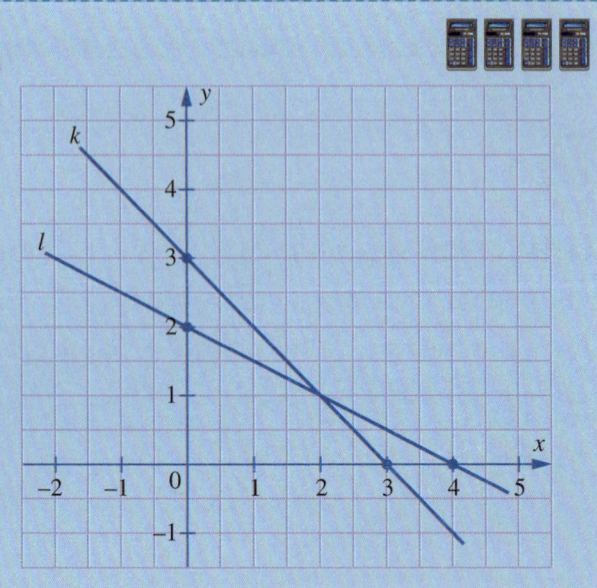

COORDINATE GEOMETRY OF THE LINE

Solution

(i) From the graph the point of intersection is (2, 1).

(ii) Label the equations ① and ②.

$$x + 2y = 4 \quad ①$$
$$x + y = 3 \quad ②$$

Make the coefficients of *x* the same but of opposite signs.

Leave ① unchanged, multiply ② by –1.

Add these new equations.

$$x + 2y = 4 \quad ①$$
$$-x - y = -3 \quad ② \times -1$$
$$y = 1$$

Put *y* = 1 into ① or ②

$$x + y = 3 \quad ②$$
$$\downarrow$$
$$x + 1 = 3$$
$$x = 2$$

key point

More examples on solving simultaneous equations may be found in *Less Stress More Success Maths Book 1*.

Therefore the point of intersection of *L* and *K* is (2, 1), which is the same answer as in part (i).

2 Geometry Theorems

aims
- To be familiar with the geometry terms listed in the glossary
- To know all theorems, corollaries and axioms
- To be able to solve problems applying the theorems, corollaries and axioms

Glossary of terms

You should be familiar with the following words and their meanings.

Axiom:	An axiom is a statement which is assumed to be true. It can be accepted without a proof and used as a basis for an argument.
Converse:	The converse of a theorem is formed by taking the conclusion as the starting point and having the starting point as the conclusion.
Corollary:	A corollary follows after a theorem and is a statement which must be true because of that theorem.
Implies:	The word implies indicates a logical relationship between two statements, such that if the first is true then the second must be true.
Is congruent to:	Two things are said to be congruent if they are identical in size and shape.
Proof:	A proof is a sequence of statements (made up of axioms, assumptions and arguments) that follow logically from the preceding one, starting at an axiom or previously proven theorem and ending with the statement of the theorem to be proven.
Theorem:	A theorem is a statement which has been proved to be true, deduced from axioms by logical argument.

You are required to know the following axioms, theorems and corollaries and must be able to apply them in answering geometric questions.

Axioms

Axiom 1: There is exactly one line through any two given points.

GEOMETRY THEOREMS

Axiom 2: **Ruler axiom**

The distance between points P and Q has the following properties:
1. The distance $|PQ|$ is never negative.
2. The distance between two points is the same, whether we measure from P to Q or from Q to P.
3. If there exists some point R between P and Q, then the distance from P to Q is equal to the sum of the distances from P to R and R to Q.

$$|PR| + |RQ| = |PQ|$$

4. Marking off a distance:

   A ray is a line which starts at a point. Given any ray from P, and given any real number $k \geq 0$, there is a unique point Q on the ray whose distance from P is k.

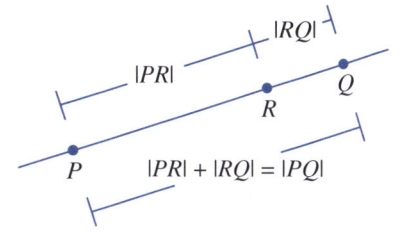

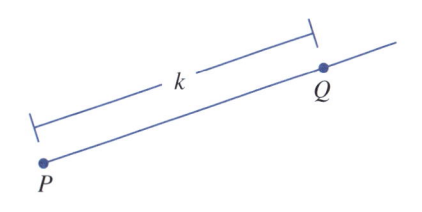

Axiom 3: **Protractor axiom**

The number of degrees in an angle (also known as its degree-measure) is always a number between 0° and 360°. It has these properties:
1. A straight angle has 180°.
2. If we know the angle $A°$, opened up at a point P, then there are two possible rays from P that form that angle.
3. If an angle is divided into two, then that angle is equal to the sum of the two angles that make it up.

$$|\angle QPR| = |\angle QPS| + |\angle SPR|$$
$$|\angle QPR| = A° + B°$$

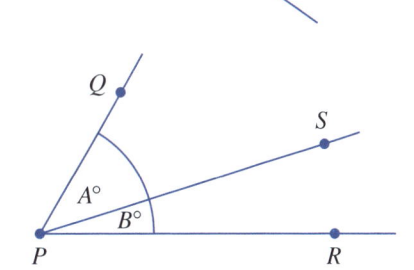

Axiom 4: **Congruent triangles**

We can say that two triangles are congruent if:
1. SAS: Two sides and the angle in between are the same in both.
2. ASA: Two angles and a side are the same in both.

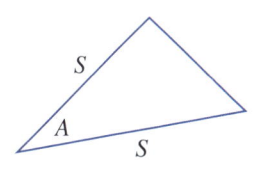

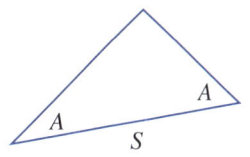

3. **SSS:** All three sides are the same in both.

4. **RHS:** The right angle, hypotenuse and another side are the same in both.

Axiom 5: Given any line l and a point P, there is exactly one line through P that is parallel to l.

Note: arrows on lines indicate that the lines are parallel.

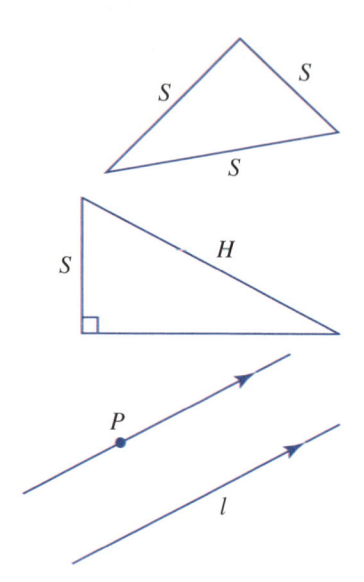

Theorems

- The application of all theorems can be examined.
- You must understand the steps involved in the proofs for theorems 1, 2, 3, 4, 5, 6, 9, 10, 13, 14, 15 and corollaries 3, 4. These proofs will be in your school textbook.

  You may be asked questions about these proofs on an exam paper, but **you are not expected to learn them off**.

- You may be asked to use these geometry theorems to prove certain things in a question.

key point
Theorems 7, 8, 11 and 12 and corollaries 1 and 2 are **not** on this course.

Theorem 1: **Vertically opposite angles**
Vertically opposite angles are equal in measure.

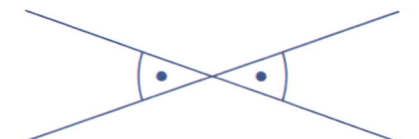

Theorem 2: **Isosceles triangles**
1. In an isosceles triangle, the angles opposite the equal sides are equal.
2. Conversely, if two angles are equal, then the triangle is isosceles.

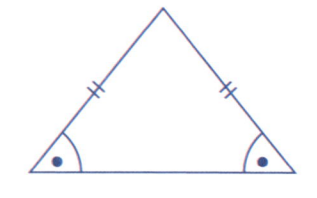

Theorem 3: **Alternate angles**
If a transversal makes equal alternate angles on two lines, then the lines are parallel (and converse).

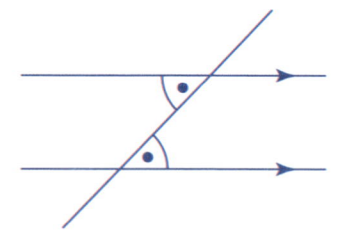

GEOMETRY THEOREMS

Theorem 4: **Angles in a triangle**

The angles in any triangle add to 180°.

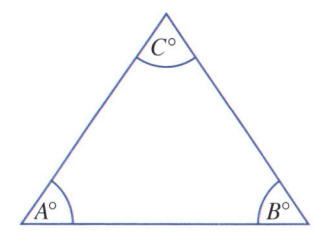

$A° + B° + C° = 180°$

Theorem 5: **Corresponding angles**

Two lines are parallel if, and only if, for any transversal, the corresponding angles are equal.

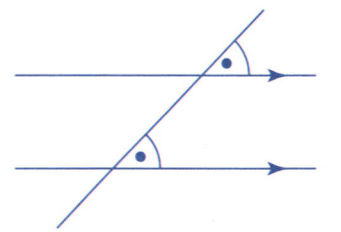

Theorem 6: **Exterior angle**

Each exterior angle of a triangle is equal to the sum of the interior opposite angles.

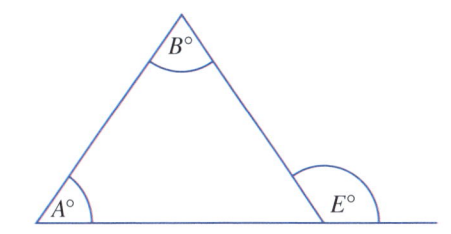

$E° = A° + B°$

Theorem 9: **Parallelograms**

In a parallelogram, opposite sides are equal and opposite angles are equal.

Two converses of this theorem are true:

1. If the opposite angles of a quadrilateral are equal, then it is a parallelogram.
2. If the opposite sides of a quadrilateral are equal, then it is a parallelogram.

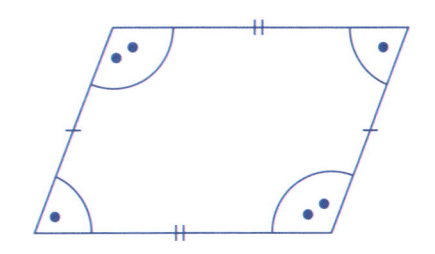

Theorem 10: **Diagonals of a parallelogram**

The diagonals of a parallelogram bisect each other.

Converse:

If the diagonals of a quadrilateral bisect one another, then it is a parallelogram.

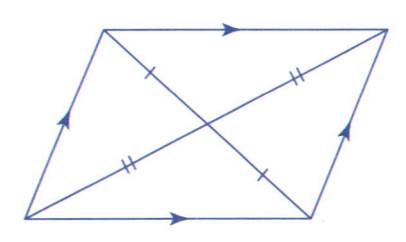

Theorem 13: Similar triangles

If two triangles are similar, then their sides are proportional, in order.

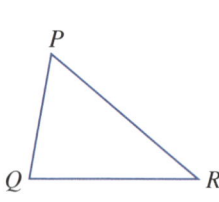

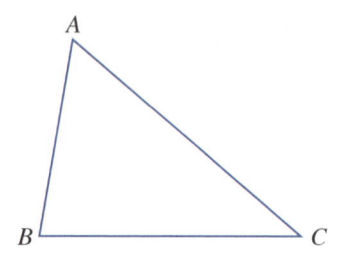

$$\left|\frac{PQ}{AB}\right| = \left|\frac{PR}{AC}\right| = \left|\frac{QR}{BC}\right|$$

Converse:

If the corresponding sides of two triangles are proportional, then they are similar.

Theorem 14: Theorem of Pythagoras

In a right-angled triangle, the square of the hypotenuse is the sum of the squares of the other two sides.

$$|AC|^2 = |AB|^2 + |BC|^2$$

Theorem 15: Converse to Pythagoras

If the square of one side is equal to the sum of the squares of the other two sides, then the angle opposite the first side is a right angle.

Corollaries

Corollary 3: Each angle in a semicircle is a right angle.

Corollary 4: If the angle standing on a chord $[BC]$ at some point on the circle is a right angle, then $[BC]$ is a diameter.

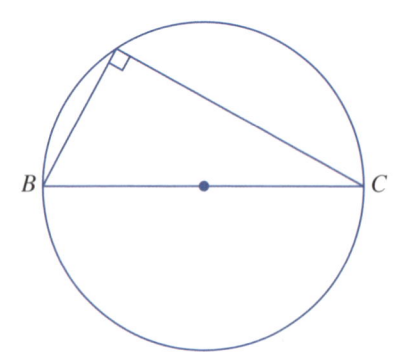

---

exam focus

When solving questions which involve diagrams, it is often helpful to do rough copies, in pencil, of the diagram on a separate piece of paper. This allows you to mark things on the diagram and to try different approaches, **without drawing on the original image**. This can be useful if you take the wrong approach the first time. You still have a clean diagram to work from.

GEOMETRY THEOREMS

Application and use of theorems

You must know all of the theorems very well and be able to apply them when solving geometric problems.

key point
- Be aware that there may be more than one method of proof for answering questions by the application of theorems.
- Many geometry problems will involve aspects of trigonometry.

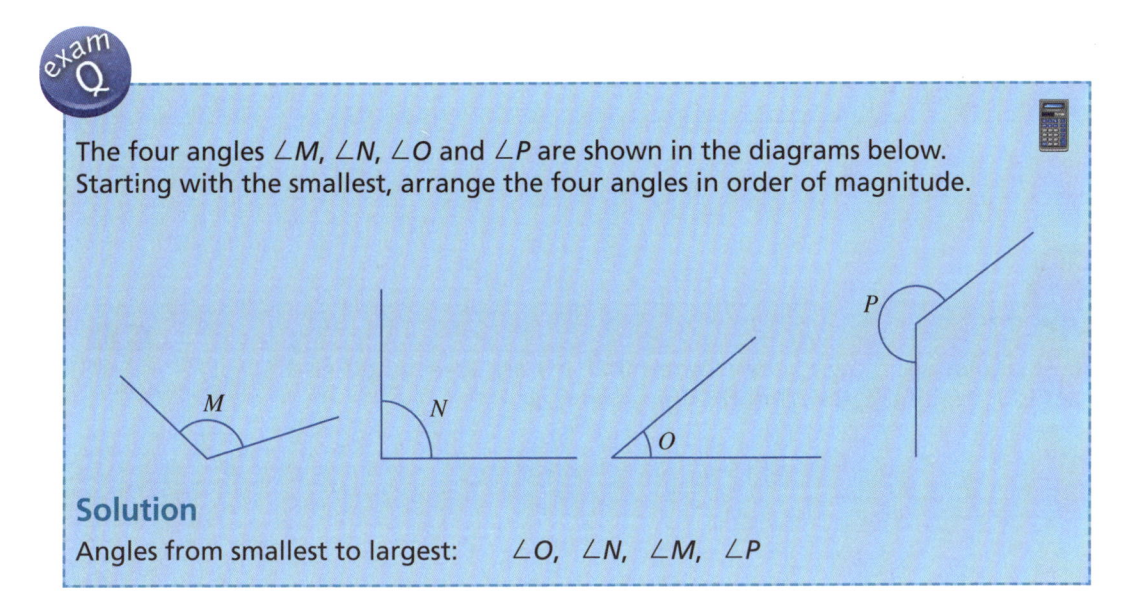

exam Q

The four angles $\angle M$, $\angle N$, $\angle O$ and $\angle P$ are shown in the diagrams below. Starting with the smallest, arrange the four angles in order of magnitude.

Solution
Angles from smallest to largest: $\angle O$, $\angle N$, $\angle M$, $\angle P$

exam Q

Cian used a protractor to measure the angle α in the diagram.
His answer was 100°.
Do you agree or disagree with Cian's measurement?
Give a reason for your answer.

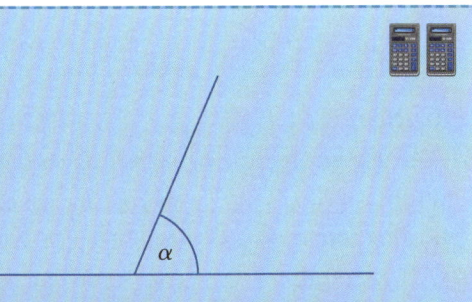

Solution
I disagree with Cian's measurement.
The angle α in the diagram is an acute angle which means it is smaller than 90°. Therefore, Cian's measurement of 100° must be wrong.

exam Q

Choose the correct terms for *A*, *B* and *C* from the following list:

        Radius
        Diameter
        Circumference
        Centre
        Chord

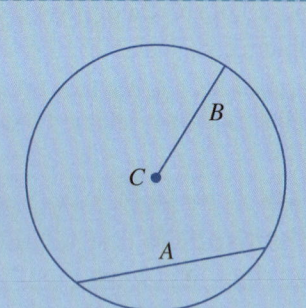

Solution
    A = Chord
    B = Radius
    C = Centre

exam Q

Four angles are shown below. Determine, in each case, whether the angle is straight, acute, obtuse, right or reflex.

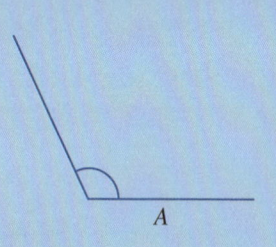

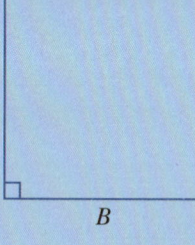

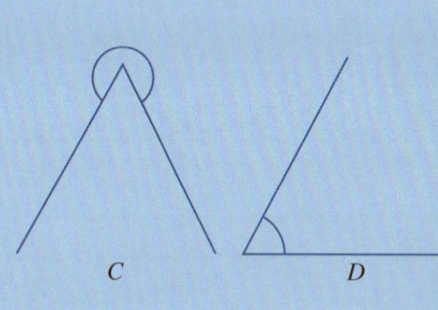

       A   B   C   D

Solution
A: Obtuse angle   (marked angle is greater than 90°)
B: Right angle   (marked angle is equal to 90°)
C: Reflex angle   (marked angle is greater than 180°)
D: Acute angle   (marked angle is less than 90°)

GEOMETRY THEOREMS

exam Q

Four triangles are shown below. Determine, in each case, whether the triangle is scalene, isosceles, equilateral or right angled.

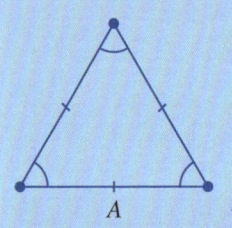

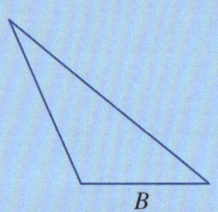

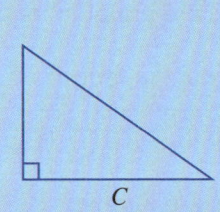

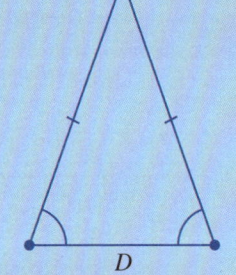

Solution

A: Equilateral triangle   (all three sides are equal and all three angles are equal)
B: Scalene triangle   (none of the three sides are equal)
C: Right-angled triangle   (one of the angles is a right angle, 90°)
D: Isosceles triangle   (two of the sides are equal and the two base angles are equal)

exam Q

The measurements of the sides of 4 triangles are as shown in the table.

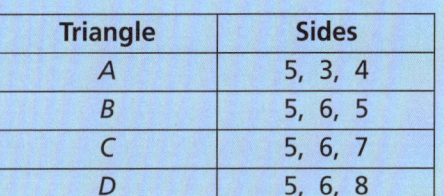

Which triangle is isosceles?
Give a reason for your answer.

Triangle	Sides
A	5, 3, 4
B	5, 6, 5
C	5, 6, 7
D	5, 6, 8

Solution
An isosceles triangle is a triangle which has two sides equal.
Triangle B is the only triangle with two sides equal. Therefore, triangle B is isosceles.

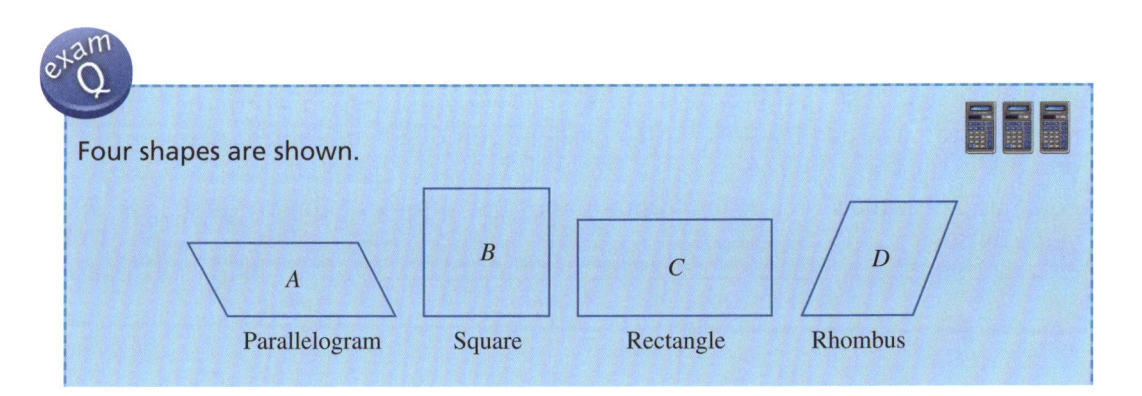

exam Q

Four shapes are shown.

A: Parallelogram   B: Square   C: Rectangle   D: Rhombus

Tick (✓) below to show the shapes for which the statements are always true.

	A	B	C	D
The diagonals bisect each other				
Opposite sides are equal in length				
All sides are equal in length				
The diagonals are equal in length				
Opposite sides are parallel				

Solution

	A	B	C	D
The diagonals bisect each other	✓	✓	✓	✓
Opposite sides are equal in length	✓	✓	✓	✓
All sides are equal in length		✓		✓
The diagonals are equal in length		✓	✓	
Opposite sides are parallel	✓	✓	✓	✓

exam focus

In a recent exam, this question was very poorly answered. Consequently, the entire question was awarded 5 marks, with a partial credit of 3 marks awarded for any **one** tick in the correct place.

You must know the structure and properties of the different geometrical shapes on your course.

Finding missing angles in a geometrical shape

Example

Two lines p and q intersect as shown in the diagram.

Find the values of angles A and B.

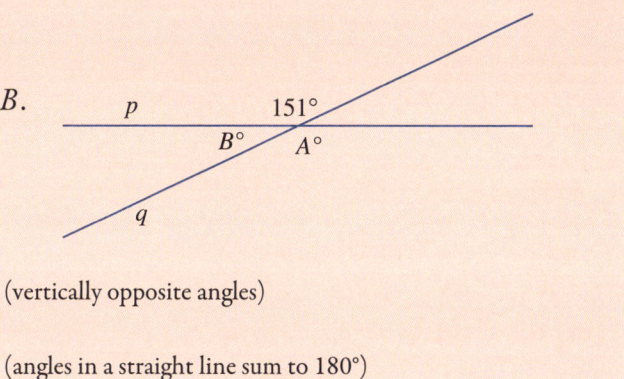

Solution

$A = 151°$ (vertically opposite angles)

$151° + B = 180°$ (angles in a straight line sum to 180°)
$B = 180° - 151°$ (subtract 151° from both sides)
$B = 29°$

Example

Find the value of angles A and B in the diagram.

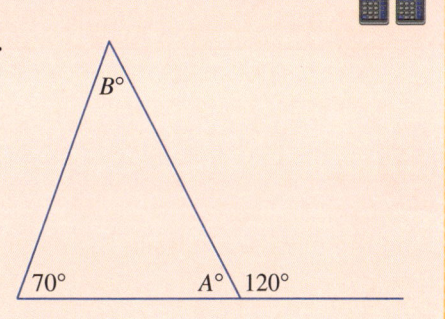

Solution

$120° + A° = 180°$ (straight angle)
$A° = 180° - 120°$ (subtract 120° from both sides)
$A° = 60°$

$70° + 60° + B° = 180°$ (angles of a triangle sum to 180°)
$130° + B° = 180°$
$B° = 180° - 130°$ (subtract 130° from both sides)
$B° = 50°$

Example

l and *m* are parallel lines.

Find the value of *x* and the value of *y*, in the diagram.

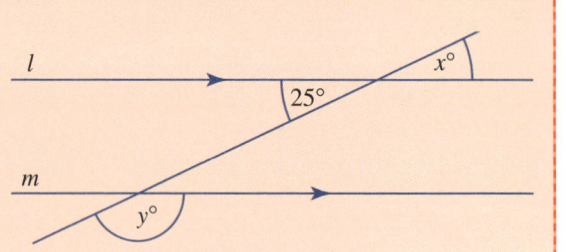

Solution

$x° = 25°$ (vertically opposite angles)

Enter the alternate angle of 25°, as shown in blue on the diagram:

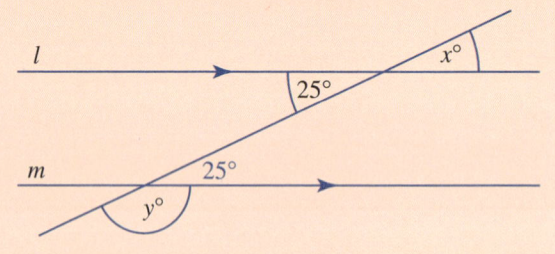

$y° + 25° = 180°$ (straight line)
$\quad y° = 180° - 25°$ (subtract 25° from both sides)
$\quad y° = 155°$

exam Q

Find the missing angles in the diagram:

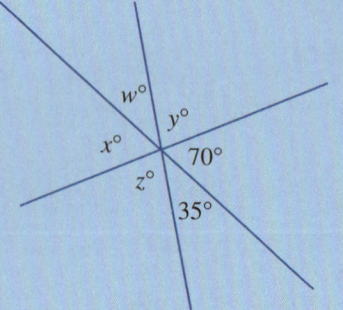

Solution

$y° + 70° + 35° = 180°$ (straight angle) $x° = 70°$ (vertically opposite)
$\quad y° + 105° = 180°$ $w° = 35°$ (vertically opposite)
$\quad\quad\quad y° = 180° - 105°$ $z° = y° = 75°$ (vertically opposite)
$\quad\quad\quad y° = 75°$

GEOMETRY THEOREMS

exam Q

In the diagram $l_1 \parallel l_2$.

Write the measure of each angle shown by an empty box into the diagram, without using a protractor.

Solution
Using the fact that some of the angles are vertically opposite, alternate, corresponding or in a straight angle, the angles can be found as follows:

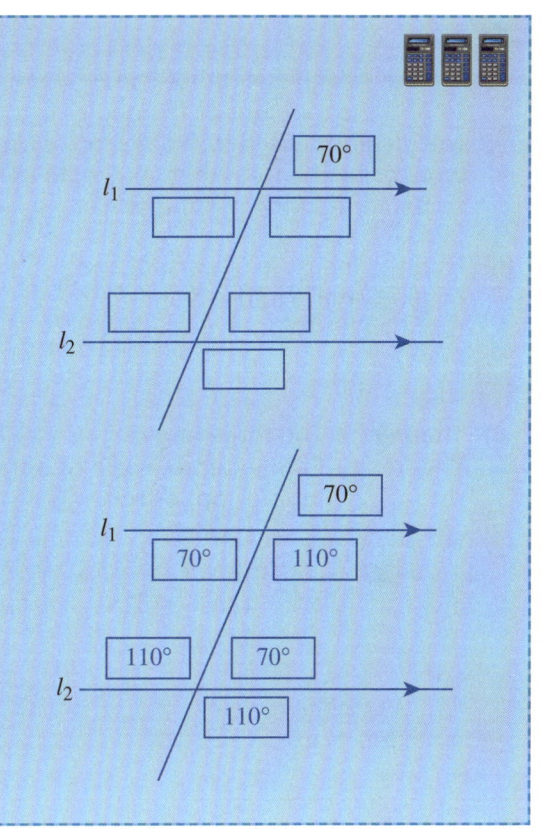

l_1 — 70°, 110° (top row with 70° given)
l_2 — 110°, 70°, 110°

Example
Find the value of x and the value of y in the diagram.

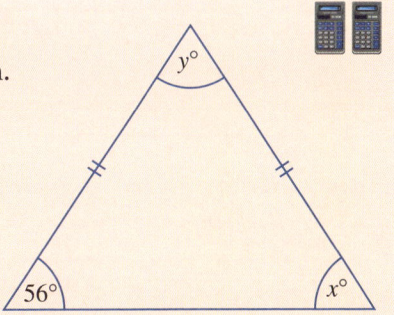

Solution
$x° = 56°$ (base angles of an isosceles triangle)

$56° + 56° + y° = 180°$ (angles of a triangle sum to 180°)
$112° + y° = 180°$
$y° = 180° - 112°$ (subtract 112° from both sides)
$y° = 68°$

exam Q

(i) Theorems on your course can be used to find the measure of the angles in the diagram. Write down, in your own words, any theorem that you could use to find one of the missing angles.

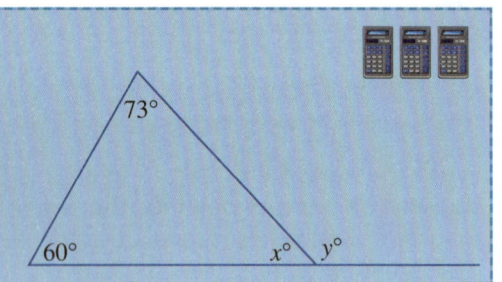

(ii) Find the measure of each of the missing angles in the diagram in part (i). Show your calculations.

Solution

(i) **Theorem:** The three angles in a triangle add up to 180°.
   Theorem: Each exterior angle of a triangle is equal to the sum of the interior opposite angles.

(ii) $60° + 73° + x° = 180°$ (three angles of a triangle sum to 180°)
   $133° + x° = 180°$
   $x° = 180° - 133°$ (subtract 133° from both sides)
   $x° = 47°$

   $60° + 73° = y°$ (exterior angle equal sum of interior opposite angles)
   $133° = y°$

Example

In the diagram, $|AB| = |BC|$ and $|AD| = |AC| = |CD|$.

Find:
(i) $|\angle BAC|$
(ii) $|\angle ADC|$
(iii) $|\angle BAD|$

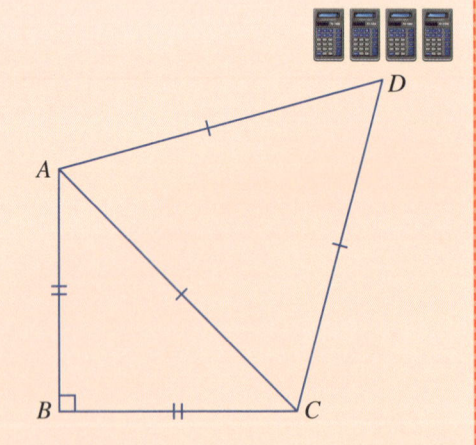

Solution

(i) In $\triangle ABC$:
   $|\angle ABC| + |\angle BAC| + |\angle BCA| = 180°$ (three angles of a triangle sum to 180°)
   $90° + |\angle BAC| + |\angle BCA| = 180°$
   $|\angle BAC| + |\angle BCA| = 90°$

   But $|\angle BAC| = |\angle BCA|$ ($\triangle ABC$ is isosceles)
   $\therefore |\angle BAC| = 45°$

GEOMETRY THEOREMS

(ii) Since $\triangle ADC$ is equilateral, the three angles are 60° each.
$$\therefore |\angle ADC| = 60°$$

(iii) $|\angle BAD| = |\angle BAC| + |\angle CAD|$
$|\angle BAD| = 45° + 60°$
$\therefore |\angle BAD| = 105°$

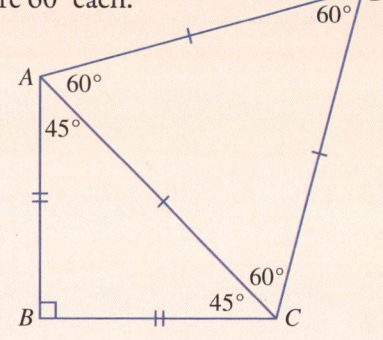

exam focus

This was a challenging question, since no numbers were given. You needed to know what equilateral and isosceles triangles are.

Reminder: The three angles in an equilateral triangle are 60° each.

exam Q

The diagram shows a parallelogram and one exterior angle. Find the value of a and the value of b.

Solution
Construction:
Label the angle 1, as in the diagram.

Proof:
$|\angle 1| + 150° = 180°$ (straight angle)
$\quad |\angle 1| = 180° - 150°$
$\quad |\angle 1| = 30°$
$\therefore 3a = 30°$ (opposite angles of a parallelogram)
$\therefore a = 10°$ (divide both sides by 3)

Opposite angles in a parallelogram are equal in measure. Therefore, the information can be entered into the diagram as shown:

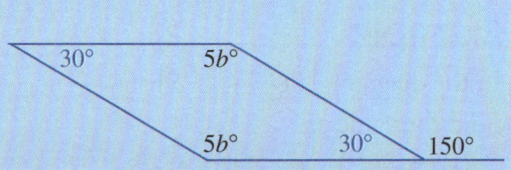

$30 + 5b + 30 + 5b = 360°$ (angles in a parallelogram sum to 360°)
$\quad\quad\quad 60 + 10b = 360°$
$\quad\quad\quad\quad\quad\quad 10b = 300°$ (subtract 60 from both sides)
$\quad\quad\quad\quad\quad\quad\quad b = 30°$ (divide both sides by 10)

Example

The diagram shows a square on top of an equilateral triangle QRS.
The point P is joined to R.

(i) Find $|\angle PQR|$.

(ii) Find $|\angle QRP|$.

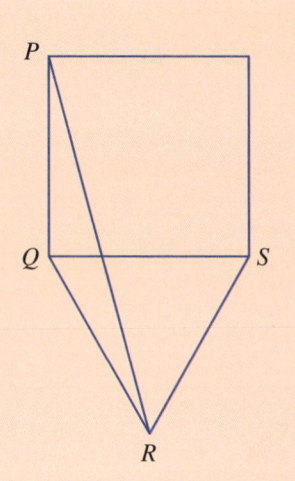

Solution

(i) $|\angle PQS| = 90°$ (one angle of a square)

$|\angle SQR| = 60°$ (one angle of an equilateral triangle)

$|\angle PQR| = |\angle PQS| + |\angle SQR|$

$|\angle PQR| = 90° + 60°$

$|\angle PQR| = 150°$

(ii) $|PQ| = |QR|$ (since the sides of the square equal the sides of the equilateral triangle)

$\therefore \triangle PQR$ is isosceles.

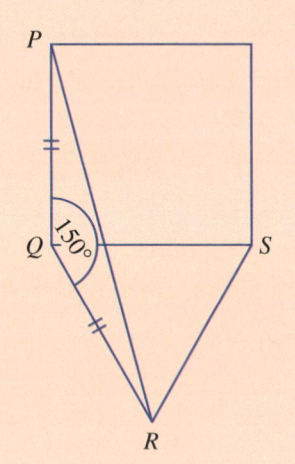

$|\angle QPR| + |\angle PQR| + |\angle QRP| = 180°$

$|\angle QPR| = |\angle QRP|$ (since $\triangle PQR$ is isosceles)

$|\angle PQR| + 2|\angle QRP| = 180°$

$\therefore 150° + 2|\angle QRP| = 180°$

$2|\angle QRP| = 30°$

$|\angle QRP| = 15°$

Example

In the diagram, $|PQ| = |PR|$.
Find the value of:

(i) x (ii) y (iii) z

In each case give a reason for your answer.

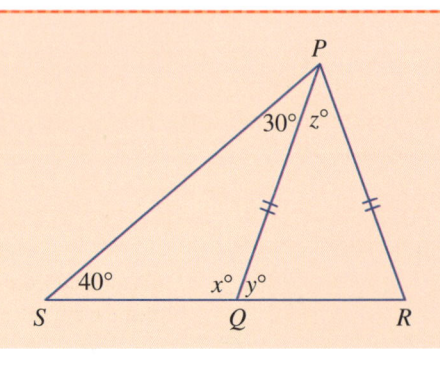

Solution:

(i) In $\triangle SQP$:
$40° + 30° + x° = 180°$ (three angles of a triangle sum to 180°)
$70° + x° = 180°$
$x° = 110°$

(ii) In $\triangle SQP$:
$40° + 30° = y°$ (exterior angle equals sum of opposite interior angles)
$70° = y°$

Alternatively:
$x° + y° = 180°$ (straight angle)
$110° + y° = 180°$
$y° = 70°$

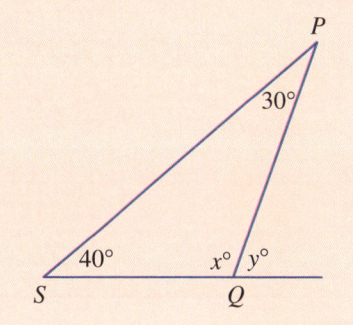

(iii) Enter the values for x and y into the diagram:
$\triangle PQR$ is isosceles

$\therefore |\angle PQR| = |\angle PRQ|$
$70° = |\angle PRQ|$

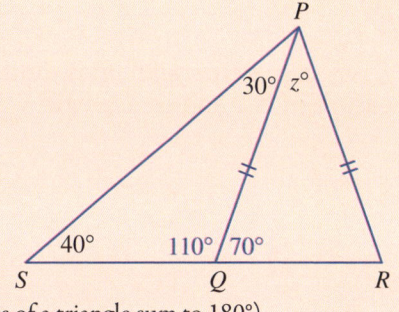

In $\triangle PQR$:
$\therefore 70° + 70° + z° = 180°$ (three angles of a triangle sum to 180°)
$140° + z° = 180°$
$z° = 40°$

Example

$[AB]$ is a diameter of a circle.
C is a point on the circle and $|\angle ABC| = 75°$.

(i) Write down $|\angle ACB|$ and give a reason for your answer.
(ii) Calculate $|\angle BAC|$.
(iii) D is another point on the circle and $|\angle ABD| = 55°$. Find $|\angle DAC|$.

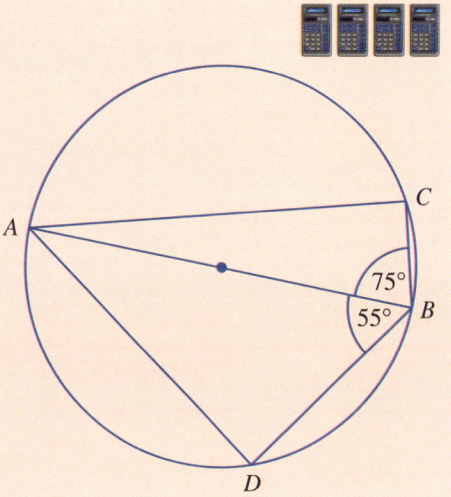

Solution

(i) $|\angle ACB| = 90°$ (angle in a semicircle is a right angle)

(ii) $|\angle BAC| + 90° + 75° = 180°$ (angles in a triangle sum to 180°)
$$|\angle BAC| + 165° = 180°$$
$$|\angle BAC| = 180° - 165° \quad \text{(subtract 165° from both sides)}$$
$$|\angle BAC| = 15°$$

(iii) $|\angle DAC| + |\angle DBC| = 180°$ (opposite angles of a cyclic quadrilateral sum to 180°)
$$|\angle DAC| + (55° + 75°) = 180°$$
$$|\angle DAC| + 130° = 180°$$
$$|\angle DAC| = 180° - 130°$$
$$|\angle DAC| = 50°$$

exam Q

If l_1, l_2 and l_3 are parallel lines, find the measure of the angles α, β and γ.

Solution

From the diagram, the three angles marked in red are corresponding angles, and so they are all equal to each other.

$\therefore \gamma = 40°$ (corresponding angles)

$40° + \beta = 180°$ (straight angle)
$\therefore \beta = 140°$

In the triangle coloured red:

The three angles of a triangle sum to 180°:

$$\alpha + 40° + 115° = 180°$$
$$\alpha + 155° = 180°$$
$$\therefore \alpha = 25°$$

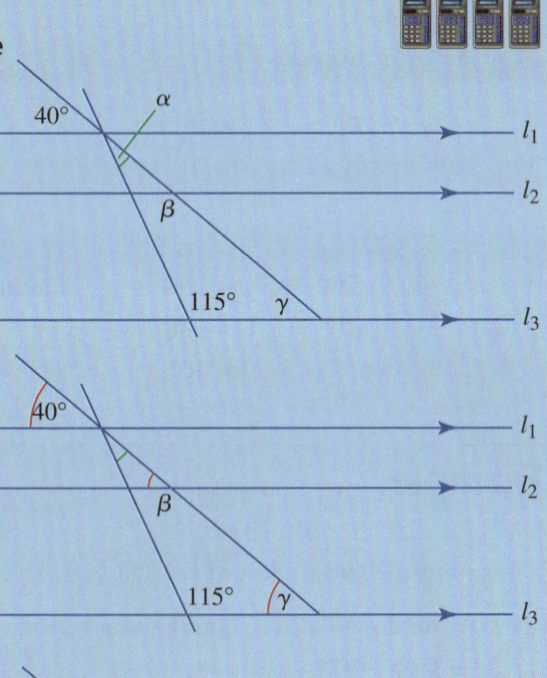

[AB] is a diameter of the circle with centre C.

D is a point on the circle as shown.

(i) Write down $|\angle ADB|$, and give a reason for your answer.

(ii) Given that $|\angle BDC| = 35°$, name another angle of 35°, and give a reason for your answer.

(iii) Write down $|\angle ACD|$, and give a reason for your answer.

(iv) Write down $|\angle CAD|$.

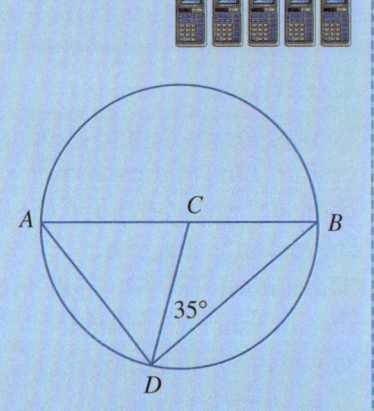

Solution

(i) $|\angle ADB| = 90°$ (angle in a semicircle is a right angle)

Reason: Angle in a semicircle is a right angle.

(ii) $|\angle CBD| = 35°$

Reason:
$\triangle CDB$ is isosceles since $|CD| = |CB|$.   (both radii)

$\therefore |\angle BDC| = |\angle DBC| = 35°$

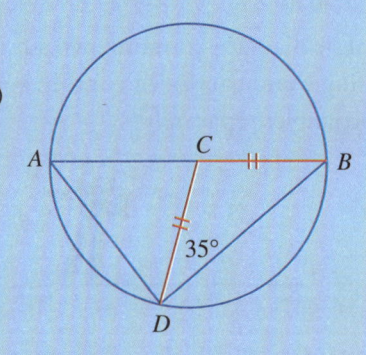

(iii) $|\angle BDC| + |\angle DBC| = |\angle ACD|$ (exterior angle equals sum of two interior opposite angles)

$$35° + 35° = |\angle ACD|$$
$$70° = |\angle ACD|$$

(iv) In $\triangle ADB$:

$|\angle ADB| = 90°$ (from part (i))
$|\angle DBA| = 35°$ (from part (ii))
$|\angle BAD| + 35° + 90° = 180°$
$|\angle BAD| + 125° = 180°$
$|\angle BAD| = 180° - 125°$
$|\angle BAD| = 55°$
$\therefore |\angle CAD| = 55°$

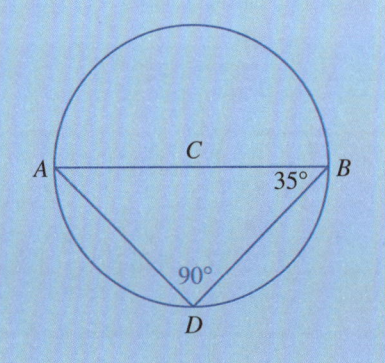

Finding missing sides or lengths in a geometrical shape

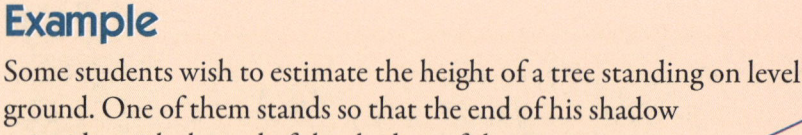

Example

Some students wish to estimate the height of a tree standing on level ground. One of them stands so that the end of his shadow coincides with the end of the shadow of the tree, as shown in the diagram.
This student is 1·62 m tall. His friend then measures the distances shown in the diagram.
Using similar triangles, or otherwise, find the height of the tree.

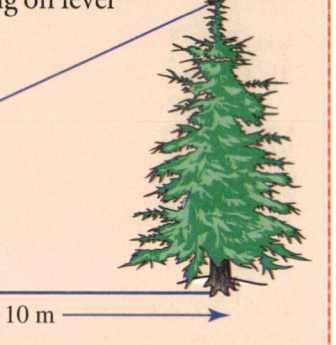

Solution

The diagram contains two similar triangles, since they have a common angle and they both contain a 90° angle. Redraw the similar triangles separately:

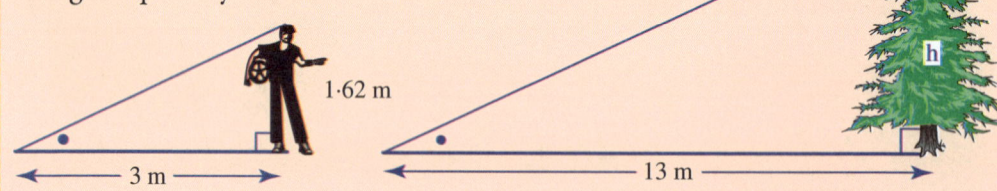

Analyse the corresponding sides:

Large triangle	Small triangle
h	1·62
13	3

Put the unknown side on the top of the left side of the fraction:

$$\frac{h}{1·62} = \frac{13}{3}$$

$$1·62\left(\frac{h}{1·62}\right) = 1·62\left(\frac{13}{3}\right) \quad \text{(multiply both sides by 1·62)}$$

$$h = 1·62\left(\frac{13}{3}\right)$$

$$h = 7·02 \text{ m}$$

exam focus

Putting the unknown quantity on the top of the left side of the equation will make the algebra easier to solve. Notice how this question unifies Algebra and Geometry.

GEOMETRY THEOREMS

exam Q

The two triangles shown are similar.

Find the value of x.

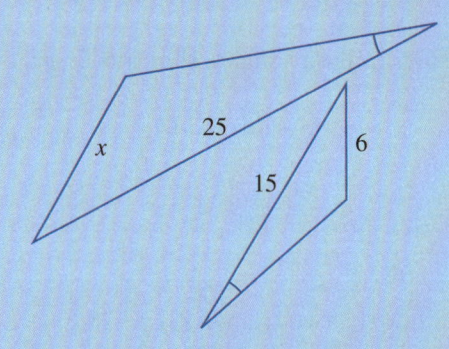

Solution

Redraw the triangles, so that they are facing the same way:

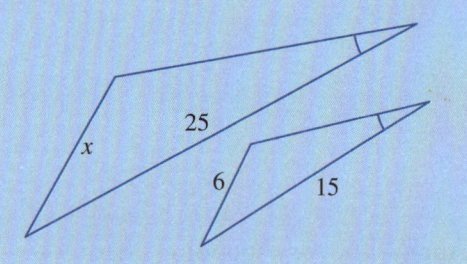

exam focus

It is not necessary to redraw similar triangles. However, this can make it easier to identify the corresponding sides. If there is not enough space to redraw the triangles on your exam paper, use different colours to highlight the corresponding sides or ask the supervisor for some extra paper.

Analyse the corresponding sides:

Large triangle	Small triangle
x	6
25	15

Put the unknown side on the top of the left side of the fraction:

$$\frac{x}{6} = \frac{25}{15}$$

$$6\left(\frac{x}{6}\right) = 6\left(\frac{25}{15}\right) \quad \text{(multiply both sides by 6)}$$

$$x = \frac{150}{15}$$

$$x = 10$$

Example

The rope on a pair of stepladders, as shown, stops the steps from opening too far.

Using similar triangles, find the length of the rope.

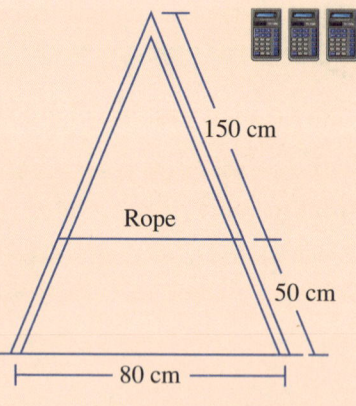

Solution

Redraw the two triangles separately and fill in all known sides:

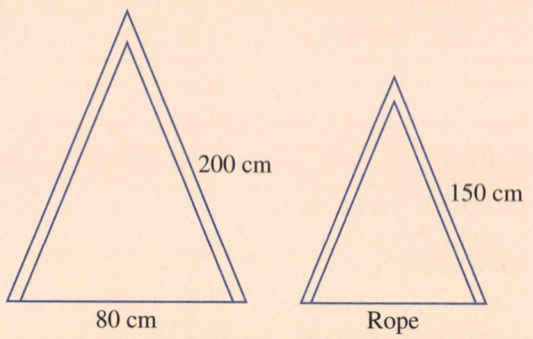

Analyse the corresponding sides:

Large triangle	Small triangle
200	150
80	Rope

Put the unknown side on the top of the left side of the fraction:

$$\frac{\text{Rope}}{80} = \frac{150}{200}$$

$$80\left(\frac{\text{Rope}}{80}\right) = 80\left(\frac{150}{200}\right) \quad \text{(multiply both sides by 80)}$$

$$\text{Rope} = \frac{12\,000}{200}$$

$$\text{Rope} = 60 \text{ cm}$$

Using geometry to prove statements

exam focus

It is important to give reasons and explanations for statements made during a proof. This shows that you understand the steps you are taking and so will help ensure that you get maximum marks in a question.

GEOMETRY THEOREMS

key point

Congruent Triangles

Two triangles are said to be congruent if they are identical in size and shape.
You must be familiar with the 4 rules for congruency.
We can say that two triangles are congruent if:

SAS
Two sides and the angle in between are the same in both.

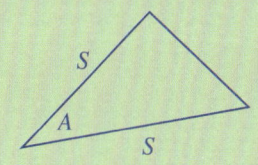

ASA
Two angles and a side are the same in both.

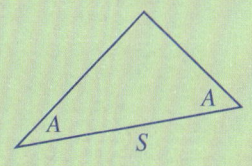

SSS
All three sides are the same in both.

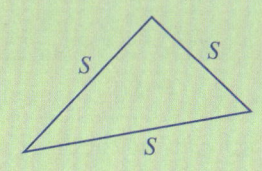

RHS
Right angle, hypotenuse and another side are the same in both.

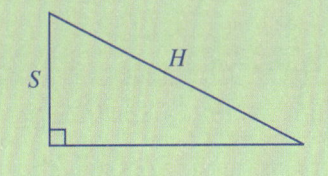

Example

Prove that the following two triangles are congruent.

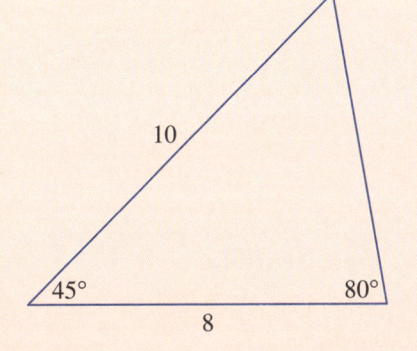

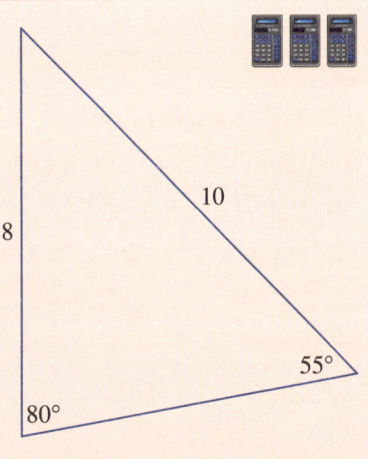

Solution

Find the measure of the angles missing in each of the triangles:

Triangle 1: Missing angle = 180° − 45° − 80° = 55°

Triangle 2: Missing angle = 180° − 55° − 80° = 45°

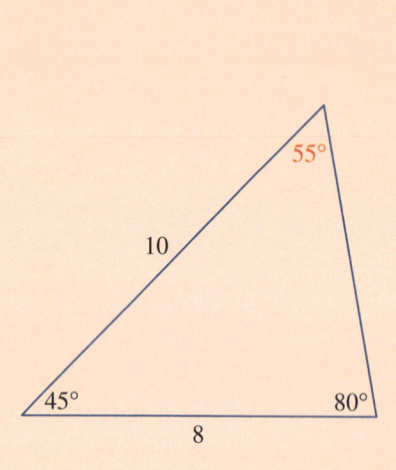

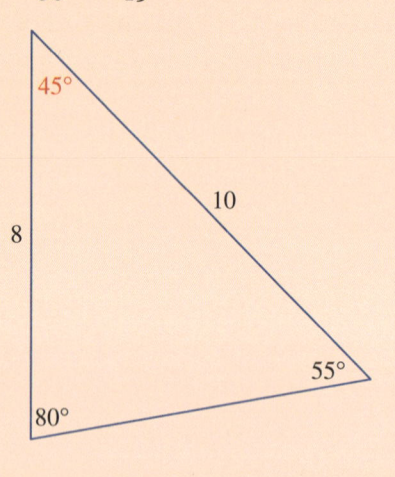

Method 1:

$8 = 8$ (side)

$10 = 10$ (side)

$45° = 45°$ (included angle)

Therefore, using the SAS rule, the triangles are congruent.

Method 2:

$8 = 8$ (side)

$45° = 45°$ (angle)

$80° = 80°$ (angle)

Therefore, using the ASA rule, the triangles are congruent.

---

exam Q

ABCD is a parallelogram.

The diagonals [*AC*] and [*BD*] intersect at the point *O*.

(i) Name an angle equal in measure to ∠*DAO*.

(ii) Prove that △*AOD* and △*BOC* are congruent.

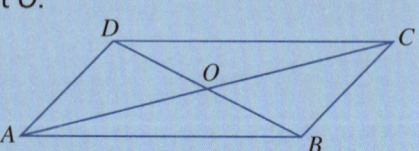

Solution

(i) ∠*DAO* = ∠*BCO*, because they are alternate angles.

(ii) |*AD*| = |*CB*| (opposite sides of a parallelogram)

|∠*DAO*| = |∠*BCO*| (alternate angles)

|∠*ADO*| = |∠*CBO*| (alternate angles)

Therefore, △*AOD* and △*BOC* are congruent. (Angle Side Angle − ASA)

GEOMETRY THEOREMS

C is the centre of the circle *k*. [AB] and [XY] are diameters of *k*.

(i) Name another line segment equal in length to [AC]. Give a reason for your answer.

(ii) Prove that △AXC and △BYC are congruent.

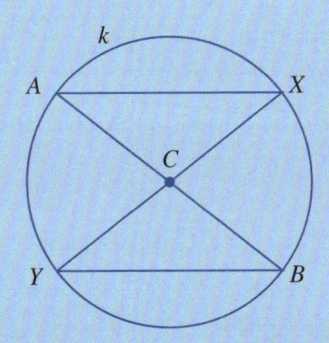

Solution

(i) |AC| = |CX| = |CY| = |CB|

Because these line segments are all radii of the circle.

(ii) |AC| = |CB| (both radii)
|CX| = |CY| (both radii)
|∠ACX| = |∠BCY| (vertically opposite angles)

Therefore, △AXC and △BYC are congruent.   (Side Angle Side – SAS)

Example

ABC is an isosceles triangle with $|CA| = |CB|$. The side $|AB|$ is extended to D and $CE \perp AB$.

(i) Name an angle equal in measure to $\angle ABC$. Give a reason for your answer.

(ii) Given that $|\angle ABC| = 58°$, find $|\angle CBD|$ and give a reason for your answer.

(iii) Given that $|AB| = 10$ cm and $|CE| = 8$ cm, find the area of $\triangle ABC$.

(iv) CE is the bisector of $\angle ACB$. Show that $\triangle ACE$ and $\triangle BCE$ are congruent.

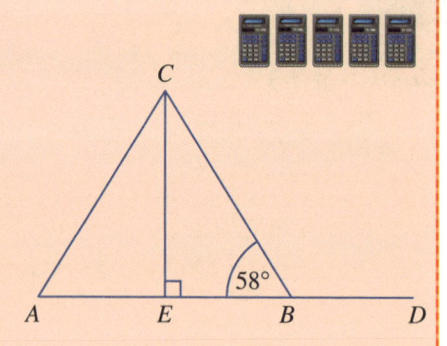

Solution

(i) $|\angle BAC| = |\angle ABC|$, since $\triangle ABC$ is isosceles.

(ii) $|\angle ABC| + |\angle CBD| = 180°$ (straight angle)
$58° + |\angle CBD| = 180°$ (given $|\angle ABC| = 58°$)
$|\angle CBD| = 180° - 58°$ (subtract 58° from both sides)
$|\angle CBD| = 122°$

(iii) Area of $\triangle ABC = \dfrac{1}{2}(\text{Base}) \times (\text{Height})$

$= \dfrac{1}{2}|AB||CE|$

$= \dfrac{1}{2}(10)(8)$

$= 40 \text{ cm}^2$

(iv) $|CE| = |CE|$ (common side)
$|CA| = |CB|$ ($\triangle ABC$ is isosceles)
$|\angle ECA| = |\angle ECB|$ (since CE is the bisector of $\angle ACB$)
$\therefore \triangle ACE$ and $\triangle BCE$ are congruent.   (Side Angle Side – SAS)

3 Constructions

aims
- ☐ To be able to complete all 13 constructions
- ☐ To be able to use your knowledge of constructions to solve practical problems

There are 13 constructions, which you must be able to perform, on the Junior Cycle Ordinary Level course. The syllabus numbers these constructions as shown in the checklist below:

Note: Constructions 3 and 7 are not shown as they are not required for the Ordinary Level course.

☐ 1. Bisector of a given angle, using only compass and straight edge.

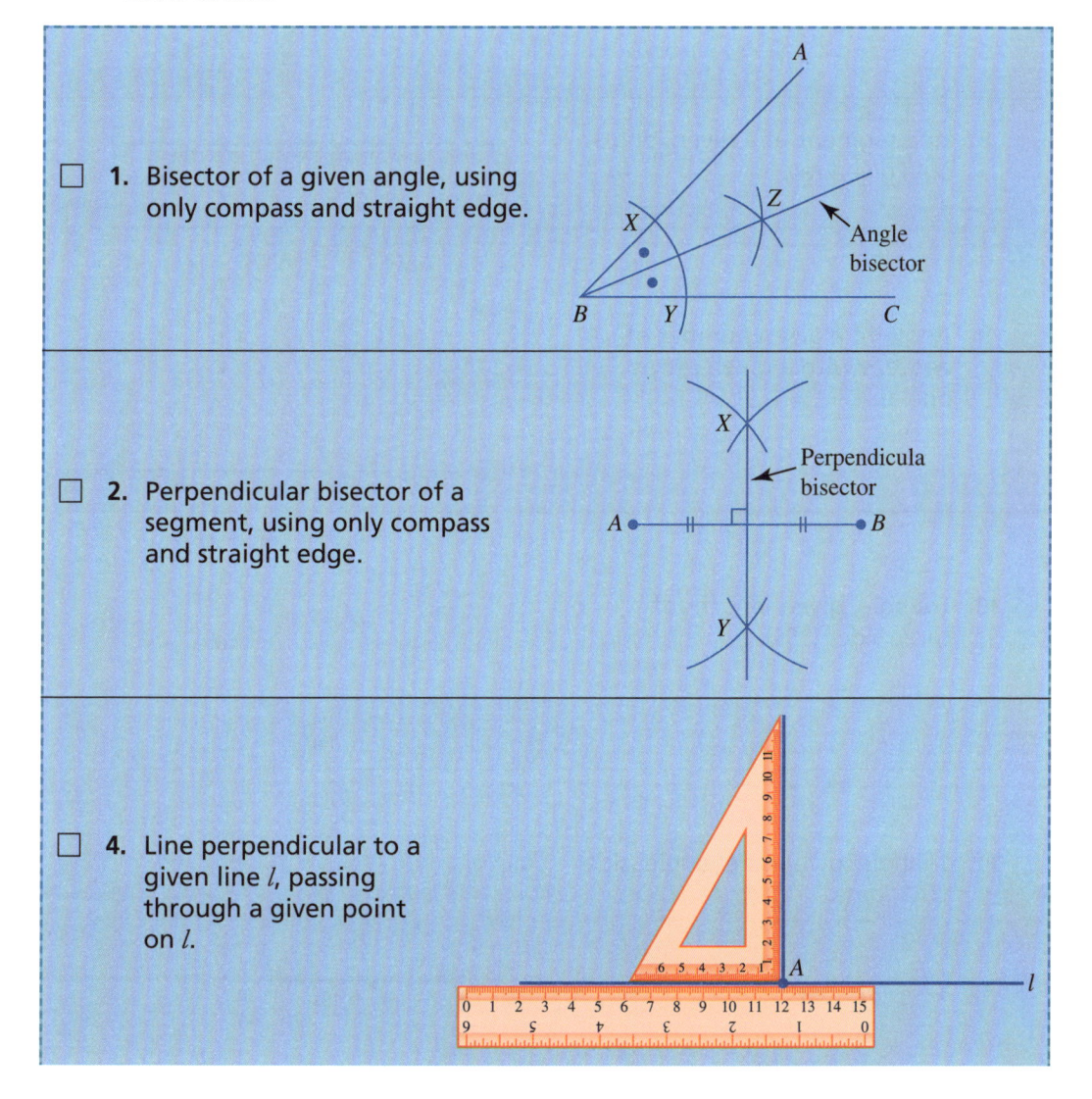

☐ 2. Perpendicular bisector of a segment, using only compass and straight edge.

☐ 4. Line perpendicular to a given line l, passing through a given point on l.

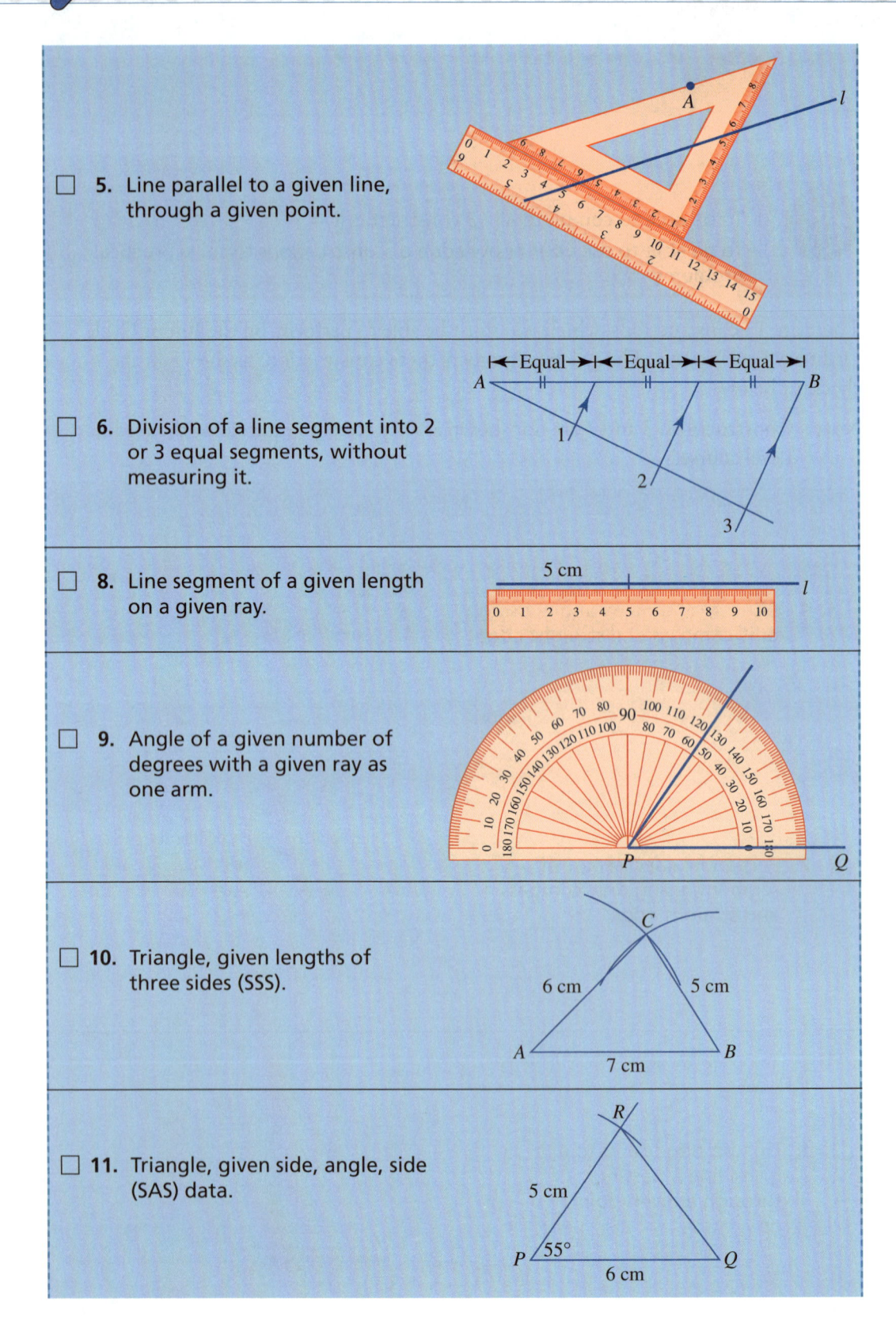

5. Line parallel to a given line, through a given point.

6. Division of a line segment into 2 or 3 equal segments, without measuring it.

8. Line segment of a given length on a given ray.

9. Angle of a given number of degrees with a given ray as one arm.

10. Triangle, given lengths of three sides (SSS).

11. Triangle, given side, angle, side (SAS) data.

CONSTRUCTIONS

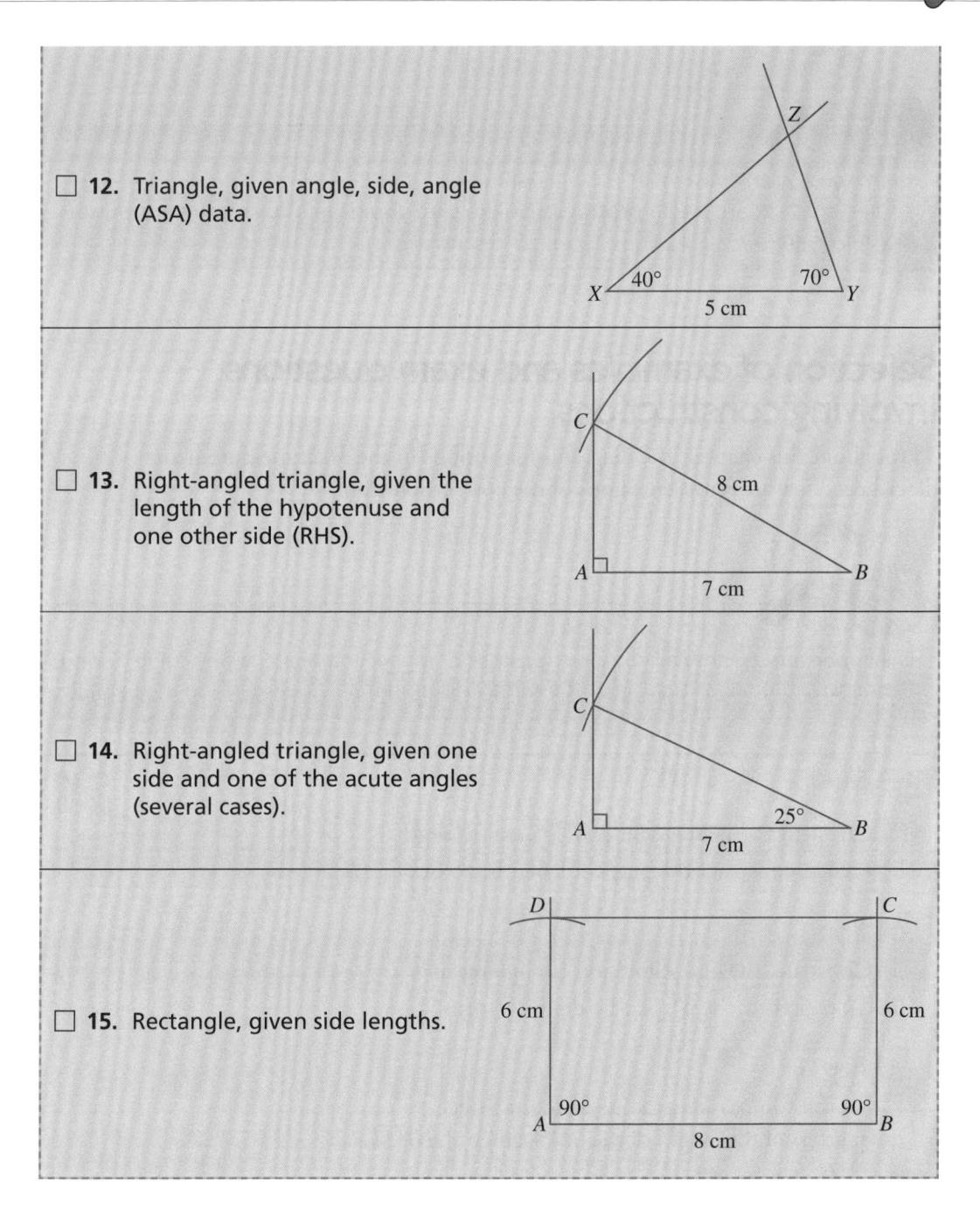

☐ **12.** Triangle, given angle, side, angle (ASA) data.

☐ **13.** Right-angled triangle, given the length of the hypotenuse and one other side (RHS).

☐ **14.** Right-angled triangle, given one side and one of the acute angles (several cases).

☐ **15.** Rectangle, given side lengths.

- Constructions numbered 3 and 7 are not listed as they are not required for the Ordinary Level course.
- The steps required for completing each of these constructions are detailed in your text book.
- Computer simulations of these constructions can be found at www.mathopenref.com.

> **exam focus**
>
> To draw accurate constructions you will need a good pencil, an eraser, a compass, a ruler, a set square and a protractor. Make sure you have a full mathematical set in your exam.

Selection of examples and exam questions involving constructions

Throughout this chapter, the diagrams may not be of the exact measurements described. They are representations of the correct solution.

> **exam focus**
>
> It is important to show **all** construction lines or marks you make at any stage during the construction. Erasing any of these may result in marks being lost in an exam.

Example

(i) Construct a line segment $[AB]$, 5 cm in length.
(ii) Hence, construct the perpendicular bisector of $[AB]$.

Solution

(i) Construct the line segment 5 cm in length: A————————B

(ii) To construct the perpendicular bisector:

Step 1:
Set the compass to a radius of about three-quarters of the length of the line segment $[AB]$.

(Any radius above half the length of the line segment will do.)

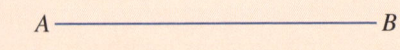

Place the compass point on A and draw arcs above and below the line segment.

Step 2:

Keep the same radius as in step 1.

Place the compass point on *B* and draw arcs above and below the line segment to intersect the other arcs.

Where the arcs intersect, label the points *X* and *Y*.

Step 3:

Draw the line through *X* and *Y*.

The line *XY* is the perpendicular bisector of the line segment [*AB*].

key point

Any point on the perpendicular bisector of a line segment [*AB*] is equidistant (same distance) from the points *A* and *B*. The perpendicular bisector of the line segment [*AB*] is always at right angles to the line segment.

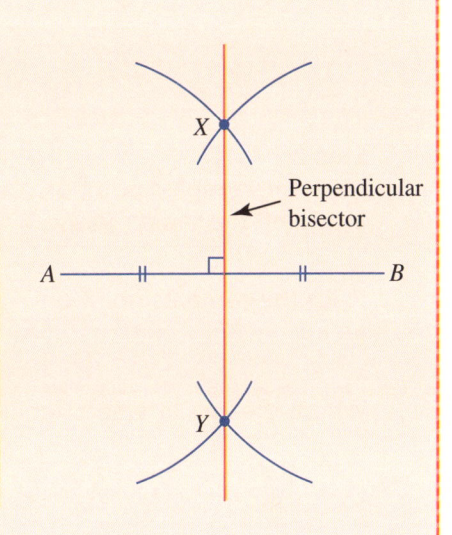

---

exam Q

(i) Construct an angle *ABC* such that $|\angle ABC| = 70°$.

(ii) Hence, without using your protractor, bisect the angle *ABC* using a compass and a straight edge.

Solution

(i) Draw the line segment [*BC*].

Place the centre of the protractor at the point *B*. Starting from the 0° mark at *C*, mark the position of 70°.

This is the position for the line segment [*BA*].

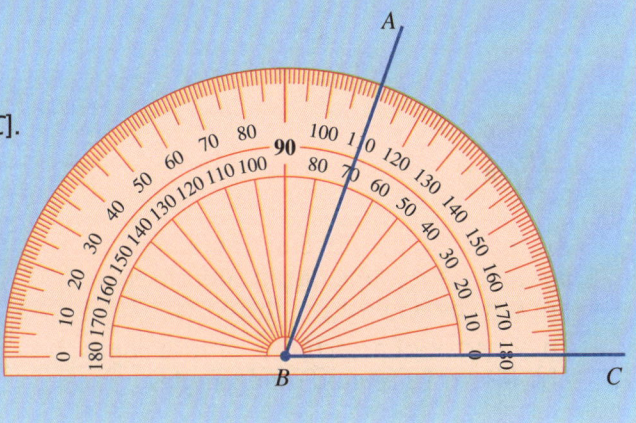

(ii) To bisect the angle ABC:

Step 1:
Set your compass to a sensible radius (neither too large nor too small).

Place the compass point on the vertex, *B*. (Corner, B)

Draw two arcs to intersect the arms at *X* and *Y*.

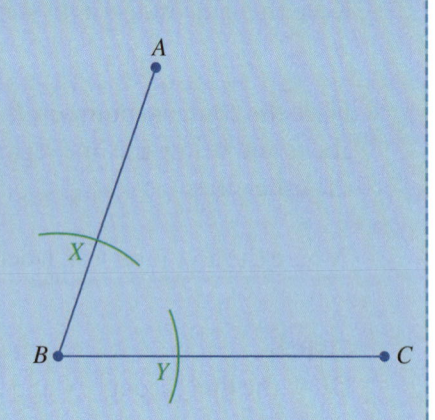

Step 2:
Place the compass point on *X* and draw an arc. Keep the same radius.

Place the compass point on *Y* and draw an arc.

Where the arcs intersect, label the point *Z*.

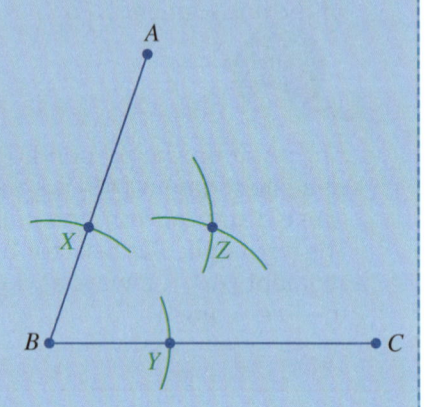

Step 3:
Draw a line from *B* through the point *Z*.

The line *BZ* is the bisector of the angle *ABC*.

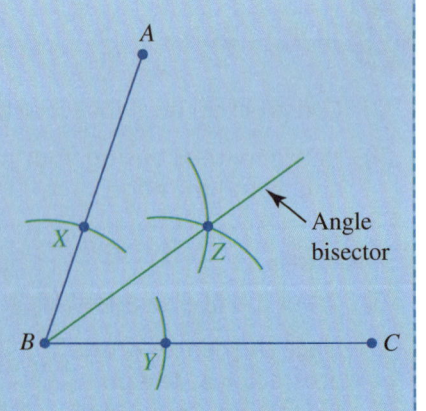

Angle bisector

key point

Any point on the bisector of an angle is equidistant (same distance) from the arms of the angle.

The bisector of an acute or obtuse angle also bisects its related reflex angle.

Example

Construct the triangle ABC such that $|AB| = 7$ cm, $|AC| = 6$ cm and $|BC| = 5$ cm.

Solution

Step 1:

Draw a rough sketch of the triangle.

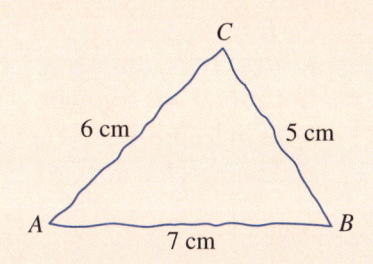

Step 2:

Using a ruler, draw a horizontal line segment 7 cm in length.
Label the end points A and B.

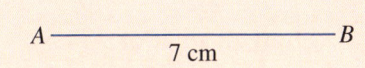

Step 3:

Set your compass to a radius of 6 cm.
Place the compass point on the point A.
Draw an arc above the line segment.

Set your compass to a radius of 5 cm.
Place the compass point on the point B.
Draw an arc above the line segment to meet the other arc.

Label the point where the arcs meet C.

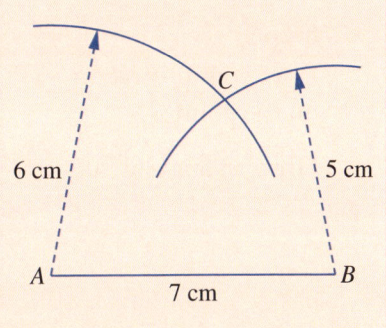

Step 4:

Using your ruler, join A to C and B to C.
The triangle ABC is now drawn as required.

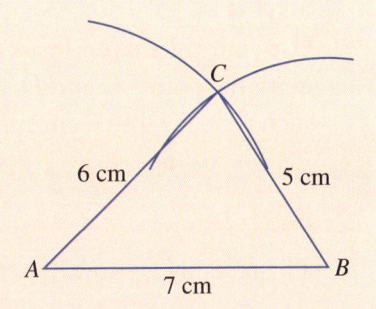

Example

(i) Construct a rectangle $ABCD$ 8 cm long and 6 cm wide.

(ii) Measure the length of the diagonal line.

Solution

(i) **Step 1:**

Using a ruler, draw a horizontal line segment 8 cm in length. Label the end points A and B.

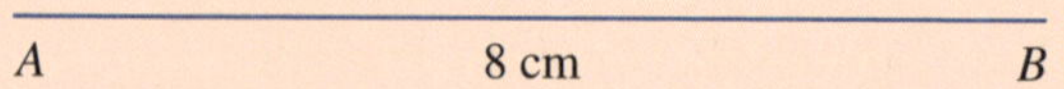

Step 2:

Place your protractor on the point A.

Draw an angle of 90°.

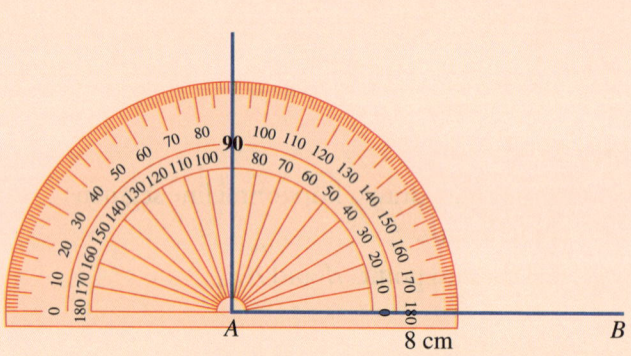

Step 3:

Place your protractor on the point B.

Draw an angle of 90°.

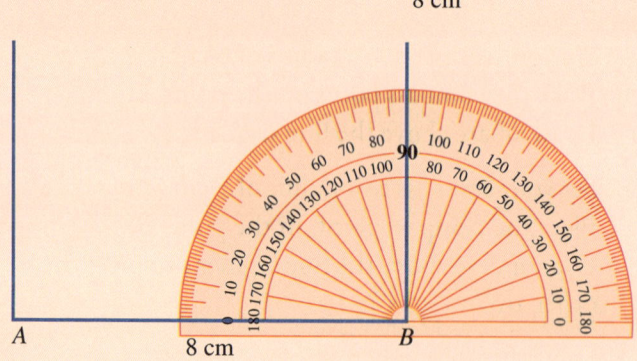

Step 4:

Use your ruler or compass to mark the points C and D such that $|AD| = 6$ cm and $|BC| = 6$ cm.

Join C to D.

The rectangle is now drawn.

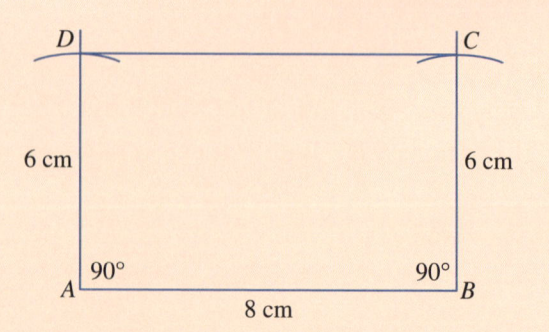

(ii) Use a ruler to measure the length of the diagonal of the rectangle. That is, measure $|AC|$ or $|BD|$.

The diagonal is measured to be 10 cm.

CONSTRUCTIONS 59

exam Q

Amy is a scout. The scoutmaster has made an equilateral triangle with pegs and a rope as shown in the diagram. Amy measures one side of the triangle. It is 6 m in length.

(i) Find the perimeter of the triangle.

(ii) Construct an accurate scale diagram of the equilateral triangle. Use a scale of 1 cm to represent 1 m.

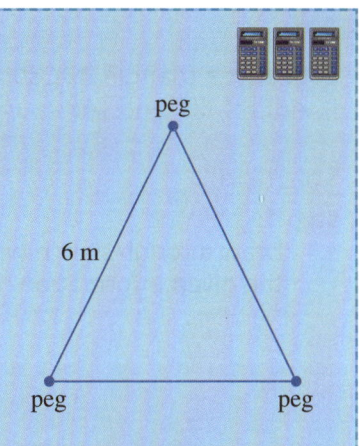

Solution

(i) Perimeter is the sum of all the sides. Since the triangle is equilateral, each side is 6 m in length.

Therefore, perimeter = 6 + 6 + 6 = 18 m.

(ii) Construct an equilateral triangle of side 6 cm:

Step 1:

Using a ruler, draw a horizontal line segment 6 cm in length.

Label the end points *A* and *B*.

Step 2:

Set your compass to a radius of 6 cm.

Place the compass point on the point *A*.

Draw an arc above the line segment.

Keep the compass at a radius of 6 cm.

Place the compass point on the point *B*.

Draw an arc above the line segment to meet the other arc.

Label the point where the arcs meet *C*.

Step 3:

Using your ruler, join *A* to *C* and *B* to *C*.

The triangle *ABC* is now drawn as required.

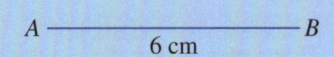

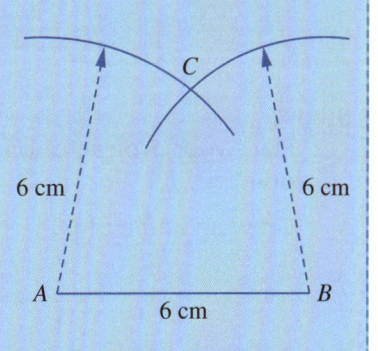

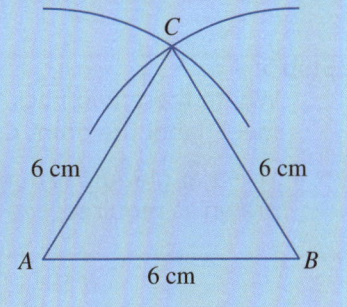

Construct a triangle ABC such that $|\angle BAC| = 45°$, $|\angle ABC| = 60°$ and $|AB| = 7$ cm.

Solution

Step 1:
Draw a rough sketch with the given information.

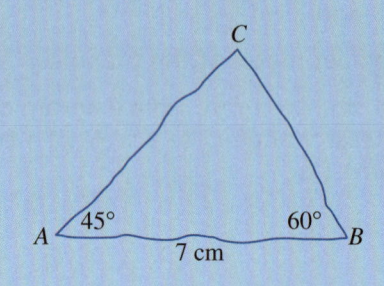

Step 2:
Using a ruler, draw a horizontal line segment 7 cm in length.

Label the end points A and B.

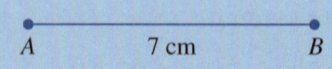

Step 3:
Place your protractor on the point A.

Draw an angle of 45°.

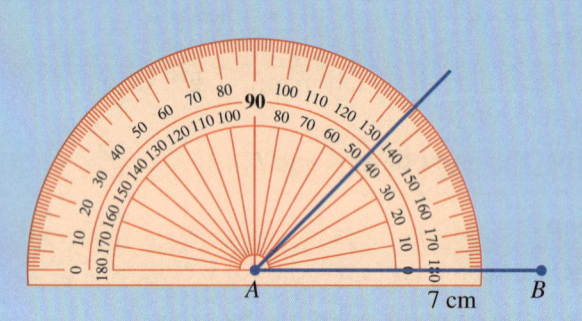

Step 4:
Place your protractor on the point B.

Draw an angle of 60°.

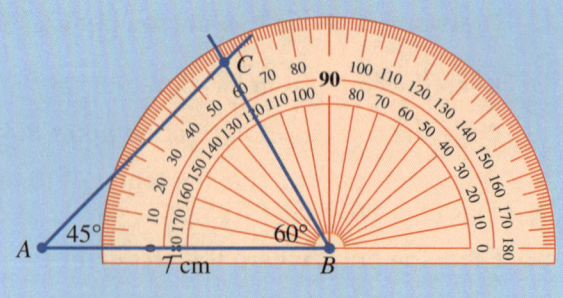

Step 5:
Where these two lines meet, label the point C.

The triangle ABC is now drawn as required.

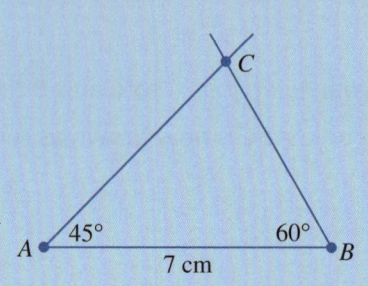

CONSTRUCTIONS

exam Q

(i) Construct a line segment [PS], 8 cm long.

(ii) Divide the line [PS] into three equal segments, without measuring it.

Solution

(i) Construct a line segment 8 cm in length and label the end points P and S:

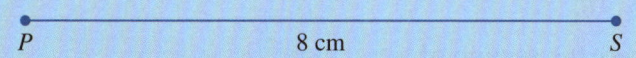

P　　　　　8 cm　　　　　S

(ii) To divide a line segment into three equal parts:

Step 1:

From P, draw a line at an acute angle to PS.

Using your compass, mark off three equal spaces, A, B and C.

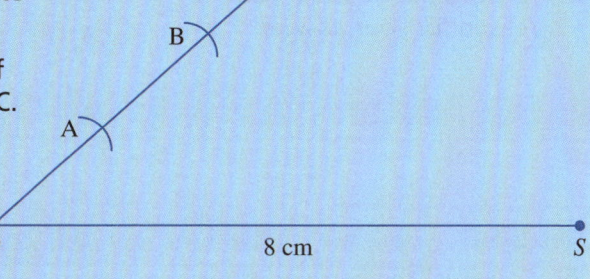

Step 2:

Join the last division, point C, to S.

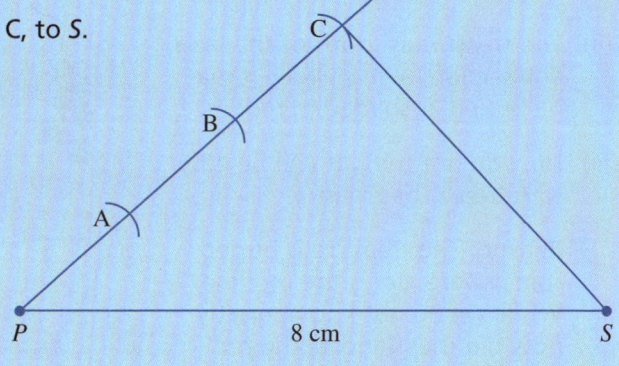

Step 3:

Draw lines parallel to [CS], from points B and A.

The line segment is now divided into three equal parts.

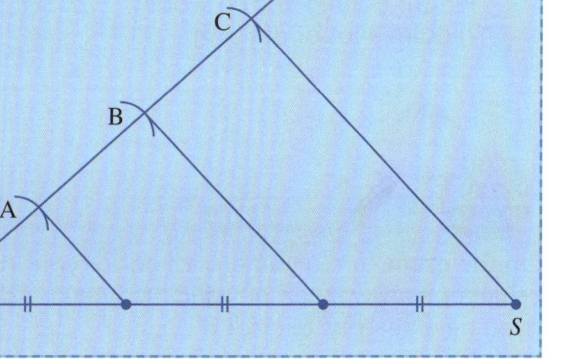

exam Q

The diagram shows an island, with a lake. Treasure is buried on the island.

The treasure is south of the lake, somewhere along the perpendicular bisector of the line joining A to B.

(i) Construct the perpendicular bisector of [AB].

(ii) Shade, in red, the section of the bisector, along which the treasure is buried.

(iii) Do you think it will be easy to retrieve the treasure? Give a reason for your answer.

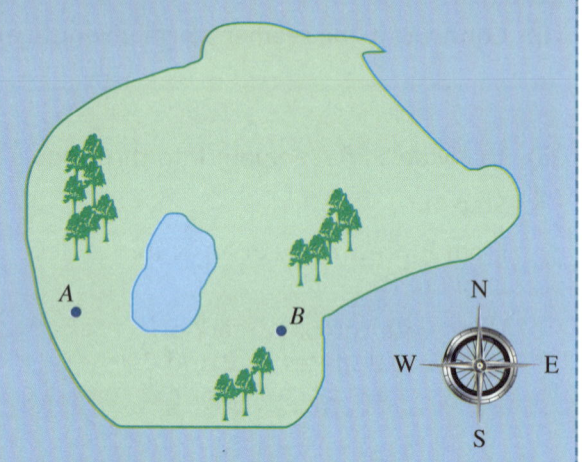

Solution

(i) Construct the perpendicular bisector of [AB]:

(ii) The treasure is south of the lake. The section, along which it may be buried, is shaded in red:

(iii) No, I do not think it will be easy to retrieve the treasure.

Reason: The treasure is buried somewhere along the red line. While we do not know exactly how big the island is, the red line is covering a substantial length of land and so would require a lot of digging.

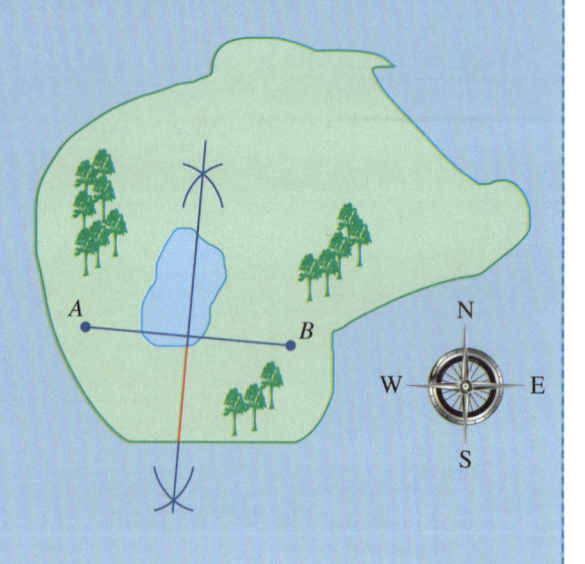

exam focus

In the exam, when you are asked for your opinion you must be aware that more than one answer can be valid. Whatever opinion you give, it is important that you have reasons to back it up.

4 Transformation Geometry

aims
- To learn how to find the image of objects under:
  - translation
  - axial symmetry
  - central symmetry
- To learn how to locate axes of symmetry in simple shapes
- To be able to recognise images of points and objects under:
  - translation
  - axial symmetry
  - central symmetry

Transformations

The word **transformation** means change. The movement of a point or a shape from one position to another is called a **transformation**. In other words, a transformation changes the position of a shape.

Object and image

The original position of a shape is called the **object**. The new position of the shape is called the **image**. The image is where the object moves to. We say that the object **maps onto** the image.

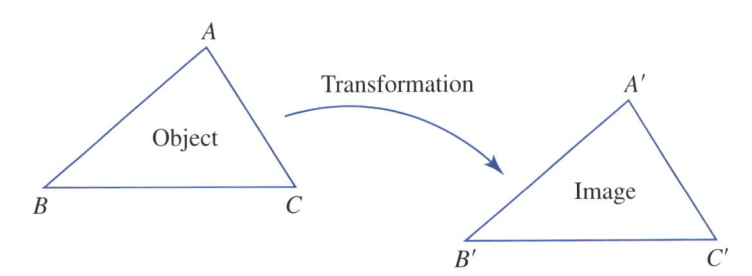

- Often the images of points are indicated by primes. A' is pronounced 'A prime'.
- A and A' are called **corresponding** points because the point A' is the image of the point A.
- Figures have **critical** points that define its shape, usually its vertices (corners).
- When constructing an image, we usually only find the image of the critical points.
- In the triangle above, the critical points are A, B and C and their images are A', B' and C', respectively. Then we join the image points to construct the image of the object.

On our course, we will meet three types of transformations:

1. Translation
2. Axial symmetry
3. Central symmetry

> Each of these transformations changes the position of a shape but not its size or shape.

Translation

Under a translation, every point in the shape is moved the same distance in the same direction. It is often called a **slide**, since the shape appears to slide from one position to another. The shape does not turn or flip over. The object and its image are congruent (identical).

To describe a translation, we need to give its direction and say by how much it has moved.

A translation is often denoted by an arrow above two letters, for example $\overrightarrow{AB}$ or $\overrightarrow{AA'}$.

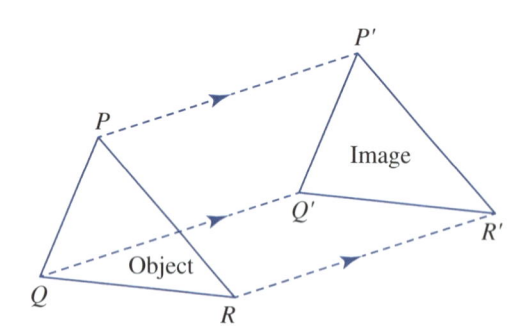

The translation on the left could be described as $P \rightarrow P'$, written as $\overrightarrow{PP'}$.

The translation could also be written as $\overrightarrow{QQ'}$ or $\overrightarrow{RR'}$.

Under a translation, lengths and angles are preserved.

key point

A translation can be described using a **column vector**.

A column vector is written in a similar way to coordinates, with the left or right (horizontal) displacement on top and the up or down (vertical) displacement on the bottom.

$\begin{pmatrix} 4 \\ -3 \end{pmatrix}$ is a translation of 4 units to the right and 3 units down.

$\begin{pmatrix} -2 \\ 5 \end{pmatrix}$ is a translation of 2 units to the left and 5 units up.

$\begin{pmatrix} -1 \\ -4 \end{pmatrix}$ is a translation of 1 unit to the left and 4 units down.

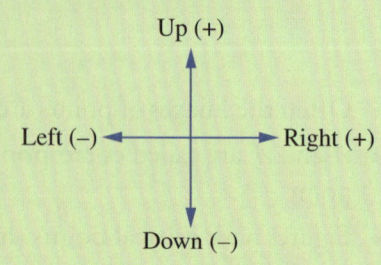

Up (+)
Left (−) ← → Right (+)
Down (−)

Example

The diagram shows triangle A.

(i) Construct the image of A under the translation 4 units right and 2 units up. Label this image B.

(ii) Construct the image of B under the translation 3 units right and 5 units down. Label this image C.

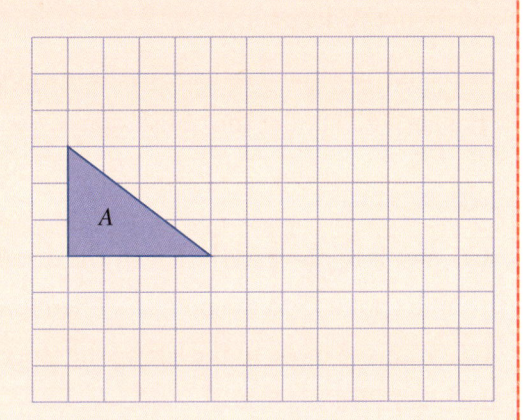

Solution

(i) Choose a point on the triangle A and move it 4 units to the right and 2 units up.

This can also be written as:

$$\begin{pmatrix} 4 \\ 2 \end{pmatrix}$$

Draw the triangle B at this new position.

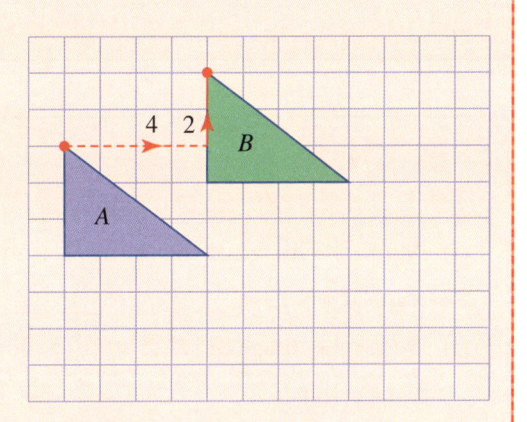

(ii) Choose a point on the triangle B and move it 3 units to the right and 5 units down.

This can also be written as:

$$\begin{pmatrix} 3 \\ -5 \end{pmatrix}$$

Draw the triangle C at this new position.

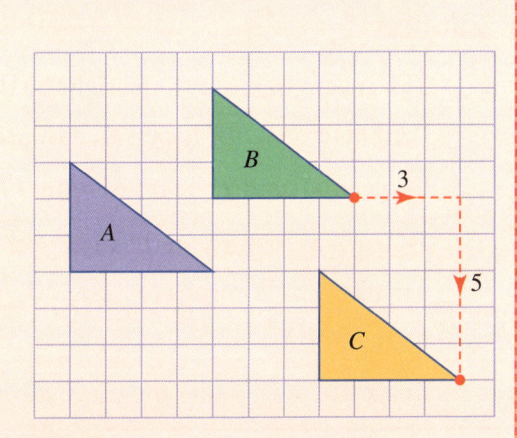

Example

$ABDE$ and $BCDE$ are two parallelograms as shown in the diagram.

Copy the diagram and shade in the image of the triangle BCD under the translation $\overrightarrow{CB}$.

Solution

$\overrightarrow{CB}$ means to move to the left by the distance from the point C to the point B. Therefore, $\overrightarrow{CB}$ means to move to the left by the length of the line $[CB]$.

Image of $\triangle BCD$ under the translation $\overrightarrow{CB}$ is $\triangle ABE$.

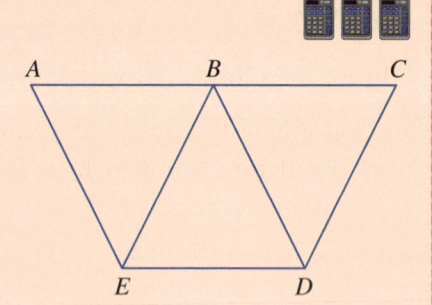

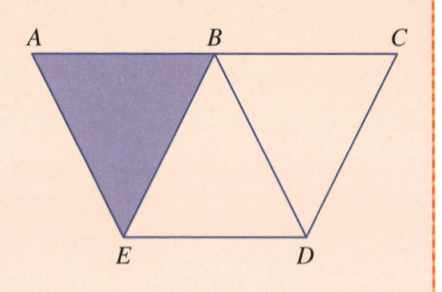

Example

$XYWT$ and $XYZW$ are two parallelograms as shown in the diagram.

(i) Name the image of the point W under the translation $\overrightarrow{TW}$.

(ii) Name the image of $[WZ]$ under the translation $\overrightarrow{WX}$.

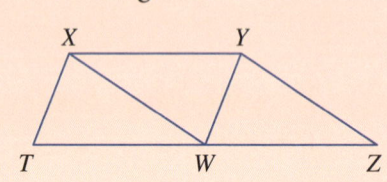

Solution

(i) $\overrightarrow{TW}$ means to move to the right by the distance from the point T to the point W. Therefore, $\overrightarrow{TW}$ means to move to the right by the length of the line $[TW]$.

Image of W under the translation $\overrightarrow{TW}$ is the point Z.

(ii) $\overrightarrow{WX}$ means to move in the direction of going from the point W to the point X. Therefore, $\overrightarrow{WX}$ means to move diagonally upwards to the left by the length of the line $[WX]$.

Image of $[WZ]$ under the translation $\overrightarrow{WX}$ is the line segment $[XY]$.

> **key point**
> It is good practice to keep the order of the images of points asked in the question.

Axial symmetry

> Axial symmetry is a reflection in a line. It involves reflecting points perpendicularly through a line.

An object reflected in a mirror creates an image. A reflection in a line is called an axial symmetry. This gives an image that looks like a reflection in a mirror (sometimes called a mirror image). The line is called the **axis of reflection** or **line of reflection** or **mirror line**. The object and the image are symmetrical about the mirror line. In other words, any point and its image are the same perpendicular distance from the axis of symmetry.

The object and the image are congruent. However, under a reflection in a line, a figure flips over.

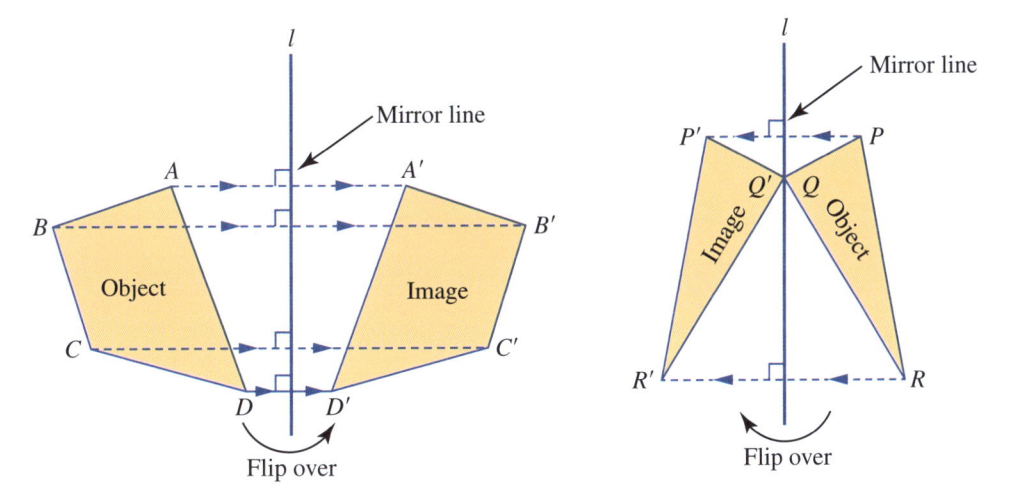

Axis of symmetry

A shape has an **axis of symmetry** or a **line of symmetry** when one half of the shape fits exactly over the other half when the shape is folded along that line. Shapes which are evenly balanced are said to be **symmetrical**. Some shapes have no axis of symmetry, some have only one axis of symmetry and others have more than one axis of symmetry.

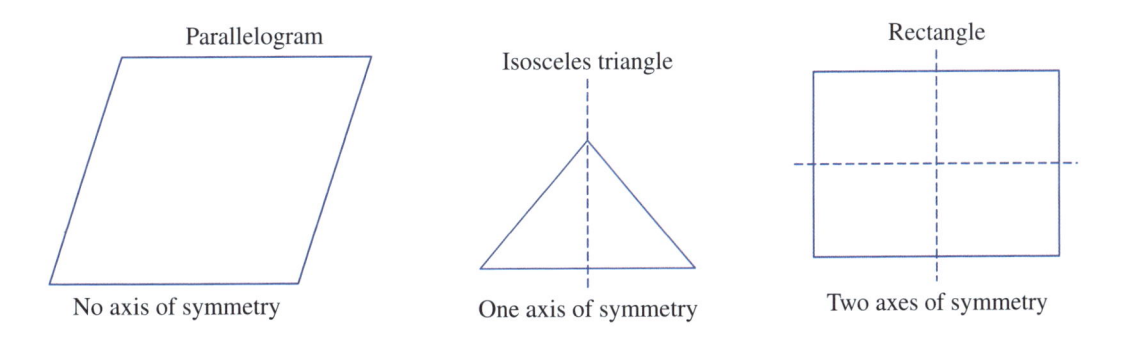

Parallelogram — No axis of symmetry

Isosceles triangle — One axis of symmetry

Rectangle — Two axes of symmetry

Equilateral triangle

Three axes of symmetry

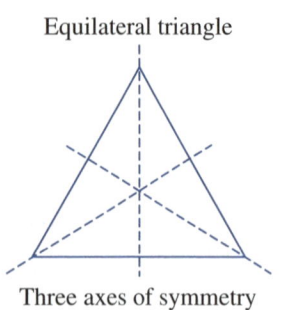

exam focus
Always draw the axes of symmetry with a dotted line.

Example

Draw all axes of symmetry on the following shapes:

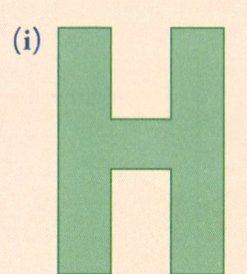

(i) H (ii) ★ (iii) ✿

Solution

(i) 2 axes of symmetry (ii) 5 axes of symmetry (iii) 6 axes of symmetry

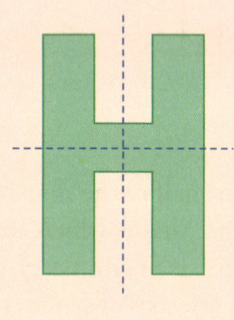

exam Q

Which of the letters in the word **DONAL** have an axis of symmetry? In each case state how many axes of symmetry the letter has.

Solution

The letter **D** has one horizontal axis of symmetry.

D

TRANSFORMATION GEOMETRY

The letter **O** has two axes of symmetry.
One is horizontal and one is vertical.

The letter **N** has no axis of symmetry.

The letter **A** has one vertical axis of symmetry.

The letter **L** has no axis of symmetry.

key point

Horizontal: ────────

Vertical: │

Example

(i) Draw the image of the blue shape, under axial symmetry in the line *m*.

(ii) Does axial symmetry change the area of the object? Give a reason for your answer.

(iii) Explain how the shape has changed under axial symmetry in the line *m*.

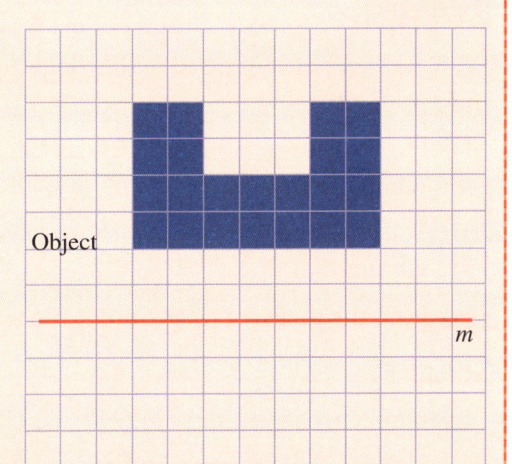

Object

m

Solution

(i) To construct the image of the blue shape in the line m:

Draw a straight line from each corner (vertex) of the object perpendicularly into the line m and continue out the same distance on the other side of m.

Join the points to construct the new shape.

The resulting shape is the image of the object under axial symmetry in the line m.

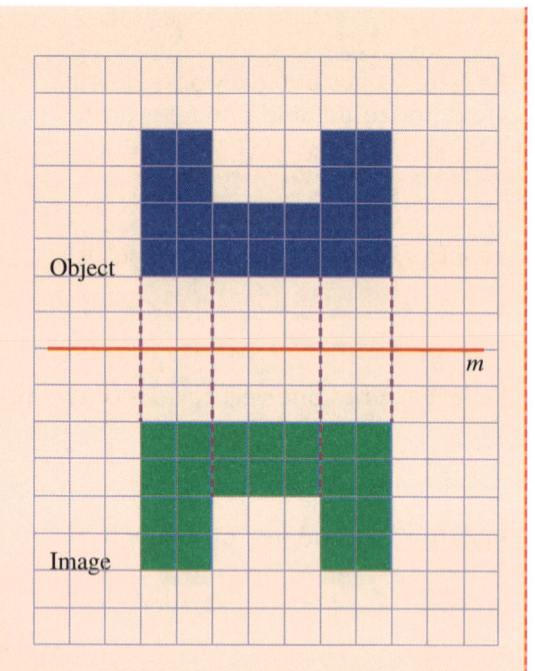

(ii) No, axial symmetry did not change the area. The lengths of the sides and the angles all remained the same. Both the object and the image are the same size. In this case, each shape covers 22 boxes of the grid.

(iii) The shape is back to front. It is the mirror image of the object.

Example

$PQRS$ is a parallelogram with diagonals intersecting at T and $PR \perp QS$.

(i) Find the image of $\triangle QRS$ under axial symmetry in QS.

(ii) What is the image of $\triangle PQR$ under axial symmetry in PR?

(iii) Find the image of $[PQ]$ under the translation $\overrightarrow{QR}$.

Solution

(i) Under axial symmetry in QS: $\triangle QRS \rightarrow \triangle QPS$

(ii) Under axial symmetry in PR: $\triangle PQR \rightarrow \triangle PSR$

(iii) Under the translation $\overrightarrow{QR}$: $[PQ] \rightarrow [SR]$

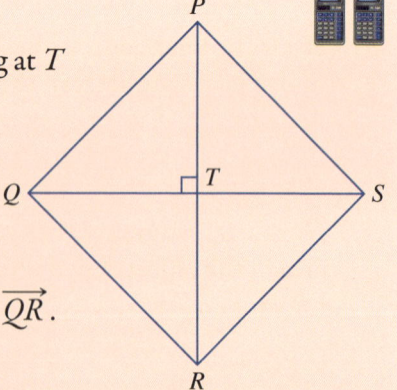

key point If a point is on the axis of symmetry (mirror line), its image is the same point.

TRANSFORMATION GEOMETRY

key point

Image of a point under:
- Axial symmetry in the x-axis: change the sign of y-coordinate.
- Axial symmetry in the y-axis: change the sign of x-coordinate.

exam Q

The diagram shows the letter F on the coordinated plane.

(i) Draw the image of the letter F under axial symmetry in the y-axis.

(ii) Write down the coordinates of the points B and C.

(iii) A, B and C are mapped onto A', B' and C' under the transformation above.

Write down the coordinates of the points A', B' and C'.

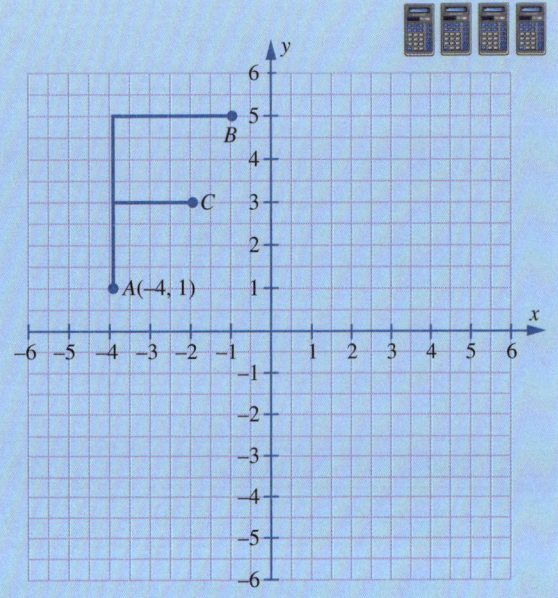

Solution

(i) Draw a straight line from each point of the letter F perpendicularly into the y-axis and continue out the same distance on the other side of the y-axis.

Join the points to construct the image of the letter F under axial symmetry in the y-axis.

(ii) B = (−1, 5) and C = (−2, 3)

(iii) A' = (4, 1), B' = (1, 5) and C' = (2, 3)

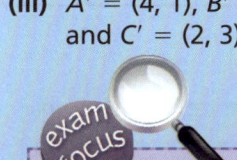

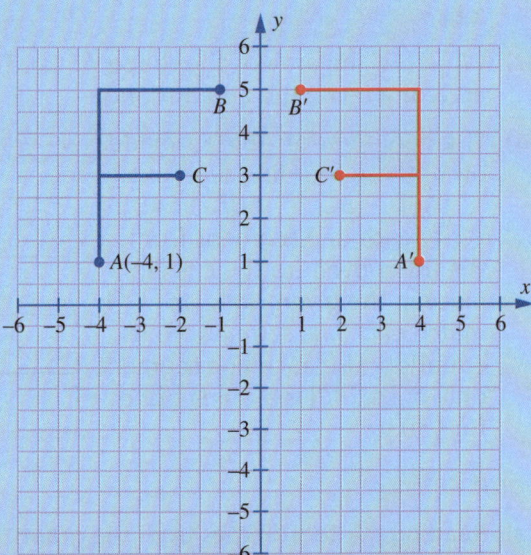

exam focus

This question requires you to be able to identify the coordinates of points on a coordinated plane. Notice the link to coordinate geometry.

72 LESS STRESS MORE SUCCESS

The quadrilateral ABCD is shown in the coordinate diagram.

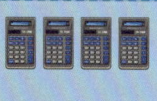

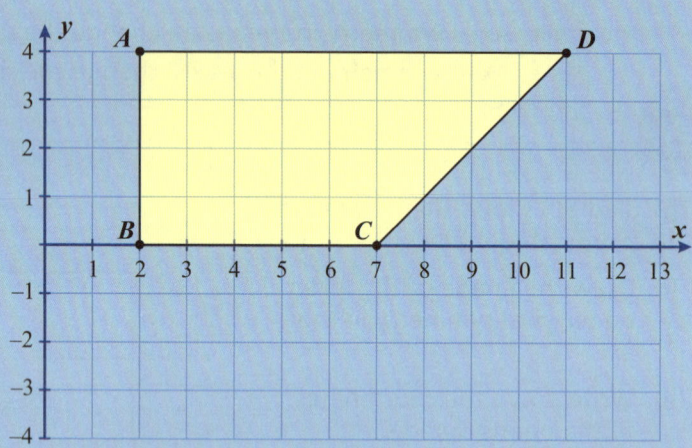

(a) Complete the table below to show the coordinates of the four corners of ABCD.

Point	A	B	C	D
Coordinates	(2, 4)	(2, 0)	(,)	(,)

(b) On the given diagram, draw the image of ABCD under axial symmetry in the x-axis.

(c) Work out the area of the shape ABCD. To do this, you might need to find the area of a rectangle and a triangle.

(d) The perimeter of ABCD is made up of these four line segments: [AB] [BC] [CD] [AD]
Write each line segment from the list above into the correct place in the given table, to match each line segment to its equation. Use each line segment only once. [BC] is already done for you.

Equation	Line segment
$x = 2$	
$y = 0$	[BC]
$y = 4$	
$y = x - 7$	

Solution

(a) Reading the coordinates from the graph, we can complete the table as shown:

Point	A	B	C	D
Coordinates	(2, 4)	(2, 0)	(7 , 0)	(11 , 4)

(b) Axial symmetry in the *x*-axis is the same as reflection in the *x*-axis. This means the *y*-values will all change sign. The *x*-values remain the same.

$A' = (2, -4)$, $B' = (2, 0)$, $C' = (7, 0)$, $D' = (11, -4)$

Plotting these on the coordinate plane gives:

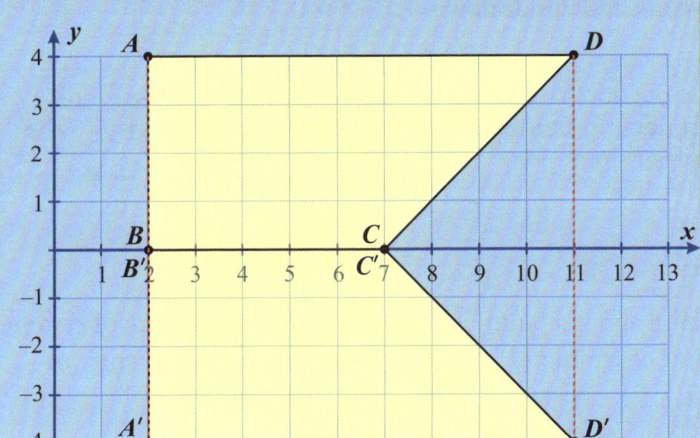

> **key point**
>
> A' is the image of A
> B' is the image of B
> C' is the image of C
> D' is the image of D

(c) Break the shape into a rectangle and a triangle. Find the area of each shape and add them to find the area of the quadrilateral *ABCD*.

Rectangle = Length × Width
= 5 × 4
= 20 square units

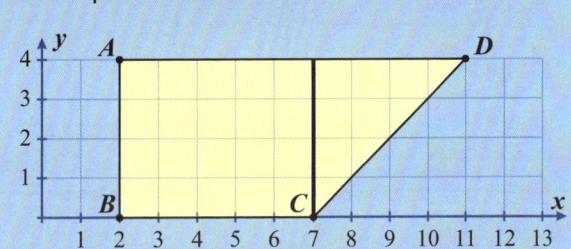

Triangle = $\frac{1}{2}$ (base)($\perp$ height)
= $\frac{1}{2}$ (4)(4)
= 8 square units

Total area = 20 + 8 = 28 square units.

(d) The line $x = 2$ is a vertical line passing through the point 2 on the *x*-axis. This is the line [AB].

The line $y = 4$ is a horizontal line passing through the point 4 on the *y*-axis. This is the line [AD].

The line $y = x - 7$, has a slope of 1, and as it is the only remaining line, it must be the equation of the segment [CD].

Equation	Line segment
$x = 2$	[AB]
$y = 0$	[BC]
$y = 4$	[AD]
$y = x - 7$	[CD]

Central symmetry

An object reflected in a point creates an image. Under central symmetry, any point and its image are equidistant from the centre of symmetry. The object and the image are congruent. However, under central symmetry, a shape is turned over. Central symmetry is exactly the same as a rotation of 180° about the centre of symmetry – the result is that the object gets turned back to front and upside down.

> Central symmetry is a reflection in a point. The point is called the **centre of symmetry**. It involves reflecting points through the centre of symmetry to the same distance on the other side.

Centre of symmetry

Some shapes are symmetrical about a point. The point is called the **centre of symmetry** (sometimes called the point of symmetry). The following shapes have a centre of symmetry, indicated by O.

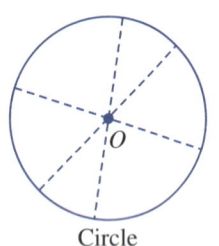

Circle 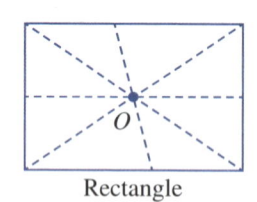   Rectangle 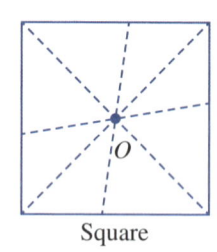   Square 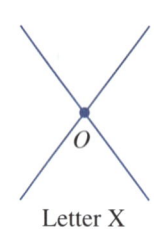   Letter X

Example

Locate the centre of symmetry of the following shapes:

(i)

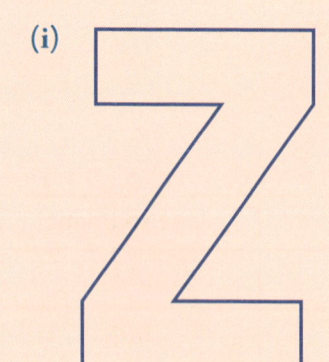

(ii)

TRANSFORMATION GEOMETRY 75

Solution

To locate the centre of symmetry for each shape:
1. Select a point on the shape and draw a line to the corresponding point on the opposite side of the shape.
2. Repeat this for many points on the shape.
3. The point where all of these lines intersect is the centre of symmetry of the shape.

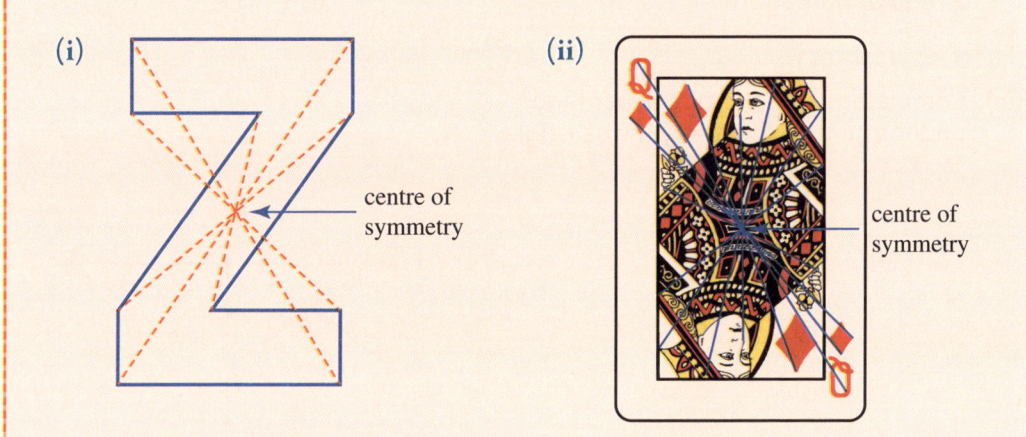

(i) centre of symmetry

(ii) centre of symmetry

Example

Construct the image of the figure under a central symmetry in the point O.

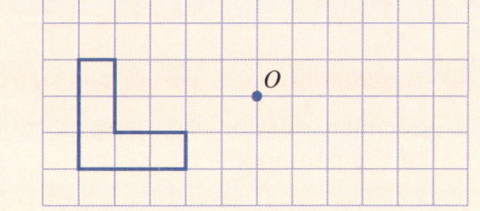

Solution

Draw a straight, dashed, line from each corner (vertex) of the object to O and continue the same distance on the other side of O.

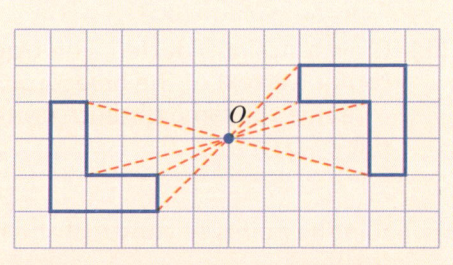

Join the points to construct the new shape.

The resulting shape is the image of the object under a central symmetry in O.

(i) Draw two axes of symmetry of the regular pentagon shown in the diagram.

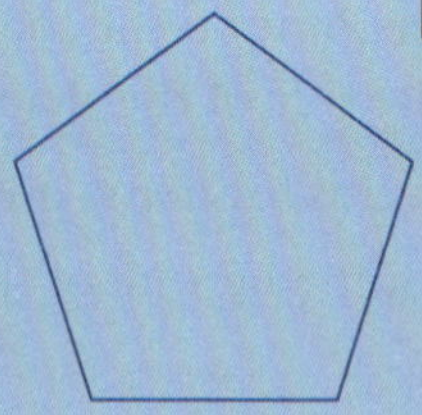

(ii) What is the total number of lines of symmetry of a regular pentagon?

(iii) Complete the image of the pentagon under a central symmetry in the origin.

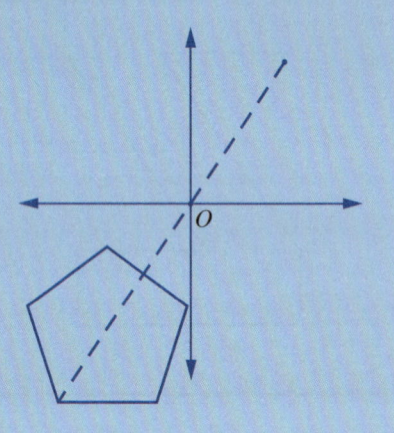

Solution

(i) Two axes of symmetry are drawn, as shown:

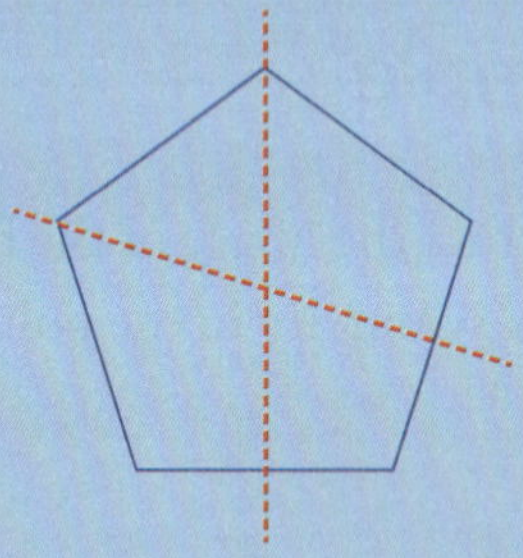

(ii) A pentagon has 5 axes of symmetry.

Each line of symmetry passes through one point of the pentagon.

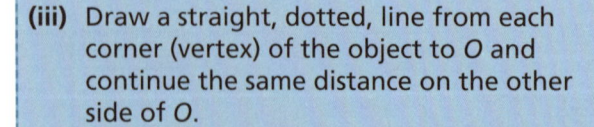

(iii) Draw a straight, dotted, line from each corner (vertex) of the object to O and continue the same distance on the other side of O.

Join the points to construct the new shape.

The resulting shape is the image of the object under a central symmetry in the origin.

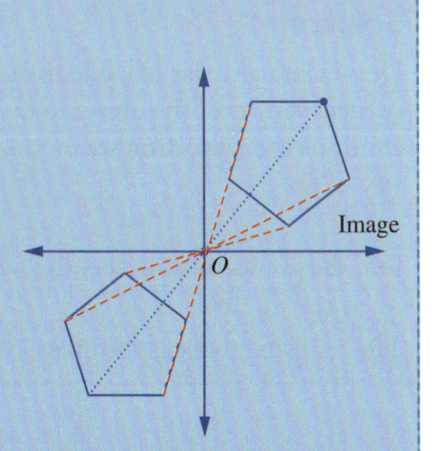

TRANSFORMATION GEOMETRY

The following diagram shows 4 points:

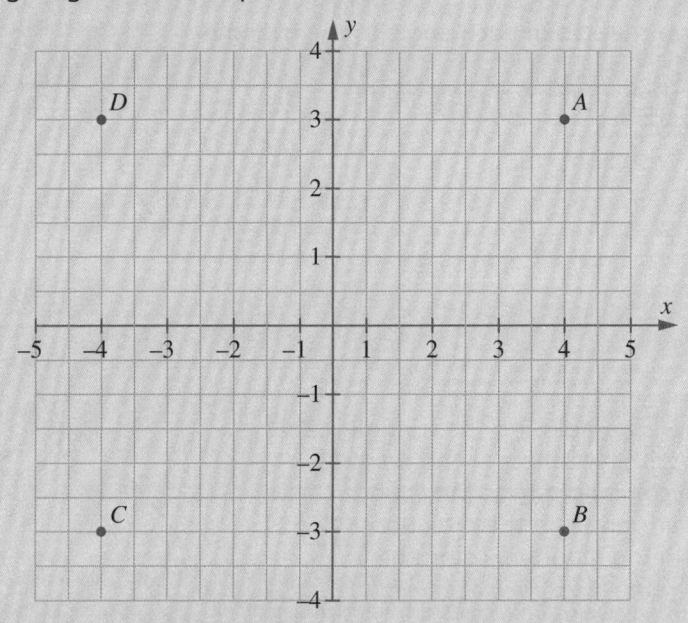

(i) List the coordinates of the points A, B, C and D.

Complete the following sentences:

(ii) B is the image of A under _____

(iii) C is the image of A under _____

(iv) D is the image of A under _____

Solution

(i) A = (4, 3)   B = (4, −3)   C = (−4, −3) and D = (−4, 3)

(ii) B is the image of A under <u>axial symmetry in the x-axis</u>.

(iii) C is the image of A under <u>central symmetry in the origin (0, 0)</u>.

(iv) D is the image of A under <u>axial symmetry in the y-axis</u>.

An equilateral triangle *XZY* has sides of length 10 cm.

(a) Write down the size of each angle in the triangle.

(b) Work out the length of the perimeter of the triangle *XZY*.
Give your answer in cm.

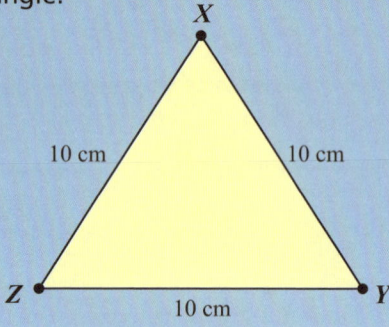

(c) Maria plays a game using the triangle *XZY*. She starts with a counter at the point *X*. She flips a coin and moves the counter around the triangle in the direction *XYZ*, as shown in the diagram, using the following rule:
  - if she gets heads (H), she moves the counter along 1 side of the triangle (e.g. *X* to *Y*)
  - if she gets tails (T), she moves the counter along 2 sides of the triangle (e.g. *X* to *Z*)

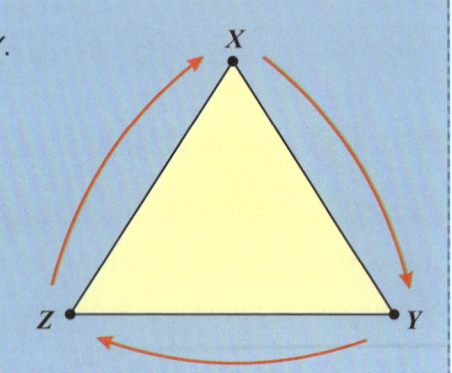

Maria's first 4 flips of the coin are H H H T. Fill in the table below to show which point the counter is at after each flip of the coin. Some are already done for you.

	Outcome of flip (H or T)	Number of sides the counter moves	After this flip, the counter is at:
Start			X
1st flip	H	1	Y
2nd flip	H		Z
3rd flip	H	1	
4th flip	T		

Solution

(a) If the triangle is equilateral, then all angles are 60°.
Therefore, $|\angle XYZ| = 60°$

(b) Perimeter = sum of all sides
Perimeter = 10 + 10 + 10
Perimeter = 30 cm

(c)

	Outcome of flip (H or T)	Number of sides the counter moves	After this flip, the counter is at:
Start			X
1st flip	H	1	Y
2nd flip	H	1	Z
3rd flip	H	1	X
4th flip	T	2	Z

Explanation:
2nd flip: H means the counter moves 1 space and lands on Z
3rd flip: H means the counter moves 1 space and lands on X
4th flip: T means the counter moves 2 spaces and lands on Z

Each of the four diagrams A, B, C and D shows the object in Figure 1 and its image under a transformation.

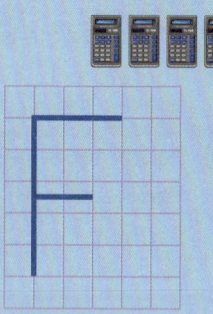

For each of A, B, C and D, state one transformation (translation, axial symmetry or central symmetry) that will map the object onto that image.

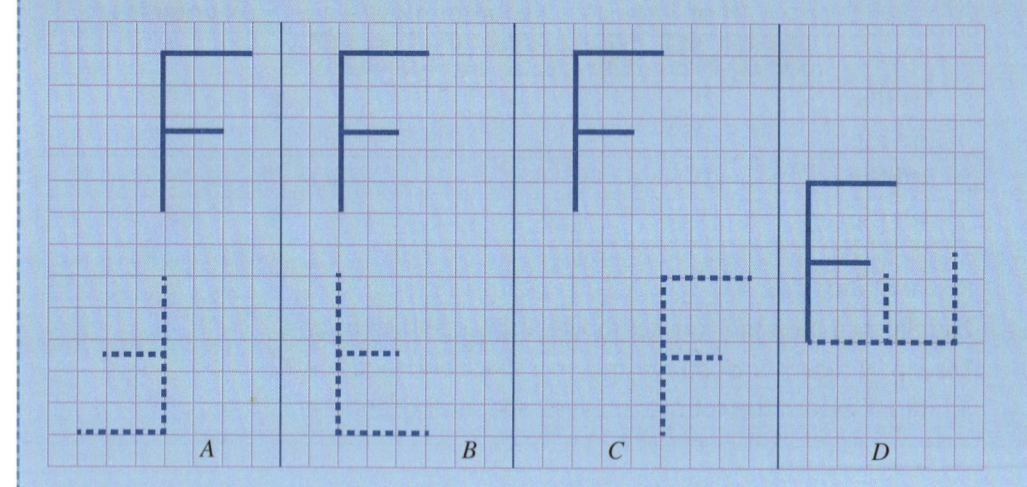

Figure 1

Solution
- **A** Central symmetry through a point (green dot).
- **B** Axial symmetry through a horizontal line (green line).
- **C** Translation: 3 units to the right and 7 units downwards.
- **D** Axial symmetry in a diagonal line (green line).

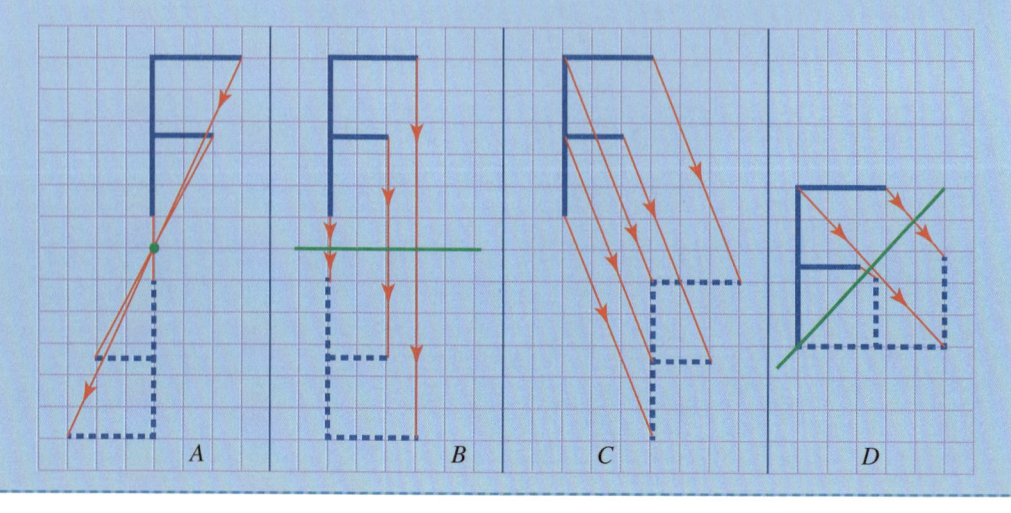

TRANSFORMATION GEOMETRY

exam Q

Each of the three figures labelled A, B and C shown below is the image of the object under a transformation. For each of A, B and C, state whether the transformation is a translation, an axial symmetry in the x-axis, an axial symmetry in the y-axis or a central symmetry.

Object   A   B   C

Solution

Image A is formed by central symmetry.

Image B is formed by axial symmetry in the y-axis. (Vertical line)

Image C is formed by axial symmetry in the x-axis. (Horizontal line)

exam Q

The diagram shows the octagon ABCDEFGH. The diagonals of the octagon intersect at the point O.

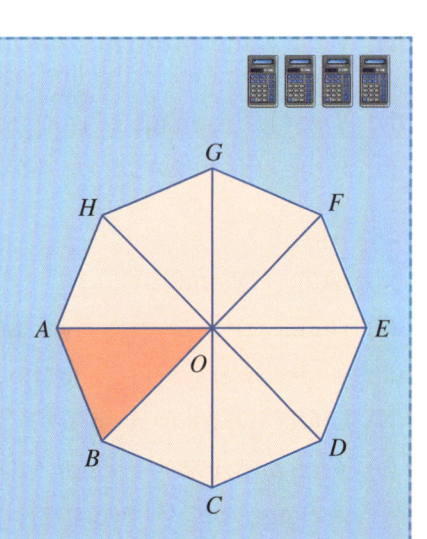

Find the image of the shaded triangle ABO under each of the following transformations:

(i) Axial symmetry in the line AE

(ii) Central symmetry in the point O

(iii) Axial symmetry in the line GC

(iv) Name the transformation which maps the shaded triangle ABO onto △GFO.

Solution

(i) Under axial symmetry in the line AE: △ABO → △AHO

(ii) Under central symmetry in point O: △ABO → △EFO

(iii) Under axial symmetry in the line GC: △ABO → △EDO

(iv) △ABO → △GFO is the result of a transformation under axial symmetry in the line HD.

> **key point**
>
> You should notice that in each case the image of the point O remained at the point O. This is because in each transformation the point O was on the line or point of symmetry.

exam Q

ABCD is a rectangle. ABDX and BYCD are parallelograms.

(i) Name three line segments equal in length to [DC].

(ii) What is the image of △BCY under the central symmetry in Z?

(iii) What is the image of △AXD under axial symmetry in the line AD?

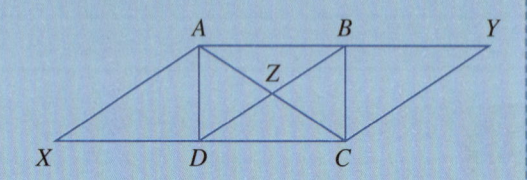

(iv) What is the image of [AX] under the translation $\vec{BY}$?

(v) If the area of △ADZ = △AZB = 5 cm², what is the area of the figure AXCY?

Solution

(i) [AB], [XD] and [BY]

(ii) Under central symmetry in point Z: △BCY → △DAX

(iii) Under axial symmetry in the line AD: △AXD → △ACD

(iv) Under the translation $\vec{BY}$: [AX] → [BD]

(v) Area of △ADZ = area of △AZB

∴ figure AXCY = 8(△ADZ)

= 8(5)

= 40 cm²

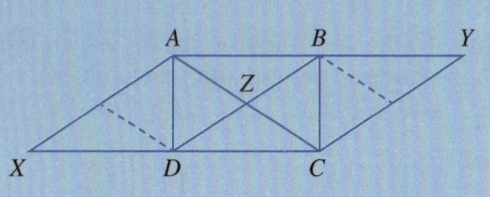

5 Trigonometry I

aims
- ☐ To learn how to use Pythagoras' theorem
- ☐ To learn how to label the sides of a right-angled triangle
- ☐ To learn how to use the trigonometric ratios to solve for missing sides and missing angles in a right-angled triangles

In trigonometry, on our course, we will only be working with right-angled triangles. A right angle can be indicated by either a box or an L shape.

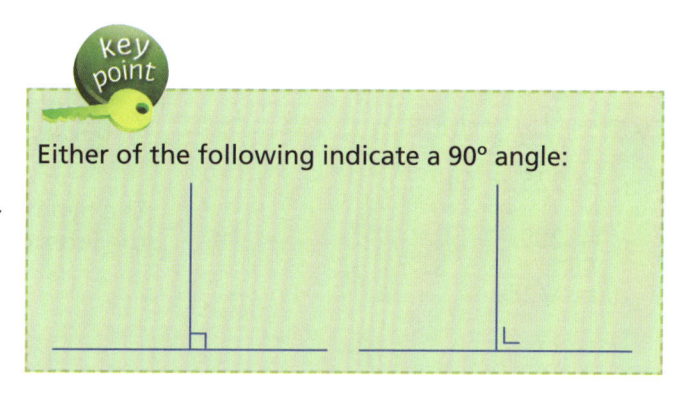

key point
Either of the following indicate a 90° angle:

Pythagoras' theorem

Pythagoras' theorem states that, in a right-angled triangle, the square of the hypotenuse equals the sum of the squares of the other two sides.

key point
The hypotenuse is the longest side, directly opposite the right angle.

Pythagoras' theorem is used:

1. To find third side in a triangle, when given the other two
2. To verify that a triangle is right angled.

(see booklet of formulae and tables, page 16)

Pythagoras' theorem:

$$c^2 = a^2 + b^2$$

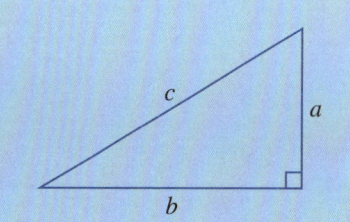

Example

In a right-angled triangle, two of the sides have length 15 and 8, as in the diagram.

Find c, the length of the hypotenuse.

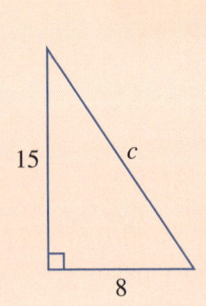

Solution

Use Pythagoras' theorem:

$c^2 = a^2 + b^2$

$(c)^2 = (15)^2 + (8)^2$

$c^2 = 225 + 64$

$c^2 = 289$

$c = \sqrt{289}$

$c = 17$

key point: The hypotenuse is on its own on the left side of the equation.

Example

In a right-angled triangle, the hypotenuse has length 5. One of the other sides has length 4.

Find x, the length of the third side.

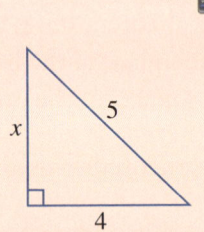

Solution

Use Pythagoras' theorem:

$c^2 = a^2 + b^2$

$(5)^2 = (4)^2 + x^2$

$25 = 16 + x^2$

$25 - 16 = x^2$

$9 = x^2$

$\sqrt{9} = x$

$3 = x$

key point: There were no units given in the question, so there are no units in the answer.

Example

$[XW]$ is a diameter of a circle with centre O. Z is a point on the circle.

Given $|OW| = 5$ cm, $|WZ| = 6$ cm, use the Theorem of Pythagoras to find $|XZ|$.

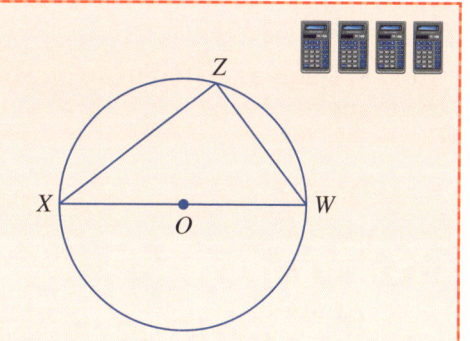

Solution

$|\angle XZW| = 90°$ (angle in a semicircle is a right angle)

$|OW| = 5$ (radius of the circle)

$\therefore |OX| = 5$ (radius of the circle)

$\therefore |XW| = 10$ and $|ZW| = 6$

Use Pythagoras' theorem:

$$c^2 = a^2 + b^2$$
$$10^2 = 6^2 + |XZ|^2$$
$$100 = 36 + |XZ|^2$$
$$100 - 36 = |XZ|^2$$
$$64 = |XZ|^2$$
$$\sqrt{64} = |XZ|$$
$$8 \text{ cm} = |XZ|$$

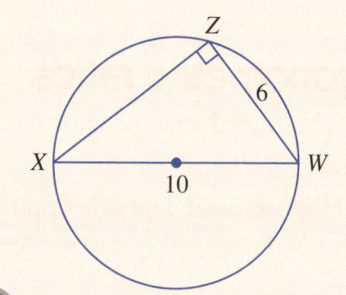

exam focus: When units are given in the question, you must give them in your answer.

---

exam Q

The isosceles triangle shown in the diagram has a base length of 10 cm and the other two sides are 13 cm in length. The perpendicular height bisects the base of the triangle.

Find, h, the perpendicular height of the triangle.

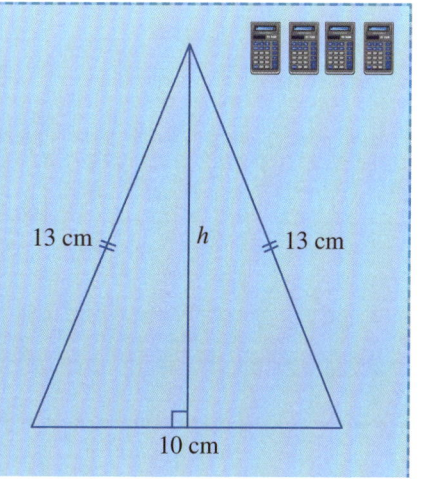

Solution
Using Pythagoras' theorem on one half of the triangle:

$$c^2 = a^2 + b^2$$
$$13^2 = h^2 + 5^2$$
$$169 = h^2 + 25$$
$$169 - 25 = h^2$$
$$144 = h^2$$
$$\sqrt{144} = h$$
$$12 = h$$

Therefore, perpendicular height, $h = 12$ cm.

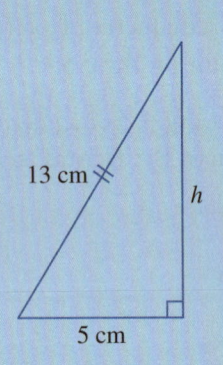

Trigonometric ratios

In a right-angled triangle with acute angle θ, we name the sides as:

- **Hypotenuse:** The side opposite the right angle. It is also the longest side.
- **Opposite:** The side opposite the angle θ.
- **Adjacent:** The side beside (adjacent to) θ.

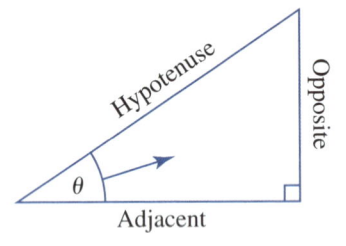

Note: θ is a Greek letter, pronounced 'theta', often used to denote an angle.
There are three trigonometric ratios. These ratios are fractions, with the length of one side over another. They are called sine, cosine and tangent and are usually abbreviated to sin, cos and tan.

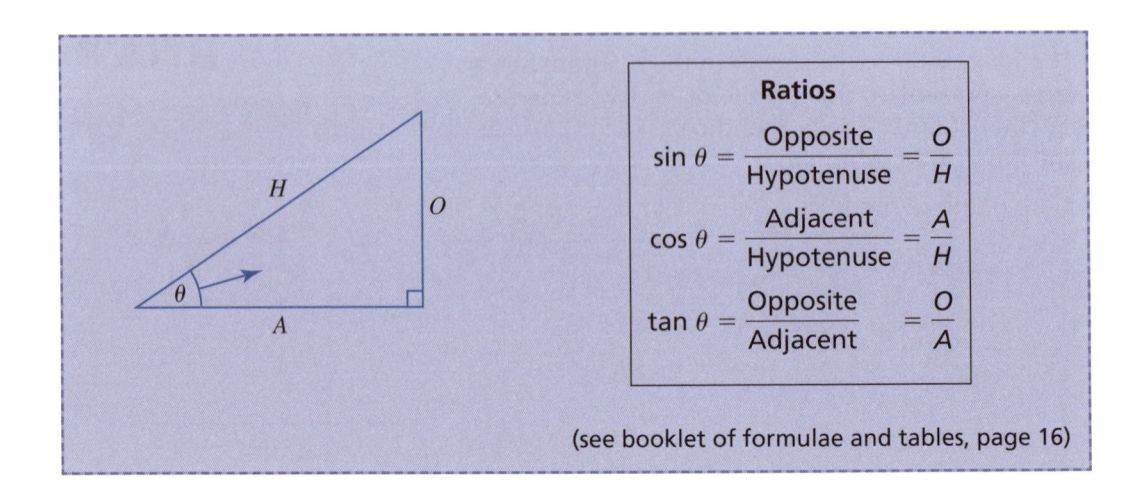

Ratios

$$\sin \theta = \frac{\text{Opposite}}{\text{Hypotenuse}} = \frac{O}{H}$$

$$\cos \theta = \frac{\text{Adjacent}}{\text{Hypotenuse}} = \frac{A}{H}$$

$$\tan \theta = \frac{\text{Opposite}}{\text{Adjacent}} = \frac{O}{A}$$

(see booklet of formulae and tables, page 16)

key point

Memory aids

Use any of these to remember the trigonometric ratios:
1. O Heck, Another Hour Of Algebra
2. Silly = $\dfrac{\text{Old}}{\text{Harry}}$ Caught = $\dfrac{\text{A}}{\text{Herring}}$ Trawling = $\dfrac{\text{Off}}{\text{America}}$
3. SOHCAHTOA

Example

The right-angled triangle ABC has measurements as shown.

(i) Write down the length of the hypotenuse of $\triangle ABC$.

(ii) Write down the value of $\sin B$, as a fraction.

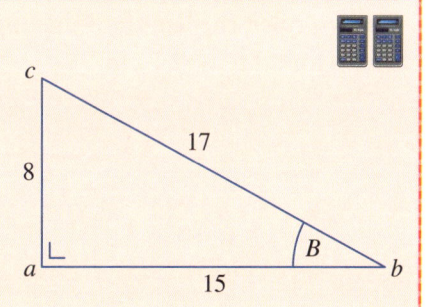

Solution

(i) Hypotenuse = 17

(ii) From the triangle we can see: Opposite = 8   Adjacent = 15   Hypotenuse = 17

$$\sin B = \dfrac{\text{Opposite}}{\text{Hypotenuse}} = \dfrac{8}{17}$$

Example

The triangle PQR has measurements as shown.

(i) Write down the value of $\sin A$, as a fraction.
(ii) Write down the value of $\cos A$, as a fraction.
(iii) Write down the value of $\tan A$, as a fraction.

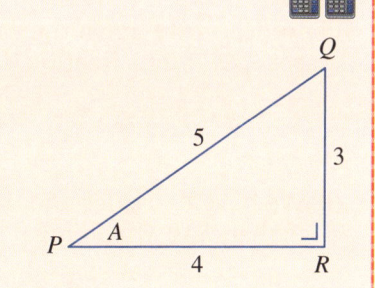

Solution

Label the sides of the triangle as shown:

(i) $\sin A = \dfrac{\text{Opposite}}{\text{Hypotenuse}} = \dfrac{3}{5}$

(ii) $\cos A = \dfrac{\text{Adjacent}}{\text{Hypotenuse}} = \dfrac{4}{5}$

(iii) $\tan A = \dfrac{\text{Opposite}}{\text{Adjacent}} = \dfrac{3}{4}$

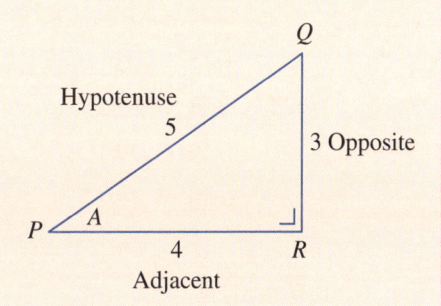

Example

The angle A is marked in the given triangle.

Measure the length of the side which is opposite to the angle A.

Solution

The side opposite to the angle A is the vertical side.

Using a ruler, the length of the opposite side is found to be 2·7 cm.

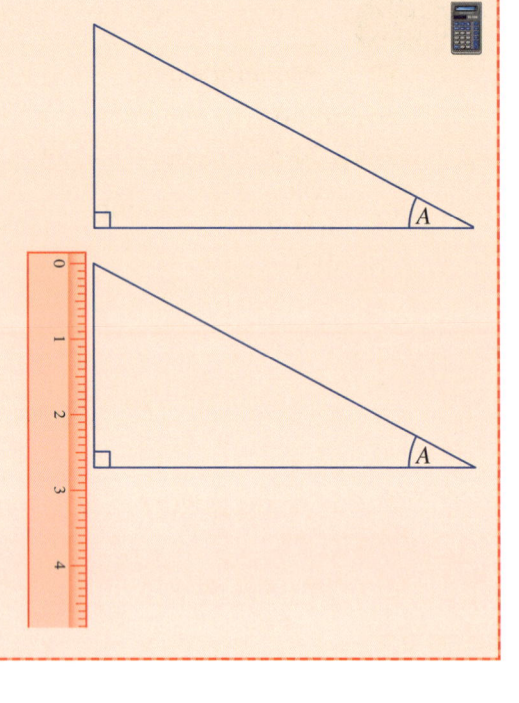

---

exam Q

In the $\triangle PQR$, $|\angle QRP| = 90°$, $|PQ| = 25$ m and $|QR| = 24$ m.

(i) Find, in metres, $|PR|$.

(ii) Hence, write down the value of $\cos \angle QPR$, as a fraction.

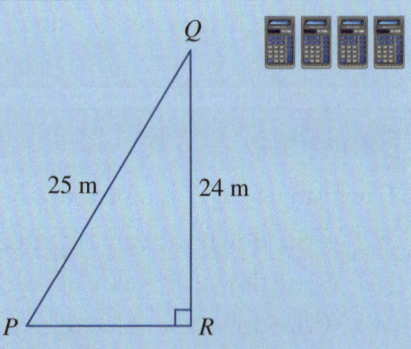

Solution

(i) We have two sides and we want to find the third side, therefore we use Pythagoras' Theorem:

$$c^2 = a^2 + b^2$$
$$25^2 = 24^2 + |PR|^2$$
$$625 = 576 + |PR|^2$$
$$625 - 576 = |PR|^2$$
$$49 = |PR|^2$$
$$\sqrt{49} = |PR|$$
$$7 = |PR|$$

Therefore, $|PR| = 7$ m.

(ii) Mark the angle $\angle QPR$ in the triangle, and label the sides.

From the triangle we can see:

Opposite = 24   Adjacent = 7   Hypotenuse = 25

$$\cos \angle QPR = \frac{\text{Adjacent}}{\text{Hypotenuse}} = \frac{7}{25}$$

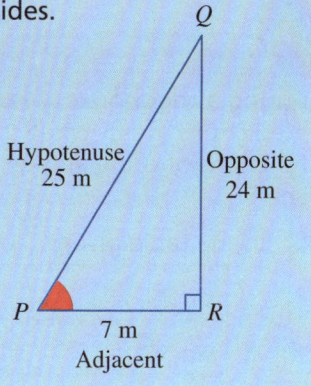

key point

Using the calculator
You must be able to use your calculator to find the value for the sin, cos and tan of angles. Your calculator is able to work in many different modes. Because of this, you **must make sure your calculator is set to do calculations in degrees**, at all times.

Example

Use your calculator to find values of the following trigonometric ratios. Give your answers to three decimal places.

(i) sin 20°   (ii) cos 55°   (iii) tan 30°   (iv) sin 72°

Solution

(i) sin 20° = 0·3420201433 = 0·342 to three decimal places
(ii) cos 55° = 0·5735764364 = 0·574 to three decimal places
(iii) tan 30° = 0·5773502692 = 0·577 to three decimal places
(iv) sin 72° = 0·9510565163 = 0·951 to three decimal places

exam focus

Make sure your calculator is set to work in degrees before starting any trigonometry question.

exam Q

During a trigonometry lesson, a group of students made some predictions about what they expected to find for the values of the trigonometric functions of some angles. They then found the sine, cosine and tangent of 25° and 50°.

(i) In the table given, show, correct to three decimal places, the values they found.

| sin 25° = | cos 25° = | tan 25° = |
| sin 50° = | cos 50° = | tan 50° = |

(ii) (a) Maria had said, 'The value from any of these trigonometric functions will always be less than 1.' Was Maria correct? Give a reason for your answer.

(b) Sharon had said, 'If the size of the angle is doubled, then the value from any of these trigonometric functions will also double.' Was Sharon correct? Give a reason for your answer.

(c) James had said, 'The value for all of these trigonometric functions will increase if the size of the angle is increased.' Was James correct? Give a reason for your answer.

Solution

(i) Completing the table with answers to three decimal places, gives:

| sin 25° = 0·423 | cos 25° = 0·906 | tan 25° = 0·466 |
| sin 50° = 0·766 | cos 50° = 0·643 | tan 50° = 1·192 |

(ii) (a) No, Maria was not correct.

The value for tan 50° = 1·192 is greater than 1, therefore the value from any of these trigonometric functions will not always be less than 1.

(b) No, Sharon was not correct.

In each case, doubling the angle did not result in the value for the trigonometric function doubling. For example, the value for sin 50° = 0·766 is not twice the value for sin 25° = 0·423.

(c) No, James was not correct.

While James's statement is correct for the sine and tangent functions, in the case of the cosine function increasing the size of the angle from cos 25° = 0·906 to cos 50° = 0·643, reduced the value for the trigonometric function.

Using trigonometric ratios to find missing sides or angles in a triangle

To use the trigonometric formula to find a missing side, or a missing angle, in a triangle, following these steps:

1. Label the sides of the triangle.
2. List the information you have and what you want.
3. Select which formula to use.
4. Substitute values into the formula.
5. Solve the resulting equation to find the missing value.

> **key point**
> In each question, write out what information you have and what information you want. This will help you to figure out which formula to use.

Example

ABC is a right-angled triangle.

$|\angle ACB| = 50°$ and $|AC| = 10$ cm.

Calculate the length of $[AB]$, correct to two decimal places.

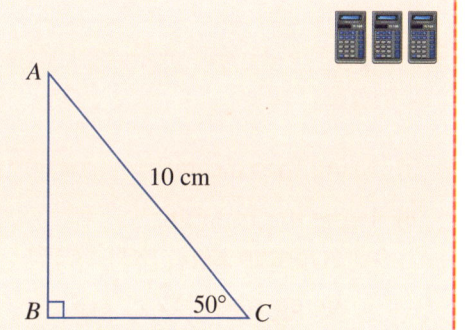

Solution

Label the sides.

    I have: hypotenuse = 10
    I have: angle = 50°
    I want: opposite = $|AB|$

Rule: $\sin \theta = \dfrac{\text{Opp}}{\text{Hyp}}$

    $\sin 50° = \dfrac{|AB|}{10}$ (substitute in known values)

    $10 \sin 50° = |AB|$ (multiply both sides by 10)

    $7 \cdot 66044 = |AB|$ (use calculator to evaluate $10 \sin 50°$)

    $7 \cdot 66 = |AB|$ to two decimal places

In the right-angled triangle XYZ, |XZ| = 13 and |∠YXZ| = 60°.

(i) Using your calculator, write down the value of cos 60°.

(ii) Using the diagram, complete the following

$$\cos 60° = \frac{|XY|}{\Box}$$

(iii) Hence, calculate |XY|.

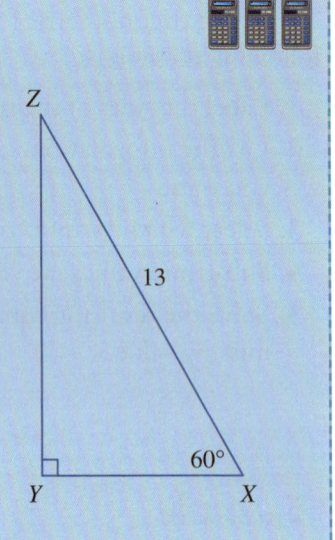

Solution

(i) Using the calculator $\cos 60° = \frac{1}{2} = 0.5$

(ii) Label the triangle:
Hypotenuse = |XZ| = 13
Opposite = |YZ|
Adjacent = |XY|

$$\cos A = \frac{\text{Adjacent}}{\text{Hypotenuse}}$$

Then, $\cos 60° = \frac{|XY|}{|XZ|}$

or $\cos 60° = \frac{|XY|}{13}$

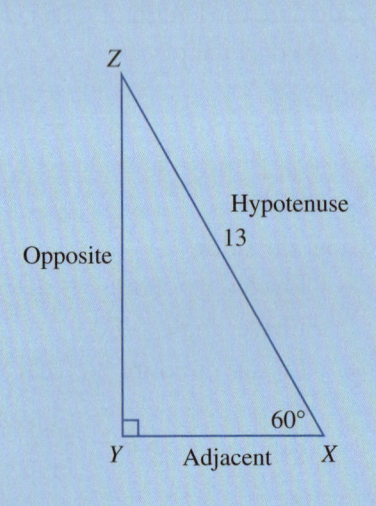

(iii) $\cos 60° = \frac{|XY|}{13}$

13(cos 60°) = |XY|

13(0·5) = |XY| (cos 60° = 0·5 from part (i))

6·5 = |XY|

In the right-angled triangle PQR, |QR| = 4 and |∠QPR| = 48°.

(i) Find |∠PQR|.

(ii) Using your calculator, write down the value of tan ∠PQR, correct to one decimal place.

(iii) Hence, or otherwise, calculate |PR| correct to one decimal place.

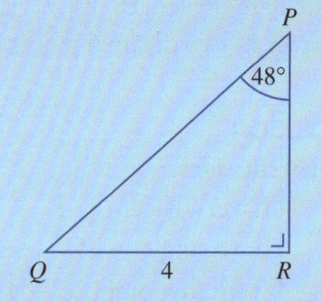

Solution

(i) The three angles of a triangle add up to 180°.

$$|\angle PQR| + 48° + 90° = 180°$$
$$|\angle PQR| = 180° - 90° - 48°$$
$$|\angle PQR| = 42°$$

(ii) tan ∠PQR → tan 42° = 0·9004 = 0·9 to one decimal place

(iii) Label the triangle in relation to ∠PQR:

I have: adjacent = 4

I have: angle = 42°

I want: opposite

Rule: $\tan \theta = \dfrac{\text{Opp}}{\text{Adj}}$

$\tan 42° = \dfrac{|PR|}{4}$ (substitute in known values)

$4(\tan 42°) = |PR|$ (multiply both sides by 4)

$4(0·9) = |PR|$ (tan 42° = 0·9 from part (ii))

$3·6 = |PR|$

Example

ABC is a right-angled triangle.
$|\angle BAC| = 35°$ and $|AB| = 8$ cm.

Calculate the length of $[AC]$, correct to two decimal places.

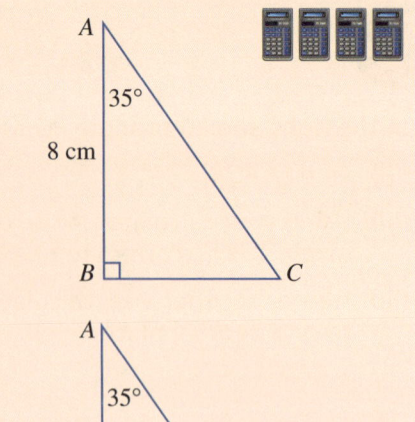

Solution

Label the sides:

I have: adjacent = 8
I have: angle = 35°
I want: hypotenuse = $|AC|$

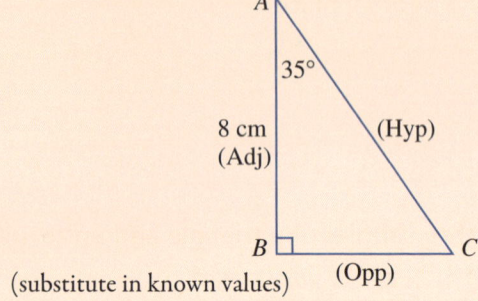

Rule: $\cos \theta = \dfrac{\text{Adj}}{\text{Hyp}}$

$\cos 35° = \dfrac{8}{|AC|}$ (substitute in known values)

$|AC|\cos 35° = 8$ (multiply both sides by $|AC|$)

$|AC| = \dfrac{8}{\cos 35°}$ (divide both sides by cos 35°)

$|AC| = 9\cdot 76619$ $\left(\text{use the calculator to evaluate } \dfrac{8}{\cos 35°}\right)$

$|AC| = 9\cdot 77$ to two decimal places.

exam Q

(i) The diagram shows the angle A in a right-angled triangle. Indicate which side is adjacent and which is opposite in relation to the angle A, and which side is the hypotenuse.

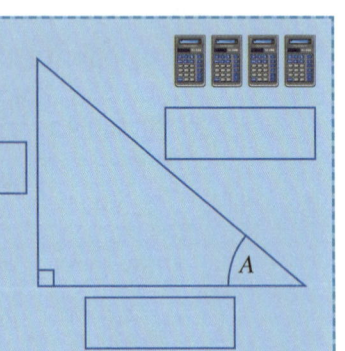

(ii) Fill in the appropriate ratios in the table below.

Trigonometric Ratio	Ratio
	$\dfrac{\text{opposite}}{\text{hypotenuse}}$
Cos A	
	$\dfrac{\text{opposite}}{\text{adjacent}}$

(iii) In the right-angled triangle

B = 35° and the opposite side is 12 cm.

Find the length of the hypotenuse correct to the nearest centimetre.

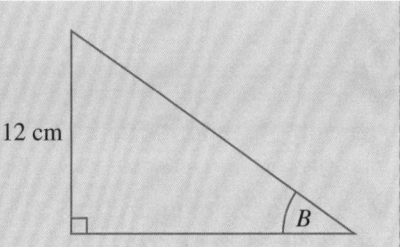

Solution

(i) **Hypotenuse:**

The side opposite the right angle. It is also the longest side.

Opposite:

The side opposite the angle A.

Adjacent:

The side beside (adjacent to) A.

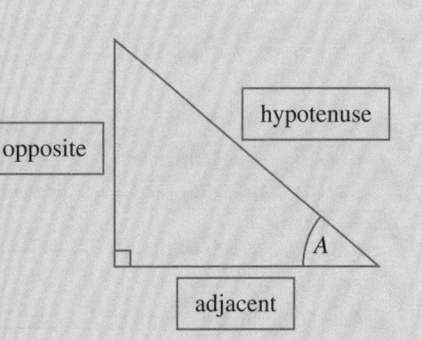

(ii) Completing the table:

Trigonometric Ratio	Ratio
Sin A	$\dfrac{\text{opposite}}{\text{hypotenuse}}$
Cos A	$\dfrac{\text{adjacent}}{\text{hypotenuse}}$
Tan A	$\dfrac{\text{opposite}}{\text{adjacent}}$

(iii) Label the sides.

I have: opposite = 12

I have: angle = 35°

I want: hypotenuse

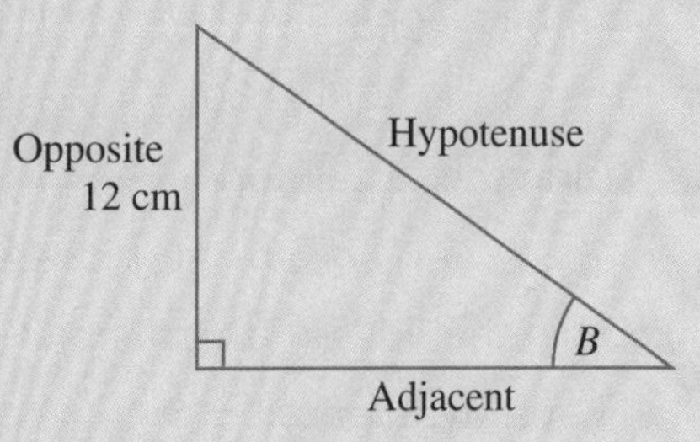

Rule: $\sin \theta = \dfrac{\text{opp}}{\text{hyp}}$

$\sin 35° = \dfrac{12}{\text{hyp}}$ (substitute in known values)

Hyp (sin 35°) = 12   (multiply both sides by hyp)

Hyp = $\dfrac{12}{\sin 35°}$ (divide both sides by sin 35°)

Hyp = 20·92136 $\left(\text{use the calculator to evaluate } \dfrac{12}{\sin 35°}\right)$

Hyp = 21 cm, to the nearest centimetre.

A group of students want to find the vertical height (h) of the triangle ABC.

Mary suggests measuring the angle at B using a protractor and using the sine function to find h.

(i) Estimate $|\angle B|$ from the diagram and, hence, find sin B.

(ii) If $|AB|$ = 8 cm, use your value of sin B to find h.
Give your answer correct to the nearest whole number.

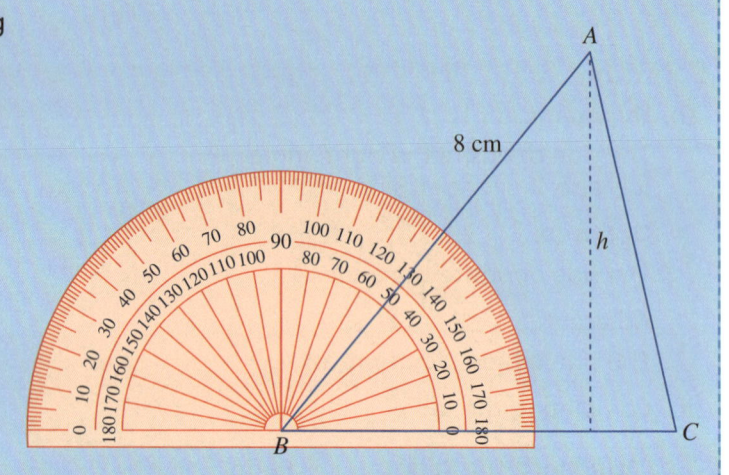

(iii) If $|BC|$ = 7·5 cm, use your answer from part (ii) to find the area of ABC.

Solution

(i) Observing the protractor: Each segment represents 10 degrees. The angle B takes up 5 segments on the protractor (shaded in green on the diagram).

Therefore, $|\angle B| = 50°$.

Using the calculator:
$$\sin \angle B = \sin 50° = 0·7660444431$$

(ii) Label the sides in the triangle:

I have: hypotenuse = 8

I have: angle = 50°

I want: opposite = h, height

Rule: $\sin \theta = \dfrac{\text{Opp}}{\text{Hyp}}$

$\sin 50° = \dfrac{h}{8}$ (put in known values)

$8(\sin 50°) = h$ (multiply both sides by 8)

$6·128 = h$ (use calculator)

Therefore, height, h = 6 cm, to the nearest whole number.

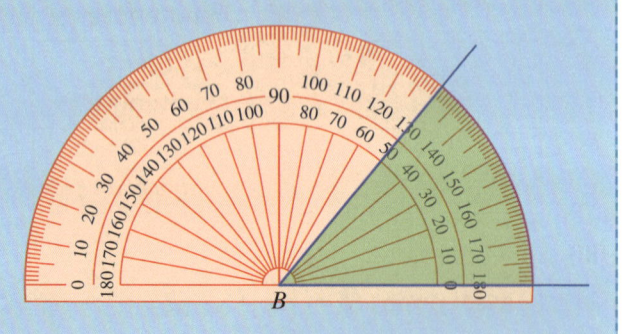

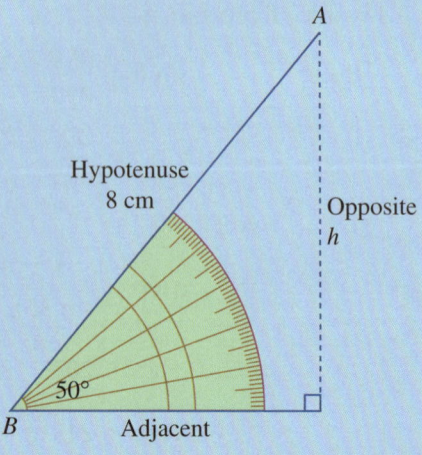

(iii) Area of triangle = $\frac{1}{2}$ (base)(height)

(see booklet of formulae and tables, page 9)

Area of triangle = $\frac{1}{2}$ (7·5)(6)

Area of triangle = 22·5 cm²

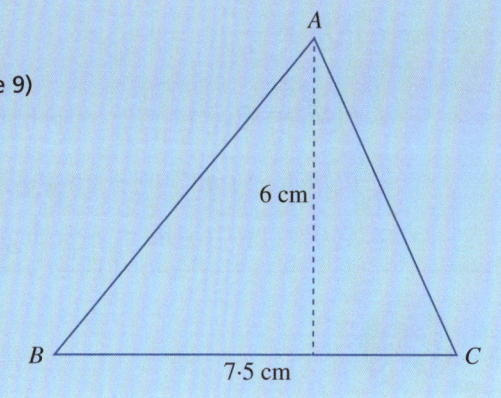

exam focus

Many students have difficulty when using the trigonometric functions to find a missing angle in a triangle. This is covered in the next two questions. Pay close attention to these questions.

Example

In the right-angled triangle PQR, $|PQ| = 10$ and $|PR| = 7$.

(i) Use the diagram to write $\sin \angle PQR$ as a fraction.

(ii) Hence, find the measure of $\angle PQR$, correct to the nearest degree.

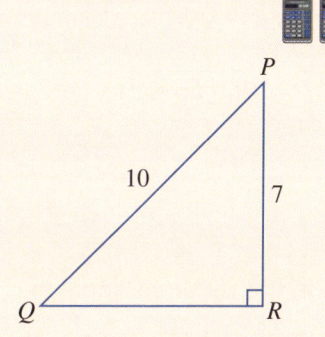

Solution

(i) Label the sides in relation to $\angle PQR$.

I have: Hypotenuse = 10
I have: Opposite = 7
I want: Angle = $|\angle PQR|$

$$\sin \theta = \frac{\text{Opp}}{\text{Hyp}}$$

$$\sin \angle PQR = \frac{7}{10}$$

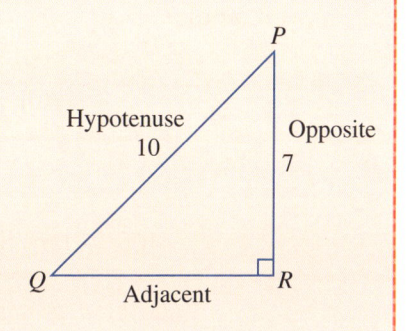

(ii) $\sin \angle PQR = \dfrac{7}{10}$

$\angle PQR = \sin^{-1}\left(\dfrac{7}{10}\right)$ (apply $\sin^{-1}$ to both sides)

$\angle PQR = 44 \cdot 427°$ (use the calculator to evaluate $\sin^{-1}(\tfrac{7}{10})$)

$\angle PQR = 44°$ to the nearest degree.

key point

Use your calculator to find $\sin^{-1}$, by pressing:

$\boxed{\text{shift}}$ then $\boxed{\text{sin}}$ (Casio calculator)

or

$\boxed{\text{2}^{\text{nd}}\text{ F}}$ then $\boxed{\text{sin}}$ (Sharp calculator)

exam Q

ABC is a right-angled triangle. $|BC| = 7$ cm and $|AB| = 5$ cm.

Find $|\angle ACB|$, correct to one place of decimal.

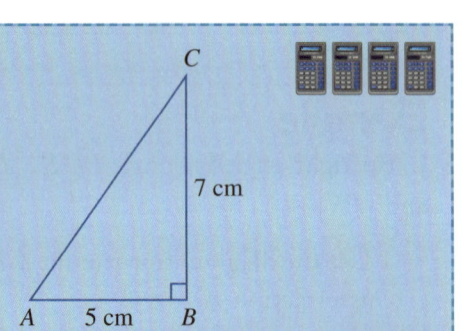

Solution
Mark in the required angle and, hence, label the sides.

I have: adjacent = 7

I have: opposite = 5

I want: angle

Rule: $\tan \theta = \dfrac{\text{Opp}}{\text{Adj}}$

$\tan |\angle ACB| = \dfrac{5}{7}$ (substitute in known values)

$|\angle ACB| = \tan^{-1}\left(\dfrac{5}{7}\right)$ (apply $\tan^{-1}$ to both sides)

$|\angle ACB| = 35 \cdot 537°$ (use the calculator to evaluate $\tan^{-1}\left(\dfrac{5}{7}\right)$)

$\angle ACB = 35 \cdot 5°$ to one decimal places.

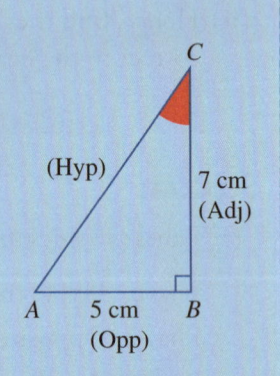

TRIGONOMETRY 1

exam Q

(i) What name is given to the longest side in a right-angled triangle?

(ii) In the case of each of the three right-angled triangles below, measure the two sides indicated and write the lengths, in millimetres, in the boxes provided.

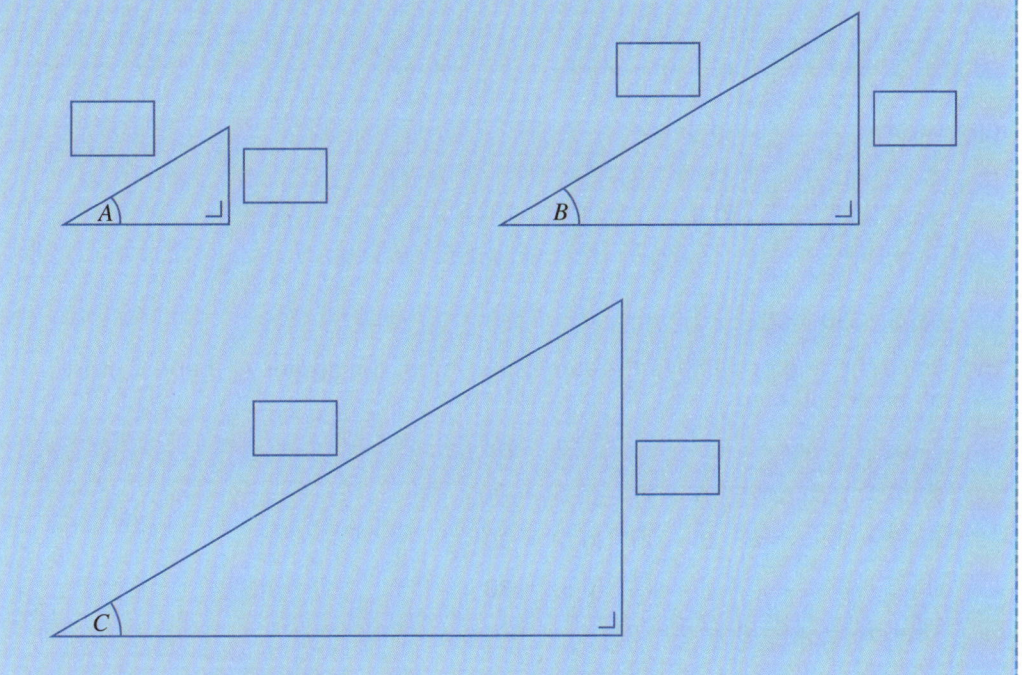

(iii) Use your measurements to write sin A, sin B and sin C as fractions and also as decimals.

(iv) From your answers for part (iii), what can you say about the angles A, B and C? Give a reason for your answer.

Solution

(i) The longest side in a right-angled triangle is called the hypotenuse.

(ii) Using a ruler to measure, the lengths of the sides are found and entered into the boxes.

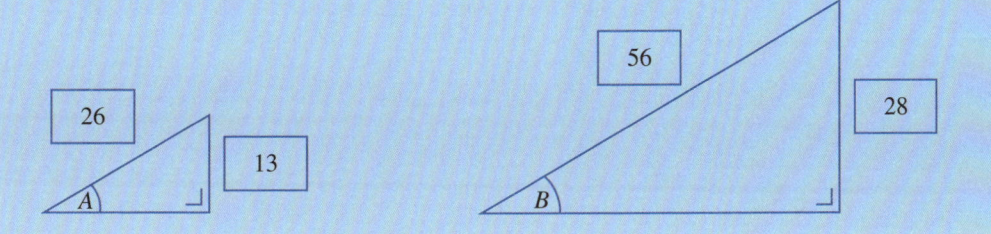

26, 13, 56, 28

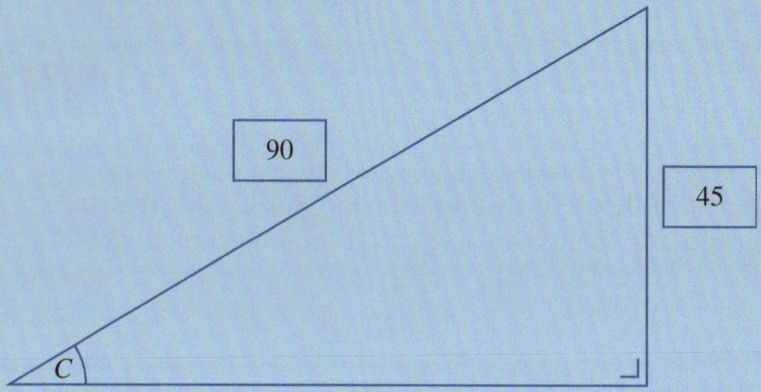

(iii) $\sin A = \frac{13}{26} = \frac{1}{2} = 0{\cdot}5$

$\sin B = \frac{28}{56} = \frac{1}{2} = 0{\cdot}5$

$\sin C = \frac{45}{90} = \frac{1}{2} = 0{\cdot}5$

(iv) Since the angles all have the same sine value, the angles *A*, *B* and *C* must all be equal.

or

$\sin A = 0{\cdot}5 \quad \Rightarrow \quad A = \sin^{-1}(0{\cdot}5) = 30°$

$\sin B = 0{\cdot}5 \quad \Rightarrow \quad B = \sin^{-1}(0{\cdot}5) = 30°$

$\sin C = 0{\cdot}5 \quad \Rightarrow \quad C = \sin^{-1}(0{\cdot}5) = 30°$

Therefore, $A = B = C = 30°$.

6 Trigonometry II: Real-World Applications

aims
- To learn how to solve triangles to find missing sides or angles
- To learn how to find the area of a triangle
- To learn how to solve trigonometric equations

Trigonometry and geometry in context

Some exam questions will require you to combine your knowledge of geometry and trigonometry to solve real-life problems. Many practical problems in navigation, surveying, engineering and geography involve solving a triangle. When solving practical problems using trigonometry, represent each situation with a right-angled triangle. Mark on your triangle the angles and lengths you know and label what you need to calculate. Use the correct ratio to link the angle or length required with the known angle or length.

key point

When a question involves a tree, tower, building, cliff, etc. we can assume that a right angle is formed between the vertical object and the ground.

exam focus

It is very important to draw a sketch of the situation. This will help you to visualise the problem and hopefully lead you to a solution.

Angle of elevation

The **angle of elevation** of an object as seen by an observer is the angle between the horizontal line from the object to the observer's eye (upwards from the horizontal).

Angle of elevation is the angle from the horizontal **up**.

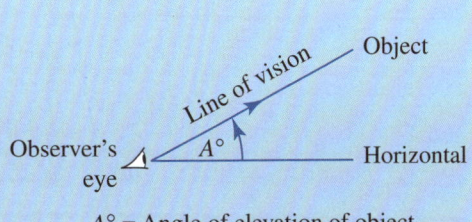

$A°$ = Angle of elevation of object

Angle of depression

If the object is below the level of the observer, the angle between the horizontal and the observer's line of vision is called the **angle of depression** (downwards from the horizontal).

Angle of depression is the angle from the horizontal **down**.

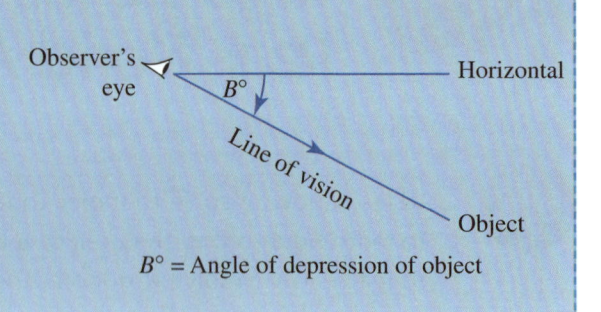

$B°$ = Angle of depression of object

key point

An angle of elevation has an equal angle of depression. The angle of elevation from A to B is equal to the angle of depression from B to A.

The angles are alternate angles, as the horizontal lines are parallel.

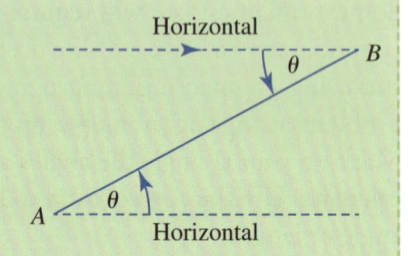

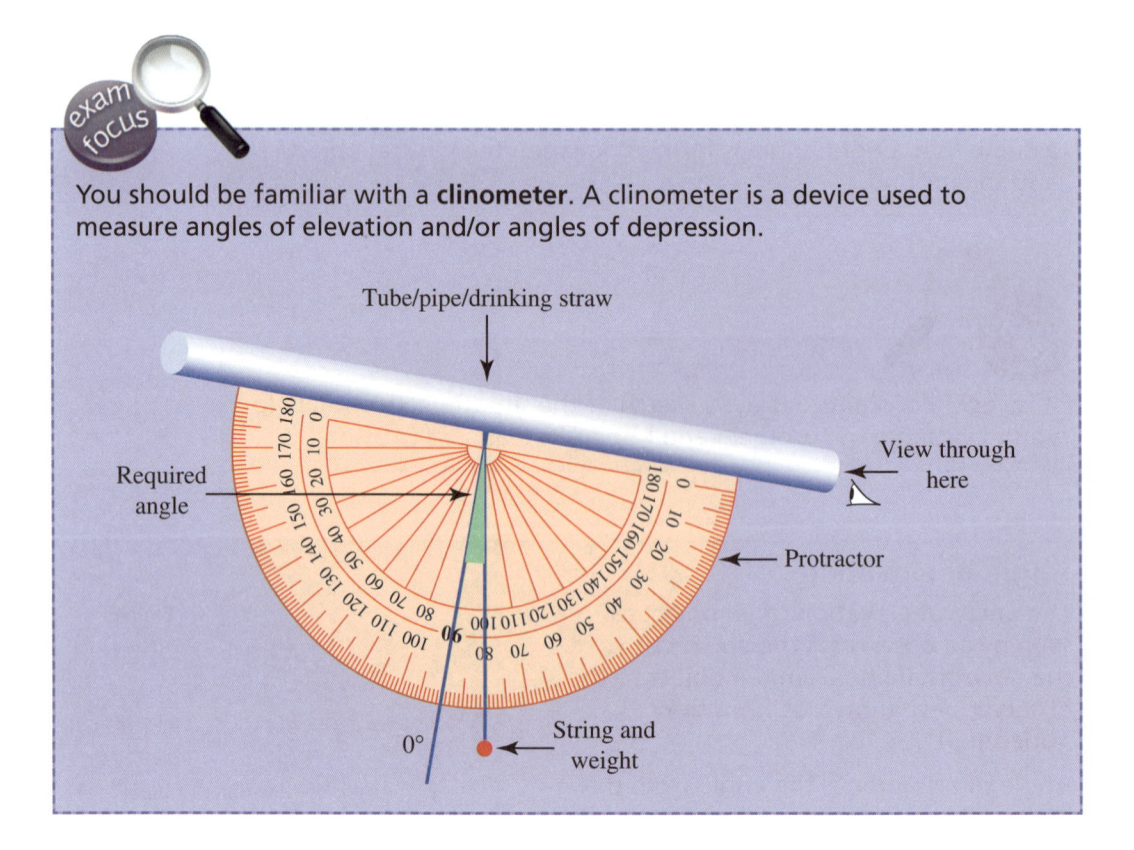

exam focus

You should be familiar with a **clinometer**. A clinometer is a device used to measure angles of elevation and/or angles of depression.

TRIGONOMETRY II: REAL-WORLD APPLICATIONS

Example

A kite on a string makes an angle of 40° to the horizontal ground (this is the angle of elevation).

The length of the string is 15 m.

How high above the ground is the kite? Give your answer to the nearest metre.

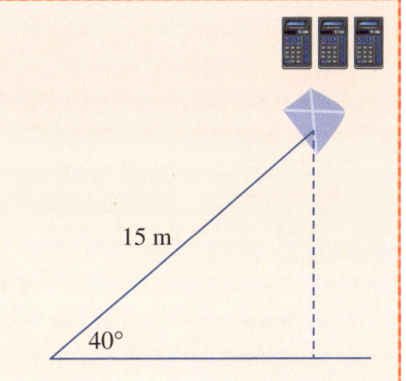

Solution

Redraw the triangle and label the sides:

I have: hypotenuse = 15
I have: angle = 40°
I want: opposite (height of the kite)

Rule: $\sin \theta = \dfrac{\text{opp}}{\text{hyp}}$

$\sin 40° = \dfrac{\text{opp}}{15}$ (substitute in known values)

$15 (\sin 40°) = \text{opp}$ (multiply both sides by 15)

$9 \cdot 6418 = \text{opp}$ (use calculator to find the value of 15 (sin 40°))

Therefore, height of the kite = 10 m, to the nearest metre.

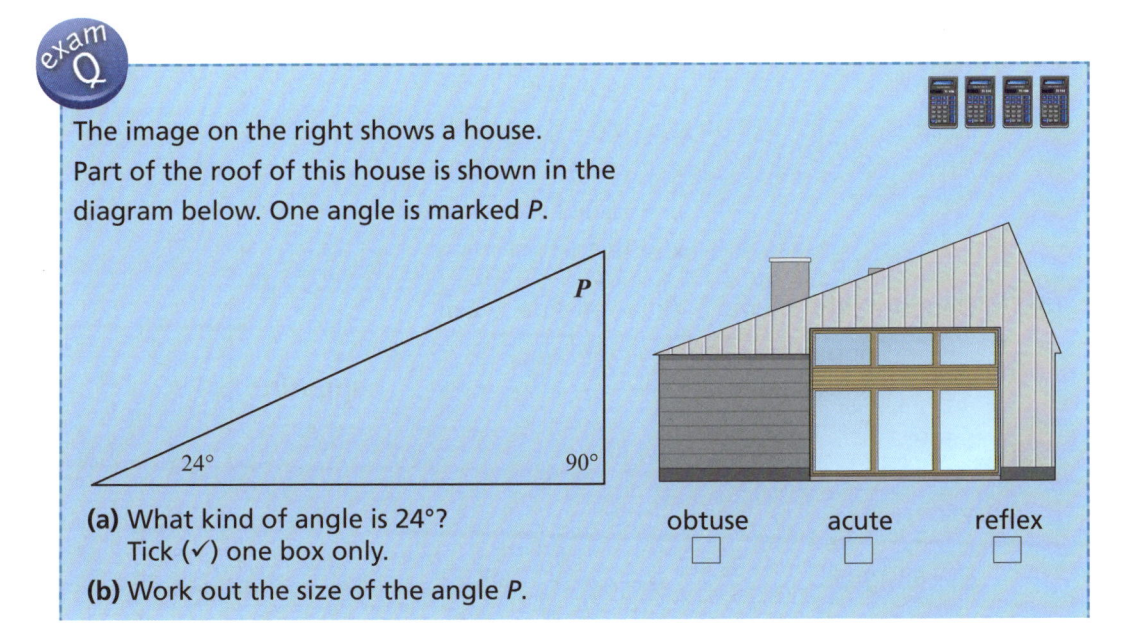

exam Q

The image on the right shows a house. Part of the roof of this house is shown in the diagram below. One angle is marked *P*.

(a) What kind of angle is 24°?
Tick (✓) one box only.

obtuse ☐   acute ☐   reflex ☐

(b) Work out the size of the angle *P*.

(c) The diagram shows more of the roof of this house.
AB is perpendicular to DC.
The lengths of some of the sides are shown on the diagram.
Note: ∠ACB is not a right angle.
Use the theorem of Pythagoras to work out the length x.
Give your answer in metres, correct to one decimal place.

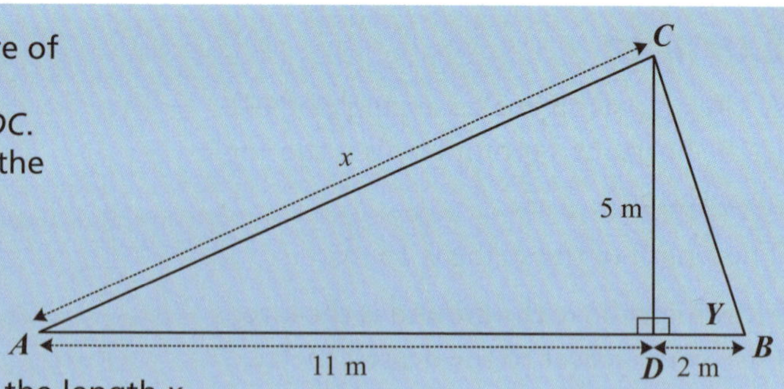

(d) Y is one of the angles in the triangle DBC.
   (i) Write down the length of the side opposite Y and the side adjacent to Y in DBC.
   (ii) Use your answer from part (d)(i) to write tan Y as a fraction.
   (iii) Hence, use a calculator to find the size of the angle Y, correct to the nearest degree.

Solution

(a) Angle 24° is less than 90°, so it is an acute angle:

obtuse ☐   acute ✓   reflex ☐

(b) The three angles in the triangle sum to 180°:
$$24° + 90° + P = 180°$$
$$114° + P = 180°$$
$$P = 180° - 114°$$
$$P = 66°$$

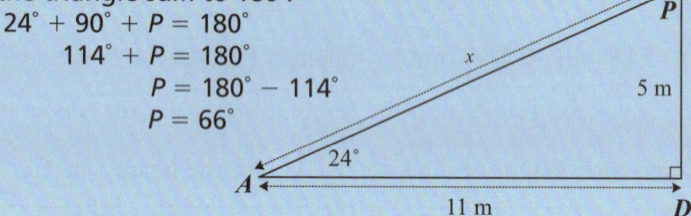

(c) Pythagoras' Theorem:
$$|AC|^2 = |CD|^2 + |AD|^2$$
$$x^2 = 5^2 + 11^2$$
$$x^2 = 25 + 121$$
$$x^2 = 146$$
$$x = \sqrt{146}$$
$$x = 12·083...$$
$$x = 12·1 \text{ m}$$

(d) (i) Opposite side = 5 m,   Adjacent side = 2 m

(ii) $\tan Y = \dfrac{\text{opposite}}{\text{adjacent}}$

$\tan Y = \dfrac{5}{2}$

(iii) $Y = \tan^{-1}\left(\dfrac{5}{2}\right)$

$Y = 68·1985...$ ⇒ $Y = 68°$

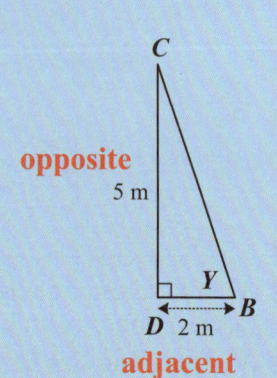

Example

The diagram shows an office block built on a river bank. From a point on the opposite river bank, the angle of elevation of the top of the office block is 30°.

(i) Find h, the height of the office block.
(ii) Find w, the width of the river, correct to 2 decimal places.

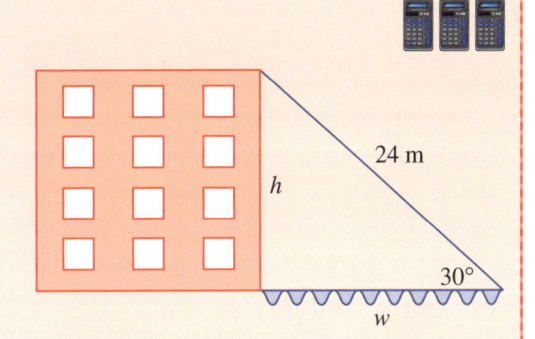

Solution

(i) Redraw the triangle and label the sides, in relation to the 30° angle.

To find h:

We have the hypotenuse = 24 m and we want the opposite = h.
Therefore, use the formula:

$$\sin \theta = \frac{\text{opp}}{\text{hyp}}$$

$$\sin 30° = \frac{h}{24}$$

$$24 \sin 30° = h$$

$$12 = h$$

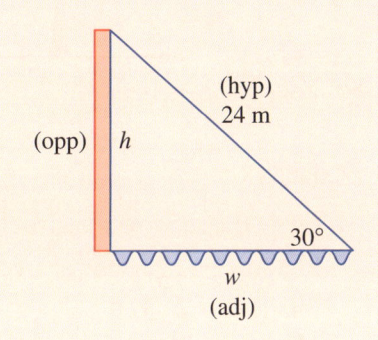

Therefore, the height of the building is 12 m.

(ii) Redraw the triangle and label the sides, in relation to the 30° angle.

To find w:

We have the hypotenuse = 24 m and we want the adjacent = w.
Therefore, use the formula:

$$\cos \theta = \frac{\text{adj}}{\text{hyp}}$$

$$\cos 30° = \frac{w}{24}$$

$$24 \cos 30° = w$$

$$20 \cdot 7846 = w$$

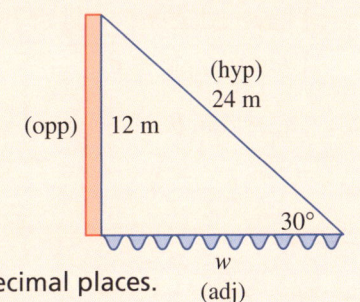

Therefore, the width of the river is 20·78 m to 2 decimal places.

exam focus

For part (ii), since we have the opposite, we could have used $\tan \theta = \frac{\text{opp}}{\text{adj}}$ or Pythagoras' theorem. However, if possible, it is good practice to avoid using values you have found in earlier parts of a question, in case you have made a mistake.

Example

A tree 32 m high casts a shadow twice its length.

(i) Write down the length of the shadow of the tree.

(ii) Calculate θ, the angle of elevation of the sun.
Give your answer to the nearest degree.

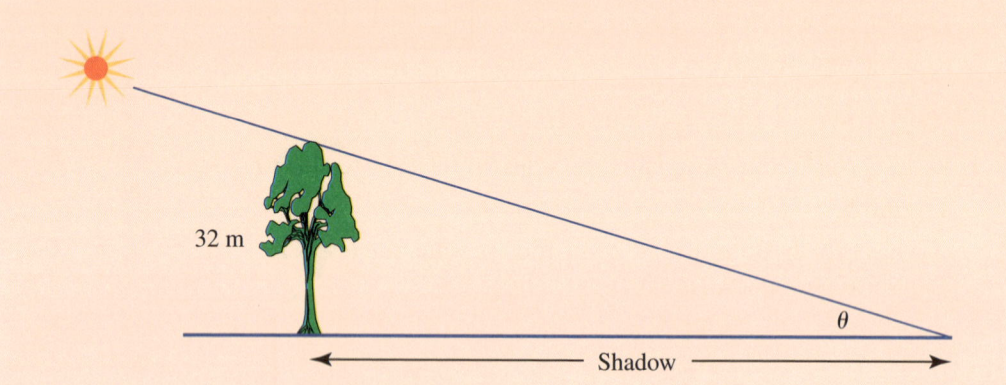

Solution

(i) Since the shadow is twice the height of the tree:
Shadow = 2 (height of tree)
Shadow = 2 (32)
Shadow = 64 m

(ii) Enter the length of the shadow of the tree.
Label the sides in relation to the angle of elevation:
I have: opposite = 32
I have: adjacent = 64
I want: angle = θ

Rule: $\tan \theta = \dfrac{\text{opp}}{\text{adj}}$

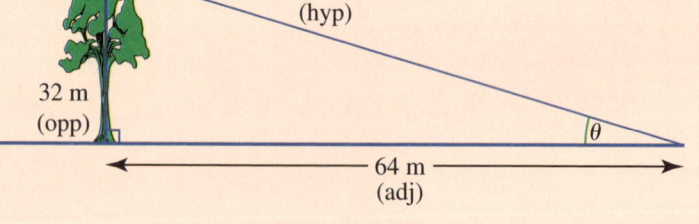

$\tan \theta = \dfrac{32}{64}$ (substitute in known values)

$\theta = \tan^{-1}\left(\dfrac{32}{64}\right)$ (apply $\tan^{-1}$ to both sides)

$\theta = 26 \cdot 565°$ (use the calculator to find the value of $\tan^{-1}\left(\dfrac{32}{64}\right)$)

Therefore, the angle of elevation is 27°, to the nearest degree.

TRIGONOMETRY II: REAL-WORLD APPLICATIONS

exam Q

Jasmine wants to find the height of her house. She measures the angle of elevation to the top of the roof using a clinometer. The angle is 30°.

She is standing 18 m from the point on the ground directly below the apex of the roof. Jasmine draws the diagram given below to show this information.

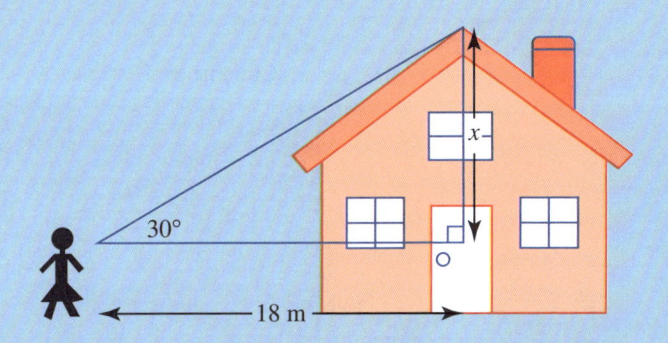

(i) Use Jasmine's measurements to find *x*. Write your answer in metres, correct to one decimal place.

(ii) What other information is needed to find the height of the house?

Solution

(i) Redraw the triangle and label the sides:

I have: adjacent = 18
I have: angle = 30°
I want: opposite = x

Rule: $\tan \theta = \dfrac{\text{opp}}{\text{adj}}$

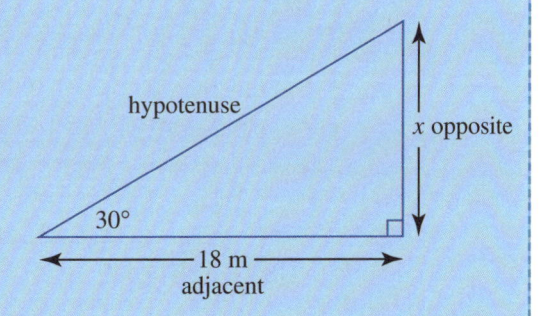

$\tan 30° = \dfrac{x}{18}$ (substitute in known values)

$18 (\tan 30°) = x$ (multiply both sides by 18)

$10 \cdot 3923 = x$ (use calculator to find the value of 18 (tan 30°))

Therefore, x = 10·4 m, to one decimal place.

(ii) Jasmine would need to measure the height from the ground up to her eyes. She would then need to add this height onto 10·4 m to get the total height of the house.

Seán makes a clinometer using a protractor, a straw, a piece of thread and a piece of plasticine (used as a weight). He stands 10 m from a tree and uses his clinometer to measure the angle of elevation to the top of the tree as shown. Seán is 1·75 m in height.

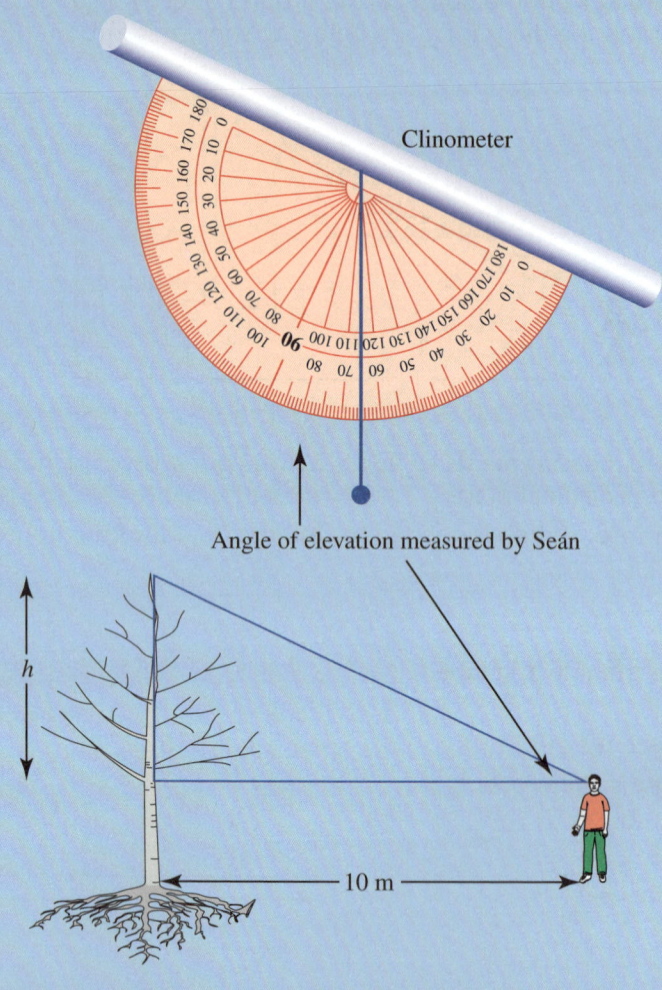

(i) Find the angle of elevation by reading the clinometer above.

(ii) Calculate the height h as shown in the diagram. Give your answer correct to two decimal places.

(iii) Find the total height of the tree.

(iv) Another student uses the same method as Seán and finds the height of the tree to be 23·1 m. Seán did not get this answer. Give one possible reason why the answers might be different.

TRIGONOMETRY II: REAL-WORLD APPLICATIONS

Solution

(i) Observing the clinometer:

Each segment represents 10°.

The angle takes up 2·5 segments on the clinometer (shaded in green on the diagram)

Therefore, the angle of elevation = 25°.

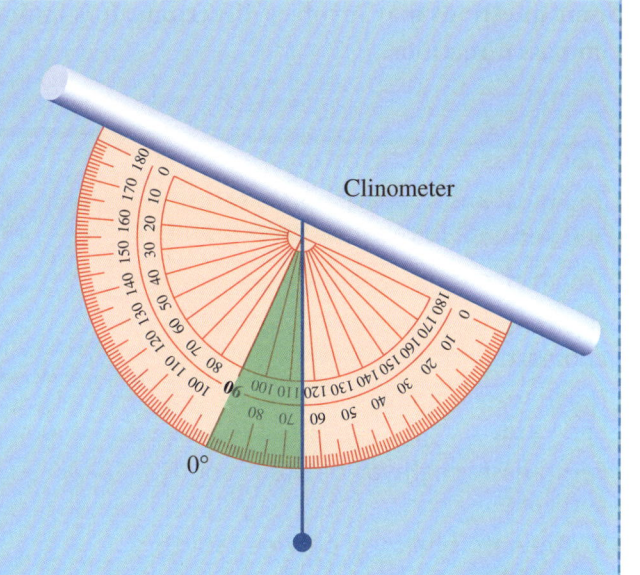

(ii) Redraw the triangle and label the sides:

I have: adjacent = 10
I have: angle = 25°
I want: opposite = h

Rule: $\tan \theta = \dfrac{\text{opp}}{\text{adj}}$

$\tan 25° = \dfrac{h}{10}$ (put in known values)

$10 (\tan 25°) = h$ (multiply both sides by 10)

$4·663 = h$ (use calculator)

Therefore, $h = 4·66$ m, to two decimal places.

(iii) Height of the tree = Height of Seán + value for h (from part (ii))

Height of the tree = 1·75 + 4·66

Height of the tree = 6·41 m

(iv) The different answers may result from inaccuracy in measuring the height of the boys, the distance 10 m or the angle on the clinometer.

For example, the other boy may have measured the angle on the wrong side of the weight on the clinometer.

exam focus

In a recent exam, this question was very poorly answered. Consequently part (i) was awarded 10 marks. Parts (ii) and (iii) **together** were awarded a total of 5 marks and part (iv) was awarded 5 marks.

Some questions may involves directions. It is important that you understand compass directions.

Compass directions

You must know where north, south, east and west are in relation to each other.

You must also be aware that:

North-east is halfway between north and east.

North-west is halfway between north and west.

South-east is halfway between south and east.

South-west is halfway between south and west.

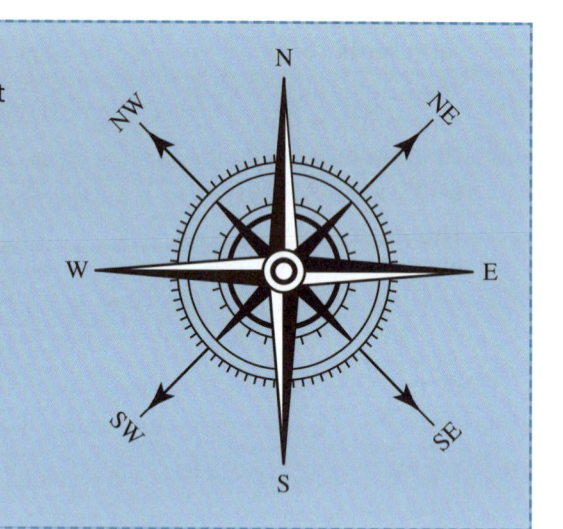

Example

Holly wished to measure the width of a river. She was at point A on the river bank, which is directly south of point B on the other bank, as shown in the diagram.

Holly walked due west, from A to C, along the river bank, at an average speed of $1 \cdot 5$ m/s.

It took Holly 40 seconds to walk from A to C.

She then measured $\angle ACB$ and found it to be 25°.

(i) Calculate $|AC|$, the distance walked by Holly.

(ii) Hence, calculate $|AB|$, the width of the river.

Give your answer correct to the nearest metre.

key point

Remember the formulae which relate distance, speed and time:

Solution

(i) Speed = $1 \cdot 5$ m/s   Distance = Speed × Time

Time = 40 sec $|AC| = (1 \cdot 5)(40)$

$|AC| = 60$ m

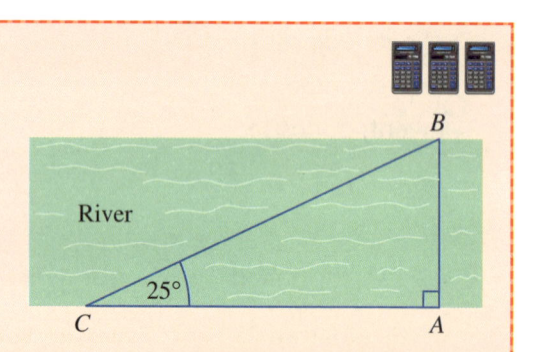

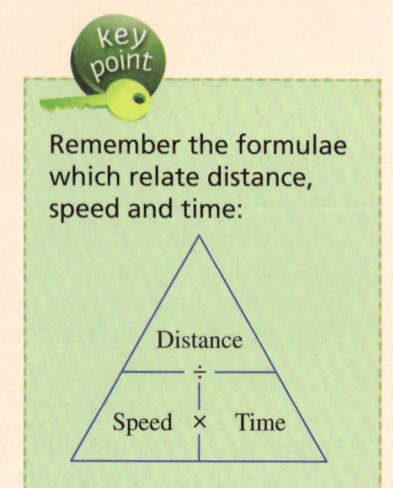

TRIGONOMETRY II: REAL-WORLD APPLICATIONS

(ii) Redraw the triangle and label the sides:

I have: adjacent = 60
I have: angle = 25°
I want: opposite

Rule: $\tan \theta = \dfrac{\text{opp}}{\text{adj}}$

$\tan 25° = \dfrac{|AB|}{60}$ (put in known values)

$60 (\tan 25°) = |AB|$ (multiply both sides by 60)

$27·978 = |AB|$ (use calculator)

$28 \text{ m} = |AB|$

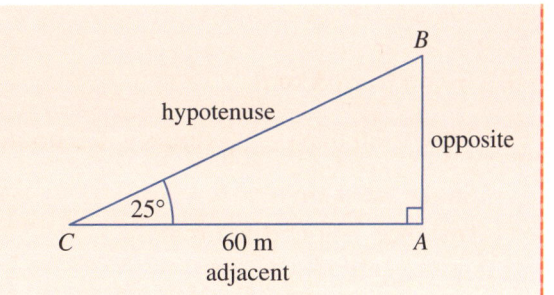

---

exam Q

A boat travels due north from A for 30 minutes at 20 km/h.

It reaches B and then travels due east for 24 minutes at 10 km/h.

It is then at C.

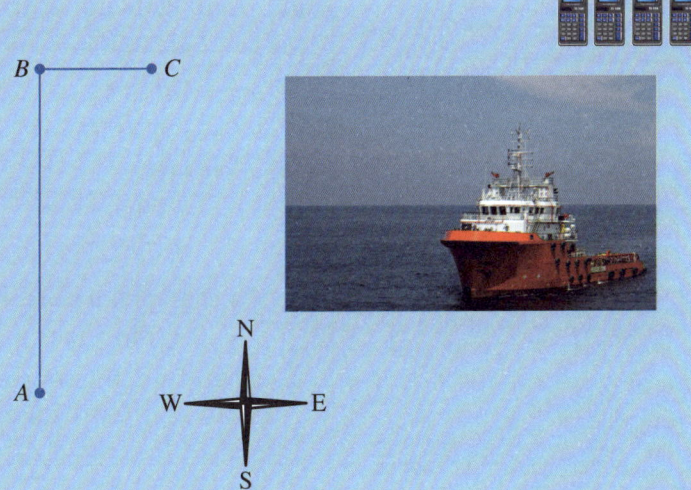

(i) How many kilometres has the boat travelled?
(ii) On the diagram, draw a line segment that shows the shortest distance from C back to A.
(iii) Use Pythagoras' theorem to calculate the shortest distance from C to A. Give your answer correct to the nearest metre.

Solution

(i) Going from *A* to *B*:

Time = 30 mins = $\frac{30}{60}$ hours = 0·5 hours

Speed = 20 km/h

Distance = Speed × Time

$|AB|$ = 20 × 0·5

$|AB|$ = 10 km

Going from *B* to *C*:

Time = 24 mins = $\frac{24}{60}$ hours = 0·4 hours

Speed = 10 km/h

Distance = Speed × Time

$|BC|$ = 10 × 0·4

$|BC|$ = 4 km

The boat has travelled 10 + 4 = 14 km

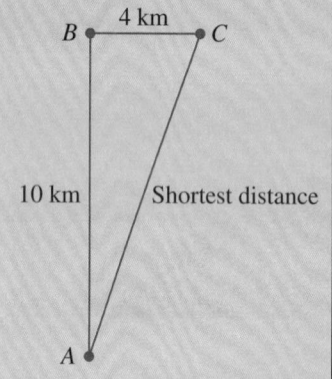

(ii)

B •———4 km———• C

10 km   Shortest distance

A •

(iii) Using Pythagoras' theorem:

$c^2 = a^2 + b^2$

$c^2 = 10^2 + 4^2$

$c^2 = 100 + 16$

$c^2 = 116$

$c = \sqrt{116}$

c = 10·77032961 km

To change km to m, multiply by 1 000:

c = 10 770·32961 m

Therefore, the shortest distance from *C* to *A* = 10 770 m, to the nearest metre.

TRIGONOMETRY II: REAL-WORLD APPLICATIONS

exam Q

Dolores is at the point C on the top of a cliff. The point B is at the base of the cliff. The height of the cliff is 35 m, as shown in the diagram.

She wishes to find |BA|, the distance from the base of the cliff to the base of the lighthouse.

Dolores measured the angle of depression from the top of the cliff to the base of the lighthouse, ∠DCA, and found it to be 41°.

CD is parallel to BA.

(i) Find |∠BAC|.
(ii) Find, to the nearest metre, |BA|, the distance from the base of the cliff to the base of the lighthouse.

Solution

(i) Since CD is parallel to BA, ∠DCA and ∠BAC are alternate angles.
Therefore, |∠BAC| = |∠DCA| = 41°.

(ii) Redraw the triangle and label the sides:

I have: opposite = 35

I have: angle = 41°

I want: adjacent = |BA|

Rule: $\tan \theta = \dfrac{\text{opp}}{\text{adj}}$

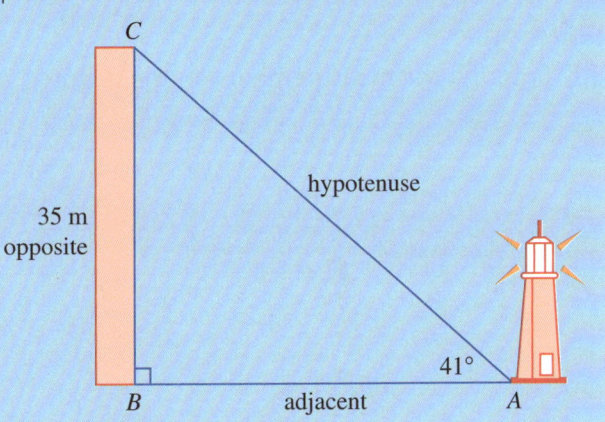

$\tan 41° = \dfrac{35}{|BA|}$ (put in known values)

$|BA| \tan 41° = 35$ (multiply both sides by |BA|)

$|BA| = \dfrac{35}{\tan 41°}$ (divide both sides by tan 41°)

$|BA| = 40·262$ (use calculator)

Therefore, |BA| = 40 m, to the nearest metre.

LESS STRESS MORE SUCCESS

On a school trip to a monastic site, Cliodhna decided to measure the height of the round tower. She stood on a mound a horizontal distance of 30 m from the tower. Using a clinometer, Cliodhna measured the angle of elevation to the top of the tower to be 18° and the angle of depression to the bottom of the tower to be 32°.

(i) Draw a diagram showing Cliodhna's measurements.
(ii) Hence, calculate the height of the tower. Give your answer to one decimal place.

Solution
(i) Entering the measurements on the picture:

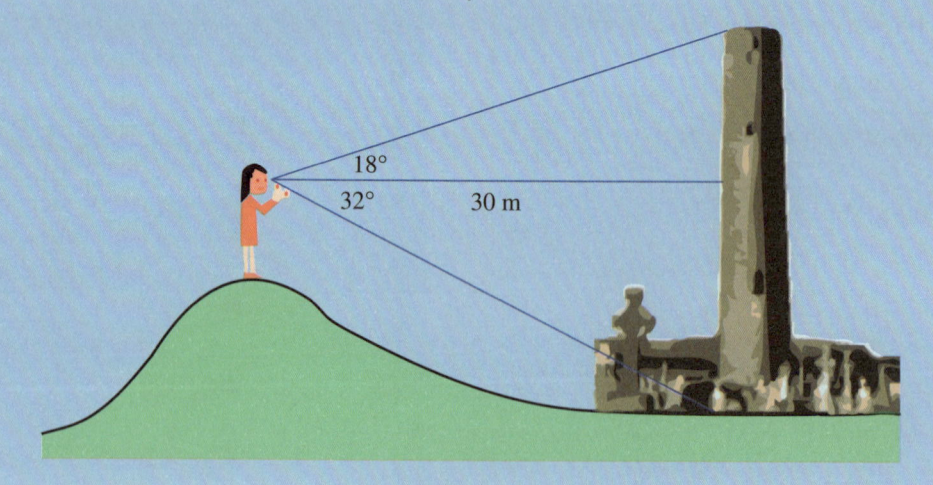

(ii) We can split the shape into two right-angled triangles:

Label the triangles ① and ②.

Label the sides of the triangles in relation to the given angles.

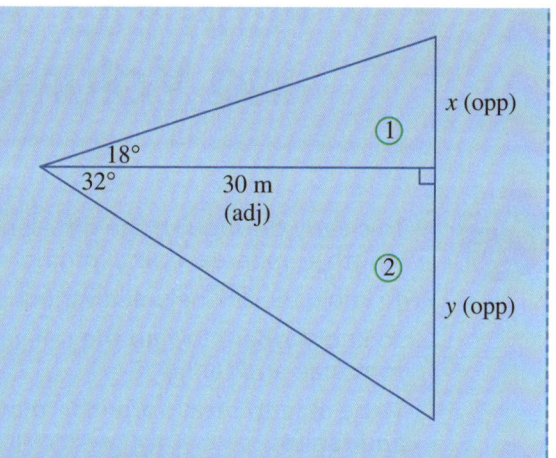

Triangle ①:
We have the adjacent and we want the opposite. Therefore, use formula:

$$\tan \theta = \frac{\text{opp}}{\text{adj}}$$

$$\tan 18° = \frac{x}{30}$$

$$30 \tan 18° = x$$

$$9 \cdot 74759 \text{ m} = x$$

Triangle ②:
We have the adjacent and we want the opposite. Therefore, use formula:

$$\tan \theta = \frac{\text{opp}}{\text{adj}}$$

$$\tan 32° = \frac{y}{30}$$

$$30 (\tan 32°) = y$$

$$18 \cdot 746 \text{ m} = y$$

Height of the tower = $x + y$
$\quad\quad\quad\quad\quad\quad\quad\;\; = 9 \cdot 74759 + 18 \cdot 746$
$\quad\quad\quad\quad\quad\quad\quad\;\; = 28 \cdot 49359$

Therefore, the height of the tower = 28·5 m, to one decimal place.

7 Perimeter, Area, Nets and Volume

aims

- To clearly distinguish the difference between the units of measure, e.g. length = m; area = m²; volume = m³
- To know the link between various units, e.g. litres and cm³ [1 l = 1 000 cm³]
- To know where to find the relevant information in the booklet of formulae and tables
- To be able to recall formulae that are not in the booklet of formulae and tables
- To know how to calculate the perimeter and areas of regular and compound 2D shapes
- To know how to calculate the surface area and volume of a cuboid, and volume of a cylinder
- To understand and be able to draw nets
- To gain the experience and confidence to apply the above knowledge in real-life exam-type questions

Perimeter and area of 2D shapes with triangles and rectangles

Example

Calculate the area of the triangle:

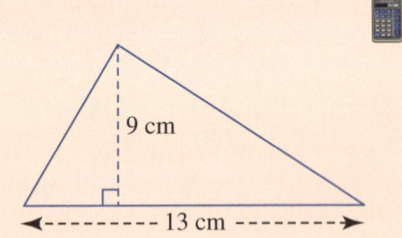

9 cm

13 cm

Solution

Area of triangle = $\frac{1}{2}$(base) × (perpendicular height)   (on page 9 in the booklet of formulae and tables)

= $\frac{1}{2}$(13)(9) = 58·5 cm²

exam focus

The perimeter of a triangle is the sum of the lengths of the three sides. This rule is **not** in the booklet of formulae and tables.

PERIMETER, AREA, NETS AND VOLUME

The perimeter and area of squares and rectangles are summarised below

Square

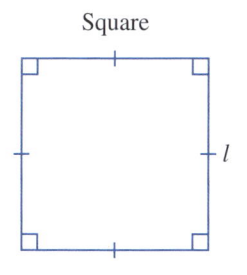

Perimeter $= l + l + l + l = 4l$
Area $= (l)(l) = l^2$

Rectangle

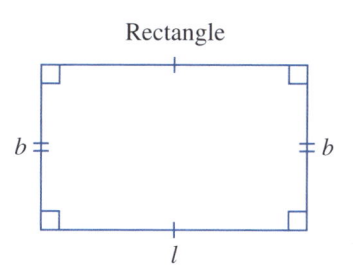

Perimeter $= l + b + l + b = 2(l + b)$
Area $= (l)(b) = lb$

key point
Where relevant, put units after your answers.

exam focus
You must know the formulae for the area of a rectangle and the perimeter of a rectangle as they are not in the booklet of formulae and tables.

exam Q

A rectangle is twice as long as it is wide. The width of the rectangle is 6 m.

(i) Find the length of the rectangle.
(ii) Find the area of the rectangle.
(iii) Find the perimeter of the rectangle.

exam focus
It is often essential to draw a diagram as an aid in understanding and answering some questions.

Solution

(i) Length = 2(width) = 2(6) = 12 m
(ii) Area rectangle = length × width
     = 12 × 6 = 72 m^2
(iii) The perimeter of a rectangle
      = 2(length + width)
      = 2(12 + 6) = 2(18) = 36 m

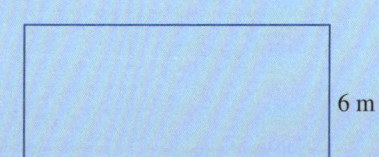

exam Q

The perimeter of a rectangular lawn is 28 m.
The length of the lawn is 9 m.

Find the width of the lawn.

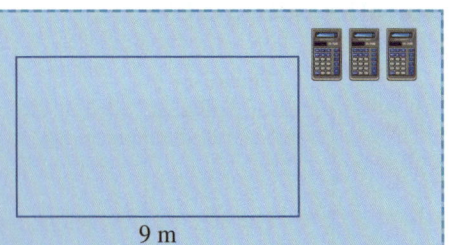

9 m

Solution

This is an equation in disguise.

Let the width of the lawn be w metres.

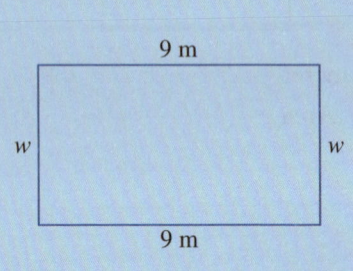

∴ The perimeter of the lawn $= w + 9 + w + 9$
$$28 = 2w + 18$$
$$28 - 18 = 2w$$
$$10 = 2w$$
$$5m = w = \text{width of the lawn}$$

exam Q

The area of a square is 49 cm². Find the length of the perimeter in millimetres.

Solution

exam focus

Good reading skills are vital in this question:
- Square → All sides equal
- Perimeter → Add all four sides
- Millimetres → 1 cm = 10 mm, always watch out for questions that combine different units of measure

Let $w =$ length of a side
Area of square $= (w)(w)$
$$49 = w^2$$
$$\sqrt{49} = w$$
$$7 \text{ cm} = w$$

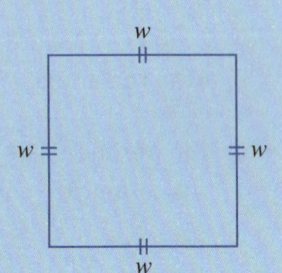

Perimeter $= 7 + 7 + 7 + 7 = 28$ cm $= 28 \times 10$ mm $= 280$ mm exam Q

Niamh wants to extend her kitchen. She has two plans.
The extension is the shaded area in each plan.

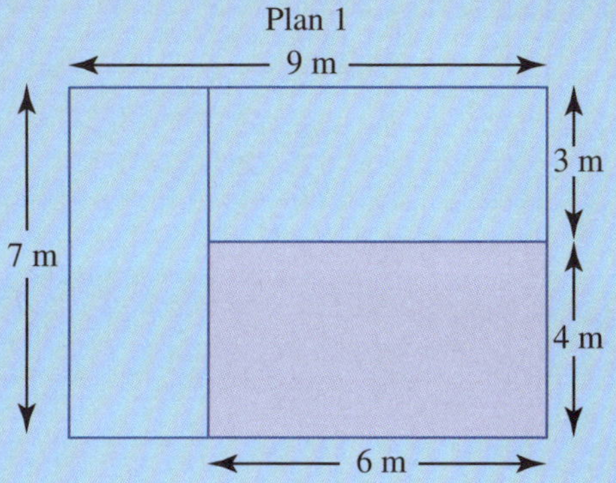

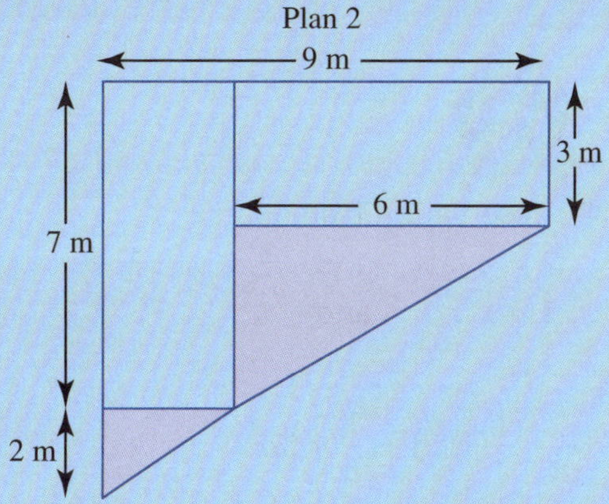

(a) Find the area of the extension for each plan.

(b) Which plan adds the biggest area to the kitchen? Tick the correct box.

Plan 1 ☐ Plan 2 ☐

(c) How many extra square metres would Niamh have if she uses this plan rather than the other plan?

Solution

(a) Area of the shaded rectangle

$= (\text{length}) \times (\text{width})$

$= 6 \times 4$

$= 24 \text{ m}^2$

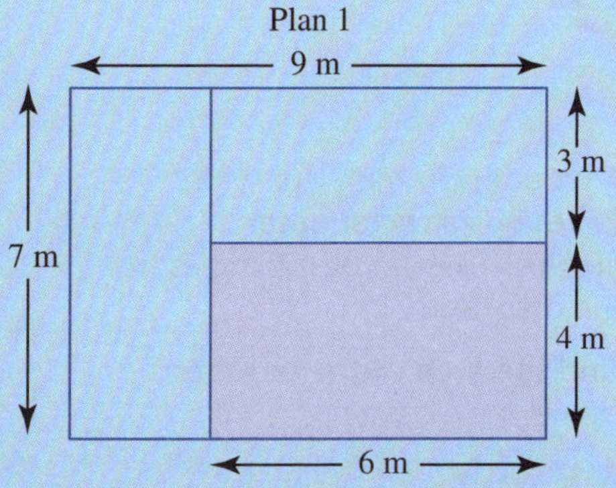

Area of shaded triangles
[both given by $\frac{1}{2}$(base)(perpendicular height)]

$= \frac{1}{2}(2)(x) + \frac{1}{2}(y)(6)$

Plan 2
9 m
3 m
6 m
7 m
y
x
2 m

key point

By observation from Plan 2:
9 = 6 + x   and   7 = y + 3
∴ 3 = x   and   4 = y

$= \frac{1}{2}(2)(3) + \frac{1}{2}(4)(6)$

$= 3 + 12$

$= 15 \text{ m}^2$

(b) Plan 1 ✓   Plan 2 ☐

(c) Extra square metres
= Area Plan 1 minus Area Plan 2
= 24 − 15
= 9 m²

exam Q

Diagram not to scale

A wooden frame 1 cm wide surrounds a rectangular picture, 18·8 cm by 12 cm, as in the diagram.

Find the area of the wooden frame.

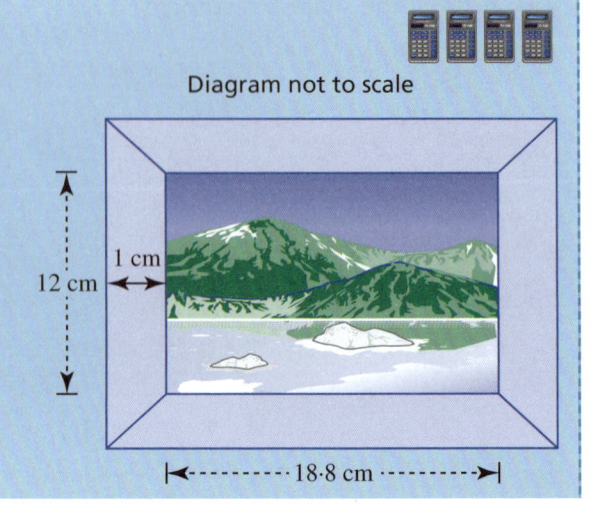

12 cm
1 cm
18·8 cm

Solution

Overall length of frame and picture = 1 + 18·8 + 1 = 20·8 cm
Overall width of frame and picture = 1 + 12 + 1 = 14 cm

Area of frame and picture = $l \times b$ = 20·8 × 14 = 291·2 cm²
Area of picture = $l \times b$ = 18·8 × 12 = 225·6 cm²

Area of wooden frame = [Area of frame and picture] − [Area of picture]
$$= 291·2 - 225·6$$
$$= 65·6 \text{ cm}^2$$

---

exam Q

A field has shape and measurements as shown in the diagram.

(i) Find, in metres, the length of the perimeter of the field.

(ii) Find, in m², the area of the field.

(iii) Ray bought the field at a cost of €40 000 per hectare. How much did Ray pay for the field?

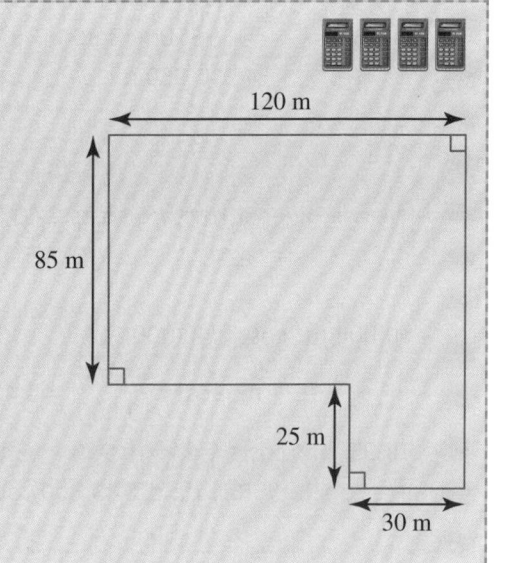

Solution

(i) Perimeter = Distance around the edges

There are two missing lengths:
120 − 30 = 90 m
85 + 25 = 110 m

∴ Length of the perimeter of the field
= 120 + 110 + 30 + 25 + 90 + 85
= 460 m

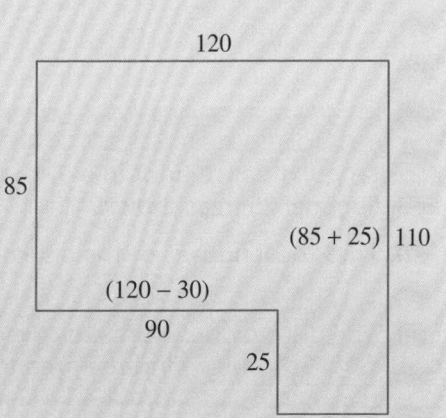

(ii) To find the area of the field we split it up into two rectangles, *A* and *B*, as shown.

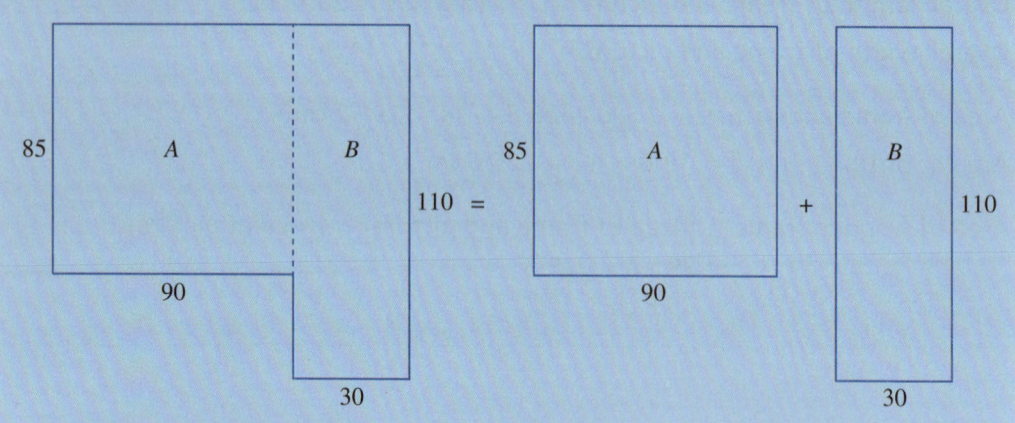

Area of field = (Area of rectangle *A*) + (Area of rectangle *B*)
= (85 × 90) + (110 × 30)
= 7 650 + 3 300
= 10 950 m²

(iii)

key point
1 hectare = 100 m × 100 m = 10 000 m²

We are given 1 hectare costs € 40 000

10 000 m² cost € 40 000

∴ 1 m² costs $\frac{40\,000}{10\,000}$ = € 4

10 950 m² costs € 4 × 10 950 = € 43 800.

We conclude Ray paid € 43 800 for the field.

exam focus
Keep the € on the right hand-side as we want our answer in euros.

---

exam Q

A rectangular dance floor in a disco has width 7 m and diagonal 25 m as shown.

(i) Find the length, *l*, of the dance floor.

(ii) The disco owner wants to cover the dance floor with tiles. Find the area to be covered.

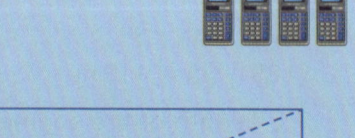

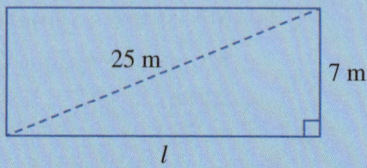

(iii) The tiles are squares of side 0·5 m. Find the number of tiles required.
(iv) She has € 2 000 to spend on tiles. The tiles cost € 2·95 each. Does she have enough money to cover the entire dance floor? Explain your answer.

Solution

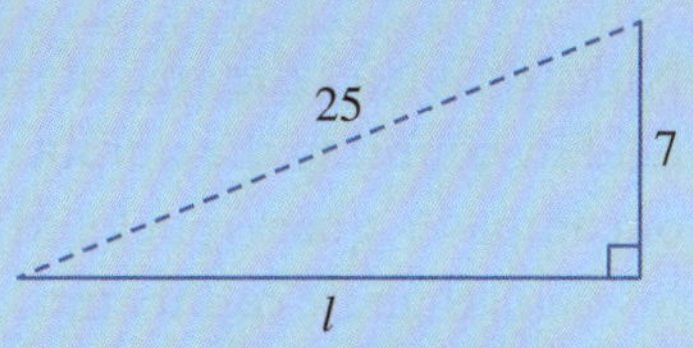

(i) Use the theorem of Pythagoras on the triangle:

$$(hyp)^2 = (opp)^2 + (adj)^2$$
$$(25)^2 = (7)^2 + (l)^2$$
$$625 = 49 + l^2$$
$$625 - 49 = l^2$$
$$576 = l^2$$
$$\sqrt{576} = l$$
$$24 \text{ m} = l$$

exam focus

Applications of Pythagoras' theorem appear in many different topics such as geometry and trigonometry.

(ii) Dance floor has area = (length) × (width)
= 24 × 7
= 168 m²

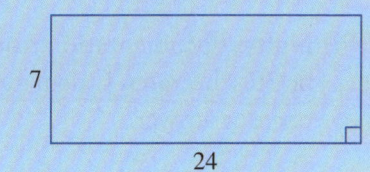

(iii) The area of one tile = 0·5 × 0·5 = 0·25 m²

Number of tiles required = $\dfrac{\text{Total area of dance floor}}{\text{Area of one tile}} = \dfrac{168}{0\cdot 25}$ = 672 tiles

(use your calculator to confirm the answer 672 tiles)

(iv) 672 tiles @ € 2·95 each = 672 × 2·95
= € 1 982·40

This amount is less than the € 2 000 she has to spend. Hence, she has enough money to cover the entire dance floor. The above work is my explanation.

exam focus

When a question asks you to explain or justify your answer, in many cases, you may write 'The above work is my explanation/justification', for full marks.

Example

Farmer Nulty has a field as outlined on the given map. Each box on the map is a 100 m by 100 m square.

Scale ⊢—⊣ equals 100 m

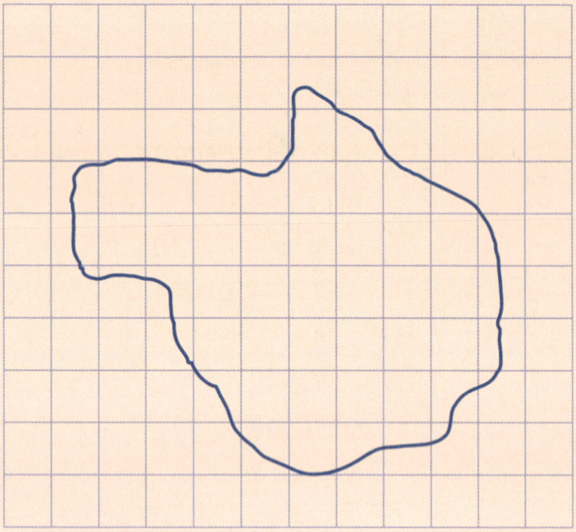

Nulty estimates the area of the field by counting the number of complete squares enclosed by his field, then he counts the number of boxes that are partially included in his field. For his estimate he counts **each** partially included box as half a box.

Find Nulty's estimate for the size of his field:

(i) in m^2

(ii) in hectares when 10 000 m^2 equal one hectare

(iii) Nultys documentation from the Land Comission states the area of the field to be 39·1 hectares. Calculate the difference between the two areas. Comment on your answer.

Solution

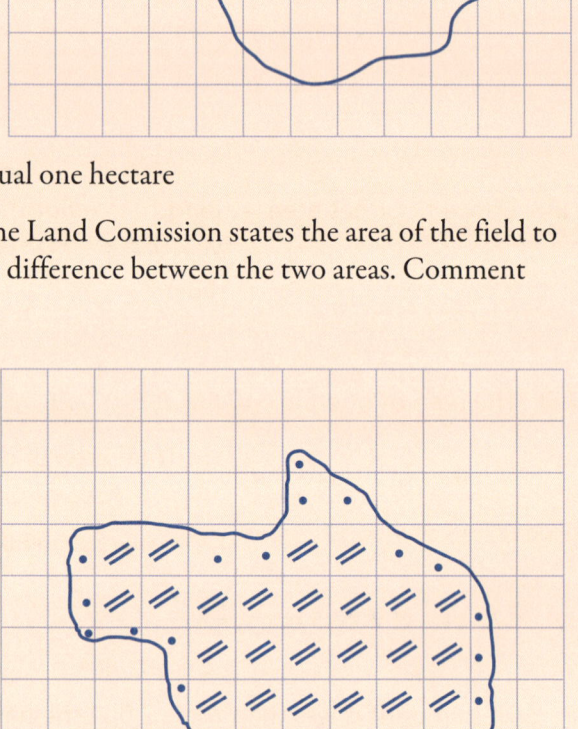

(i) Let ⫽ indicate a complete 100 × 100 m^2 box inside the field.

And let • indicate a part of a box in the field.

We count 28 complete boxes ⫽ plus 24 parts of a box •.

key point

Each • = $\frac{1}{2}$ Box

Total area = 28 [100 × 100] + $\frac{1}{2}$ (24 [100 × 100])

= 280 000 + 120 000

= 400 000 m^2

PERIMETER, AREA, NETS AND VOLUME

(ii) $400\,000\,\text{m}^2 = \dfrac{400\,000}{10\,000} = 40$ hectares

(iii) Difference $= 40 - 39 \cdot 1 = 0 \cdot 9$ hectares

There is a very small difference between the two areas, so Nulty's estimate was very accurate.

Perimeter and area of circles

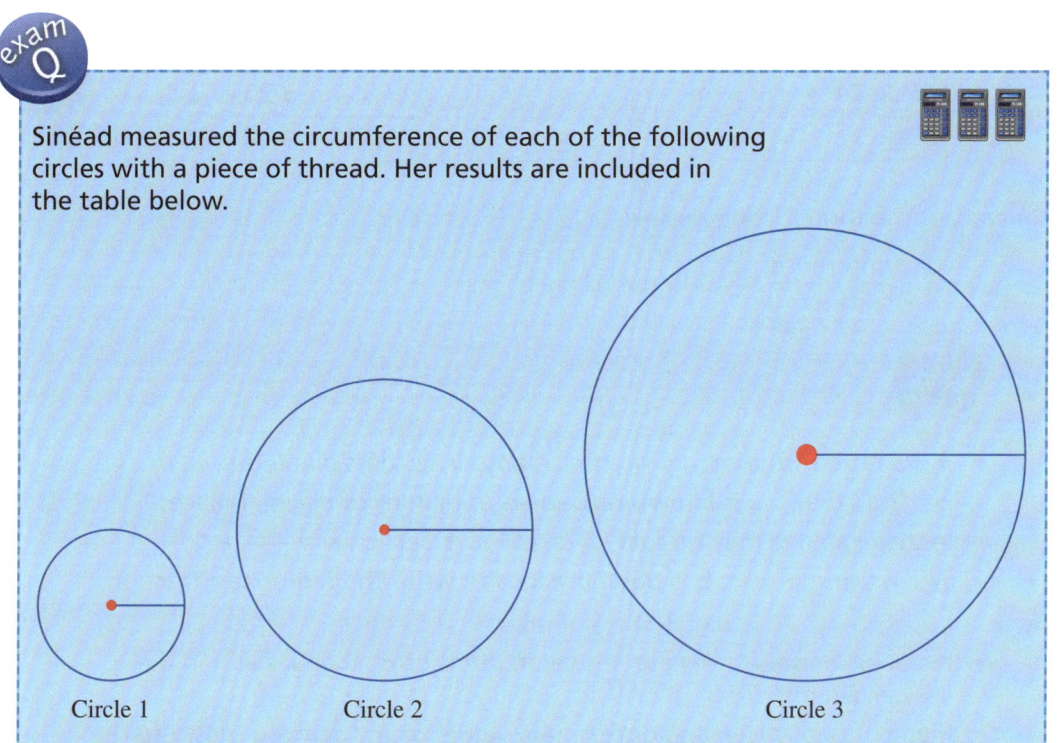

exam Q

Sinéad measured the circumference of each of the following circles with a piece of thread. Her results are included in the table below.

Circle 1   Circle 2   Circle 3

Using a ruler, measure the diameter of each circle and record your answers in the space provided.

Hence, fill in the table.

What do you notice?

	Circumference as measured by Sinéad	Diameter	Circumference ÷ Diameter (1 decimal place)
Circle 1	6·3 cm		
Circle 2	13 cm		
Circle 3	18·5 cm		

Solution

Measuring each diameter with a ruler we find:

- Circle 1 has diameter 2 cm.
- Circle 2 has diameter 4 cm.
- Circle 3 has diameter 6 cm.

Fill in the table using a calculator to evaluate circumference ÷ diameter:

	Circumference as measured by Sinéad	Diameter	Circumference ÷ Diameter (1 decimal place)
Circle 1	6·3 cm	2	6·3 ÷ 2 = 3·15 ⇒ 3·2
Circle 2	13 cm	4	13 ÷ 4 = 3·25 ⇒ 3·3
Circle 3	18·5 cm	6	18·5 ÷ 6 = 3·08 ⇒ 3·1

In each of the three circles we see:

$$\frac{\text{Circumference}}{\text{Diameter}} = \text{A number close to } \pi.$$

key point

- π is a ratio of the circumference of any circle to its diameter.
- $\pi = 3\cdot141592\ldots$ is known nowadays to billions of decimal places.
- In the exam we may be told to take π as a particular value, e.g. $\frac{22}{7}$, 3·14.
- When using $\pi = \frac{22}{7}$, it is good practice to write the radius as a fraction, e.g. $3\cdot5 = \frac{7}{2}$ or $18 = \frac{18}{1}$.
- If a question says 'give your answer in terms of π', then leave π in the answer. Do not use 3·14 or $\frac{22}{7}$ for π.
- If you are not given an approximate value for π, then you must use the value given by the calculator.

exam Q

The front wheel of Colman's bike has a diameter of 52·5 cm.

(i) Calculate, in cm, the length of the radius of the wheel.

(ii) Calculate, in cm, the length of the circumference of the wheel. Take $\pi = \frac{22}{7}$.

(iii) A cycling track has two equal parallel sides [PQ] and [SR]. It also has two equal semicircular ends with diameters [PS] and [QR] as shown.

|PQ| = [SR] = 88 metres and |PS| = |QR| = 70 metres.

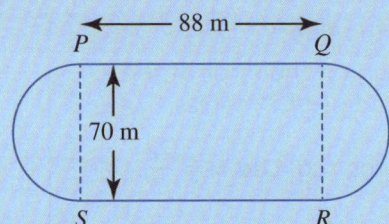

Calculate the total length, in m, of one lap of the track. Take $\pi = \dfrac{22}{7}$.

(iv) How many complete turns does the front wheel of Colman's bike make when making one complete lap of the track?

Solution

(i) Diameter = 52·5 $\Rightarrow$ Radius = $\dfrac{52\cdot 5}{2}$ = 26·25 cm

(ii) Circumference = $2\pi r = 2\left(\dfrac{22}{7}\right)(26\cdot 25)$ = 165 cm

(iii) Total length of one lap of the track
= Two straight lengths of 88 m each + Two semicircular ends each of radius 35 m
= $2(88) + 2(\pi r)$
= $176 + 2\left(\dfrac{22}{7}\right)(35)$
= 176 + 220
= 396 m

key point: $r = \tfrac{1}{2}(70) = 35$ and length of a semicircle = $\tfrac{1}{2}(2\pi r) = \pi r$

(iv) From part (ii) we had the circumference (length) of the wheel as, 165 cm.
However, 165 cm = 1·65 m.
The number of complete turns of the wheel in one lap
= $\dfrac{\text{Total length of one lap}}{\text{Circumference of the wheel}}$
= $\dfrac{396}{1\cdot 65}$
= 240 complete turns

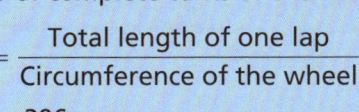

key point: 100 cm = 1 m

exam Q

The floor of the lobby in a hotel was in the shape of a square with perimeter 88 m.

(a) Calculate the area of the floor.

(b) There was a circular rug on the floor of the hotel lobby. It had a radius of 7 metres.

Calculate the area of the rug. Use $\pi = \dfrac{22}{7}$.

(c) Hence, find the fraction of the lobby floor covered by the circular rug.

Solution

(a) Let x = Length of the hotel lobby

Perimeter of the lobby $= x + x + x + x$

$88 = 4x$

$22\,m = x$

Area of the floor $= (x)(x) = (22)(22) = 484\ m^2$

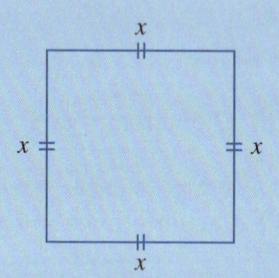

(b) Area of circle $= \pi r^2$ (on page 8 in the booklet of formulae and tables)

Area of rug $= \left(\dfrac{22}{7}\right)(7)^2$

$= (22)(7)$

$= 154\ m^2$

(c) The fraction of floor covered by the rug $= \dfrac{\text{Area rug}}{\text{Area floor}} = \dfrac{154}{484} = \dfrac{7}{22}$

PERIMETER, AREA, NETS AND VOLUME

exam Q

Four identical discs each of diameter 5 cm fit exactly on a square of side 10 cm. Take 3·14 as an approximation of π.

What is the area of that part of the square which is not covered by the discs?

What percentage of the area of the square is covered by the discs? Give the answer to the nearest percentage.

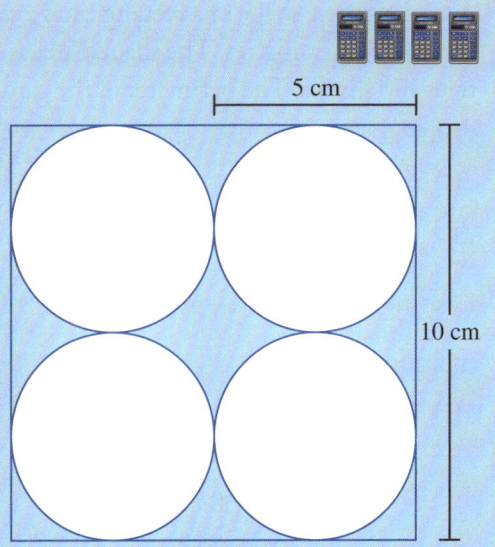

Solution

Area of the square = 10 × 10 = 100 cm²

key point

4(radius of disc) = 10
4r = 10
r = 2·5 cm

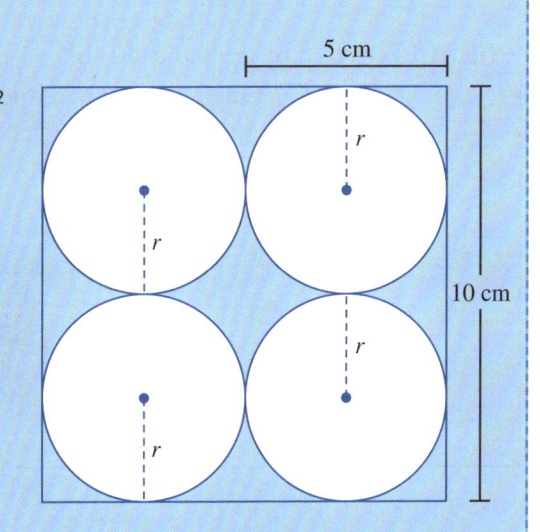

Area of four discs = $4(\pi r^2)$
 = 4(3·14)(2·5)²
 = 78·5 cm²

Area not covered by discs = Area square − Area four discs
 = 100 − 78·5
 = 21·5 cm²

Percentage covered by discs = $\dfrac{\text{Area covered by discs}}{\text{Total area}} \times 100\%$

 = $\dfrac{78\cdot 5}{100} \times 100$ = 78·5% = 79%

Example

A garden in the shape of a rectangle has a semicircular lawn of radius r metres. The shaded area is covered by trees and shrubs. The perimeter of the garden is 84 m.

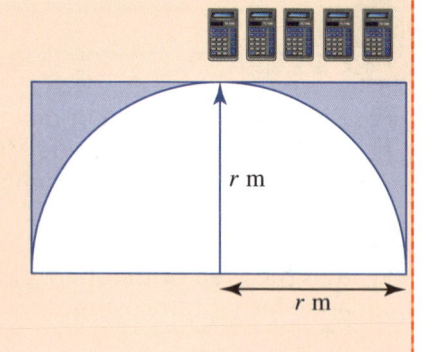

Calculate:

(i) the value of r

(ii) the area covered by trees and shrubs.

Take $\pi = \dfrac{22}{7}$.

Solution

(i) Equation given in disguise:

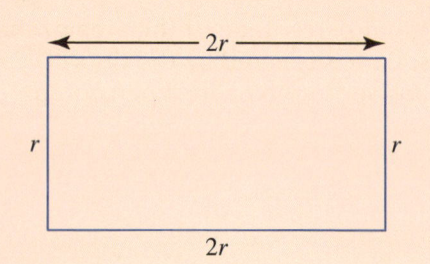

Perimeter $= 2r + r + 2r + r = 6r$

Perimeter $= 84$

$\therefore \quad 6r = 84$

$\quad\quad r = 14$ m

(ii) Area covered by trees and shrubs

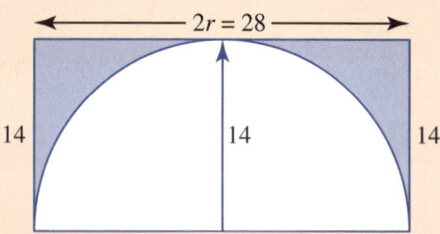

$= $ Area of rectangle $-$ Area of semicircle

$= (l \times b) - \dfrac{1}{2}(\pi r^2)$

$= (28 \times 14) - \dfrac{1}{2}\left(\dfrac{22}{7}\right)(14)^2$

$= 392 - 308$

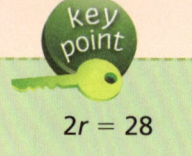

$= 84$ m^2

key point

$2r = 28$

Nets of 3D shapes

When a 3D shape is opened out, the flat shape is called the **net**.

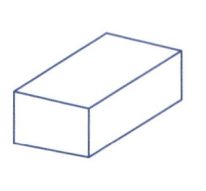

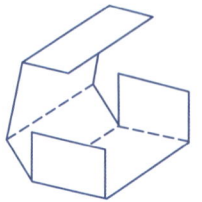

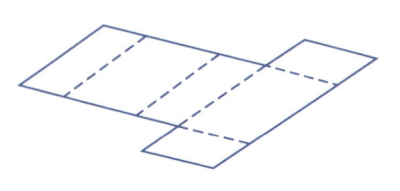

PERIMETER, AREA, NETS AND VOLUME

This is a possible **net** of a solid cube.

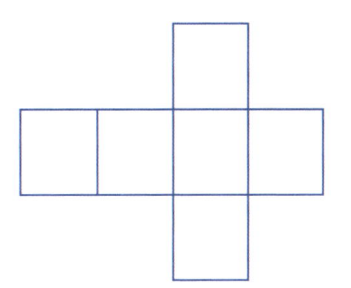

This is how it folds up to make the cube.

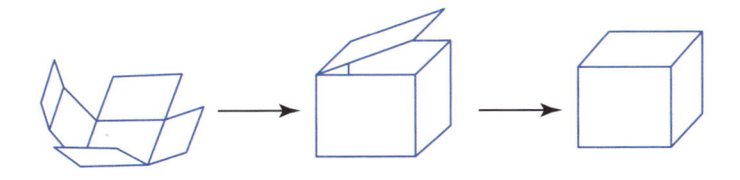

Here are two more nets for a cube.

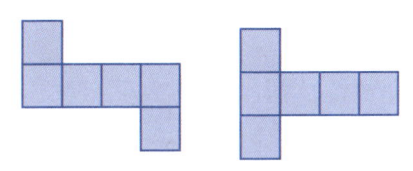

key point

There are 11 possible different nets of a cube.

An **open** rectangular box has no top. Here is its net:

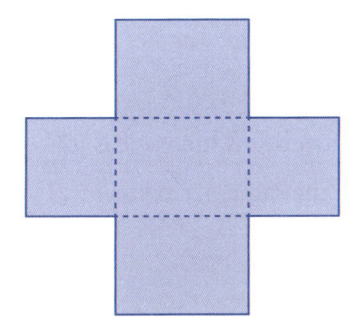

A **closed** rectangular box has a top. Here is its net:

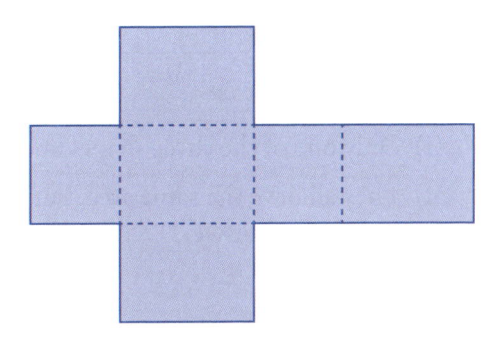

exam Q

The net of a fair six-sided die is shown. Write down:

(i) The probability of a score of 5.
(ii) The probability of a score of 6.

Solution

key point
- A fair die is equally likely to land on any side.
- A score of 5 is on two sides of the fair die.
- A score of 6 is on four sides of the fair die.

(i) The probability of a score of 5 = $\frac{2}{6} = \frac{1}{3}$

(ii) The probability of a score of 6 = $\frac{4}{6} = \frac{2}{3}$

exam focus
Here the question combines the topics, probability and nets. We constantly see this type of exam question, combining different topics from our course.

Example

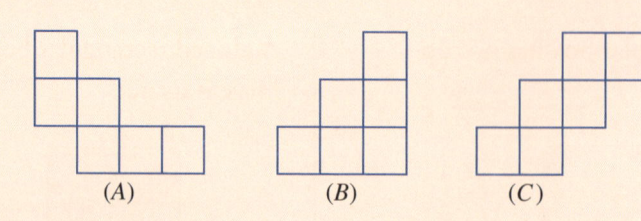

(A) (B) (C)

(i) Only one of the three shapes above is the net of a cube. Which one is it?

(ii) They all have the same area, but do they all have the same perimeter? Justify your answer.

PERIMETER, AREA, NETS AND VOLUME

Solution

(i) (C) is the net of a cube as it is the only one that folds into a six-sided shape.

> **exam focus**
> If you cannot 'see' that this shape (C) folds into a cube you should choose one by making your best guess.

> **key point**
> As an exercise, it is worthwhile to draw and cut out the shapes and puzzle out why (A) and (B) above do not form a cube when folded.

(ii) Simply counting the width of each box as one unit, we find the perimeter of $A = 14$ units, of $B = 12$ units and of $C = 14$ units.

They do not all have the same perimeter.

The above work is my justification.

---

exam Q

The shape on the right consists of 6 squares. Each side is 2 cm long. It can be folded to form a cube. Find the surface area of the cube.

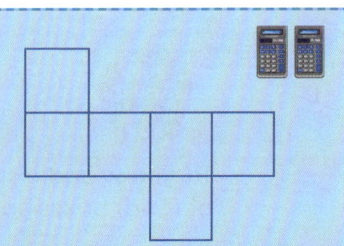

Solution

Each square has area $= l \times l = 2 \times 2 = 4$ cm^2

The net of the cube has six sides

$\Rightarrow$ Surface area of the cube $= 4 \times 6 = 24$ cm^2

> **key point**
> Surface area of 3D shapes usually only refers to the 'outside', i.e. one side of the net.

> **exam focus**
> In the exam, the above question had a suggested maximum time of 2 minutes. There is no time to waste. Get into the question, attempt everything and keep moving through the questions.

The net for a figure with a square base is shown. Each grid unit represents 5 mm.

(a) Find w, the length of the base, and d, the height of each triangular side.
(b) Find the area of the base of the figure.
(c) Find the total surface area of the figure.

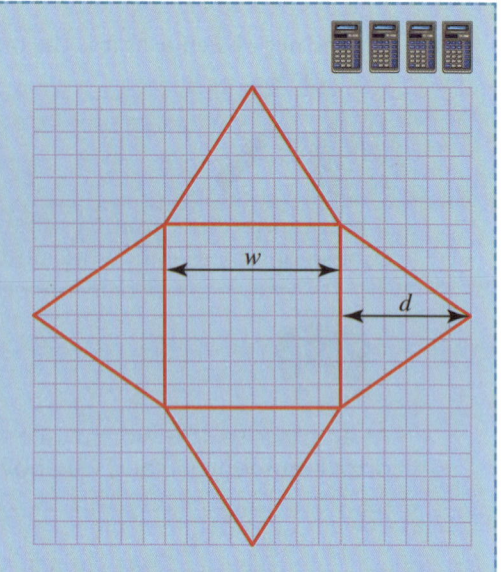

exam focus

Drawing to scale can be very useful when dealing with a shape. In a scale of 1 to 5, every one unit on the diagram represents five units in real life. Scale may be examined in many different topics. This question incorporates scale with nets and area. It is vital that you develop the skill to work with scale wherever you meet it.

Solution

(a)

key point

To find w and d simply count the number of (grid) boxes and multiply by 5 mm.

∴ w = 8 boxes × 5 mm = 40 mm
d = 6 boxes × 5 mm = 30 mm

(b) Area of base = w × w = 40 × 40 = 1 600 mm²

(c) Total surface area of the figure

= Area of the square base + 4(Area of one triangle)

$= 1\ 600 + 4\left[\dfrac{1}{2}(\text{Base} \times \text{Perpendicular height})\right]$

$= 1\ 600 + 4\left[\dfrac{1}{2}(40 \times 30)\right]$

= 1 600 + 2 400 = 4 000 mm²

PERIMETER, AREA, NETS AND VOLUME

Volume

Volume is the space occupied by a solid. It is measured in cubic units, e.g. m³, which we say as **one cubic metre**.

Rectangular objects

1. **Rectangular solid (cuboid)**

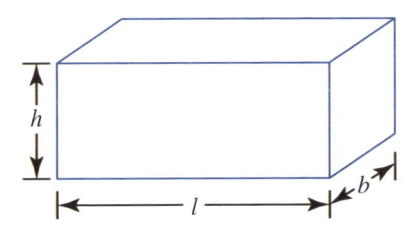

   Volume = lbh
   Surface area = $2lb + 2lh + 2bh$

2. **Cube**

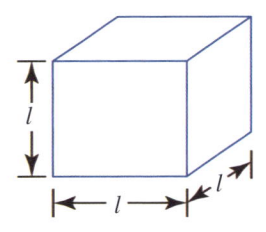

   Volume = l^3
   Surface area = $6l^2$

> **exam focus**
>
> The formulae on the previous page are **not** in the booklet of formulae and tables. You must know them.

Example

By counting the number of 1 cm³ cubes, find the volume of each of the following shapes.

= 1 cm³

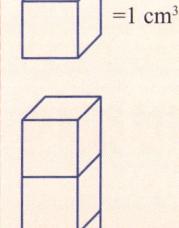

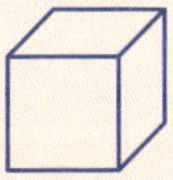

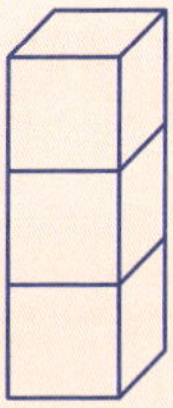

Figure 1 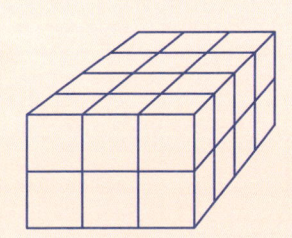   Figure 2    Figure 3

Solution

key point

Using volume = $(l)(b)(h)$ in each case
Figure 1 has = $(1)(1)(3) = 3$ cubes
Figure 2 has = $(3)(4)(2) = 24$ cubes
Figure 3 has = $(4)(5)(3) = 60$ cubes

Hence, we can write:
Figure 1 has volume $3 \times 1 \text{ cm}^3 = 3 \text{ cm}^3$
Figure 2 has volume $24 \times 1 \text{ cm}^3 = 24 \text{ cm}^3$
Figure 3 has volume $60 \times 1 \text{ cm}^3 = 60 \text{ cm}^3$

---

exam Q

The surface area of a cube is 96 cm². Calculate its volume.

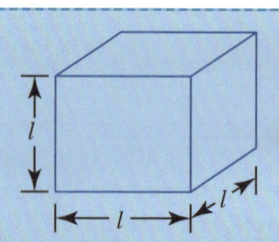

Solution

Let the length of one side of the cube be *l* cm.

Equation given in disguise:

Surface area = 96 cm²
$\therefore \quad 6l^2 = 96$
$l^2 = 16$
$l = 4$ cm

Volume = l^3
       = 4^3
       = 64 cm³

Therefore, the volume of the cube is 64 cm³.

---

exam Q

A jeweller buys a rectangular block of gold of length 4 cm, width 3 cm and height 2 cm. 1 cm³ of gold costs €400.

(i) Calculate the cost of the block of gold.

The jeweller needs 0·25 cm³ of gold to make a gold ring.

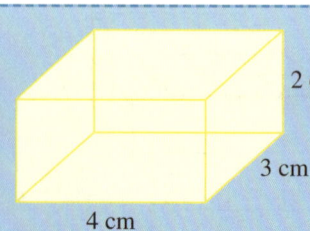

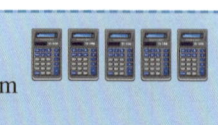

PERIMETER, AREA, NETS AND VOLUME

(ii) How many rings can be made from the block?

(iii) Each ring is sold for €120. Calculate the amount of profit the jeweller makes on each ring.

Solution

(i) Volume of block
$= l \times b \times h$
$= 4 \times 3 \times 2 = 24 \text{ cm}^3$
1 cm³ costs €400
$\Rightarrow$ 24 cm³ costs €400 × 24 = €9 600

(ii) Number of rings $= \dfrac{\text{Total volume of block}}{\text{Volume of one ring}} = \dfrac{24}{0\cdot 25} = 96$ rings

(use your calculator to check this)

(iii) Total cost = €9 600
Total number of rings = 96

Cost of one ring $= \dfrac{\text{Total cost}}{\text{Number of rings}} = \dfrac{9\ 600}{96} = $ €100

We know profit = Selling price − Cost price
$= 120 - 100$
$= $ €20 per ring

Example

The volume of a rectangular block is 560 cm³. If its length is 14 cm and its breadth is 8 cm, find (i) its height and (ii) its surface area.

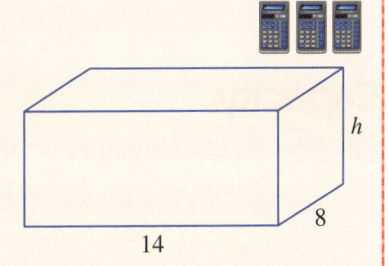

Solution

(i) Equation given in disguise:
Volume = 560 cm³
$\therefore (l)(b)(h) = 560$
$(14)(8)(h) = 560$
$112\,h = 560$
$h = \dfrac{560}{112} = 5$ cm

(ii) Surface area
= Area of (top + bottom + front + back + side + side)
$= 2lb + 2lh + 2hb$
$= 2(14)(8) + 2(14)(5) + 2(5)(8)$
$= 224 + 140 + 80$
$= 444 \text{ cm}^2$

> **exam Q**
>
> Clive estimates the dimensions of a rectangular tank to be 5 m by 4 m by 3 m.
>
> (a) Use Clive's values to work out the volume of the tank, in m³.
>
> (b) Clive's estimates are all correct to the nearest metre. The actual volume of the box is K m³, where $K \in \mathbb{N}$. Work out the largest value that K could have.
>
> **Solution**
>
> (a) Volume = Length × Width × Height
> Volume = 5 × 3 × 4
> Volume = 60 m³
>
> (b) If each of the sides was rounded to the nearest metre, they each must be smaller than the following:
> Length = 5·5 m, Width = 3·5 m, Height = 4·5 m
> We will find the volume at these maximum values:
> Volume = Length × Width × Height
> Volume = 5·5 × 3·5 × 4·5
> Volume = 86·625 m³
> The volume must be less than 86·625 m³, therefore the largest whole number value the volume can be is 86 m³.　So, $K = 86$.

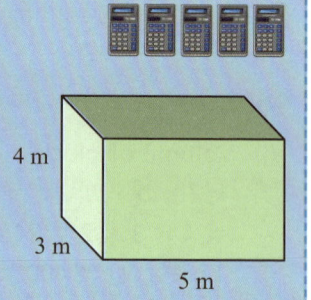

Capacity

The capacity of a container is the amount of liquid it can hold.
The most commonly used measure is the litre.

> **key point**
>
> - 1 litre = 1 000 cm³, i.e. a one-litre bottle of water contains 1 000 cm³ of liquid.
> - To convert litres to cubic centimetres (cm³) multiply by 1 000.
> - 1 l = 1 000 millilitres (ml) $\Rightarrow$ 1 cm³ = 1 ml

PERIMETER, AREA, NETS AND VOLUME

Example

Using the clues below, write the correct capacity below each item using the information given.

Item	Spoon	Cup	Mug	Jug	Bucket	Watering can
Capacity			380 ml			

- 50 spoonfuls will fill the mug.
- The cup holds 80 ml less than the mug.
- The jug holds $3\frac{1}{2}$ times as much as the cup.
- The bucket holds as much as the mug and two jugs.
- The watering can holds twice the total of the first five containers plus an extra 2·15 litres.

Solution

- 50 spoonfuls fill mug $\Rightarrow \dfrac{380}{50} = 7\cdot6$ ml in spoon.
- Cup hold 80 ml less than the mug $\Rightarrow 380 - 80 = 300$ ml in cup.
- Jug holds $3\frac{1}{2}$ times as much as the cup $\Rightarrow 300 \times 3\frac{1}{2} = 1\,050$ ml $= 1\cdot05\,l$ in jug.
- Bucket holds as much as the mug and two jugs
  $\Rightarrow 380 + 2(1\,050) = 380 + 2\,100 = 2\,480$ ml
  $\qquad\qquad = 2\cdot48\,l$ in bucket
- Watering can holds twice the total of the first five containers plus an extra 2·15 l
  $\Rightarrow 2(7\cdot6 + 300 + 380 + 1\,050 + 2\,480) + 2\cdot15\,l$
  $= 2(4\,217\cdot6) + 2\cdot15\,l$
  $= 8\,435\cdot2$ ml $+ 2\cdot15\,l$
  $= 8\cdot4352\,l + 2\cdot15\,l$
  $= 10\cdot5852\,l$

Answer

Item	Spoon	Cup	Mug	Jug	Bucket	Watering can
Capacity	7·6 ml	300 ml	380 ml	1·05 l	2·48 l	10·5852 l

Volume of a cylinder

exam Q

Cement is stored in a silo in the shape of a cylinder on a cone as shown in the diagram.

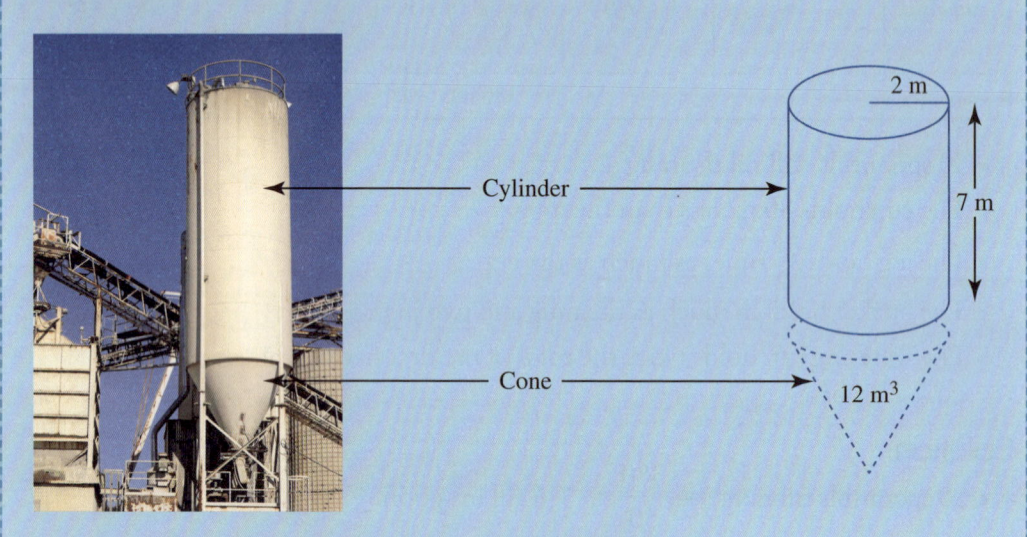

(a) The height of the cylinder is 7 m and the radius is 2 m.
Find the volume of the cylinder. Use $\pi = 3\cdot 142$.
Give your answer correct to the nearest m^3.

(b) The volume of the cone is 12 m^3.
Find the total volume of cement in the silo when it is full.
Give your answer correct to the nearest m^3.

(c) If 1 m^3 of cement weighs 2·5 tonnes, what is the total weight of the cement in the silo?

Solution
(a) Volume of cylinder = $\pi r^2 h$ (see page 10 in the booklet of formulae and tables)
$= (3\cdot 142)(2)^2(7)$
$= 87\cdot 976$
$= 88$ correct to nearest m^3

(b) Volume when full = Volume cone + Volume cylinder
$= 12 + 88$
$= 100$ m^3

(c) 1 m^3 weighs 2·5 tonnes
100 m^3 weighs 2·5 × 100 = 250 tonnes total weight.

Example

(i) A hot water cylinder in a café has dimensions as shown. Find, in terms of π, the volume of the cylinder.

(ii) The café serves hot drinks in very large cylindrical mugs with dimensions of height 14 cm and radius 5 cm. They are filled to exactly 2 cm below the rim of the mug. Find, in terms of π, the volume of hot water in a mug.

(iii) Hence, calculate how many mugs can be filled from the full hot water cylinder when each mug is filled as in part (ii).

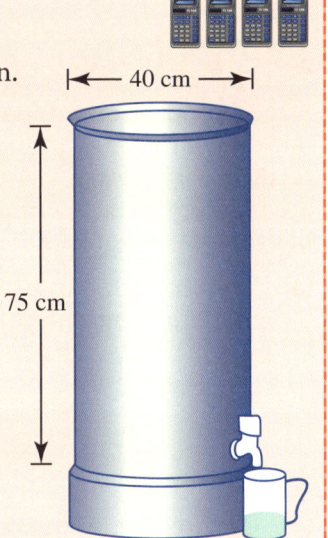

Solution

(i) Volume of cylinder

$= \pi r^2 h = \pi(20)^2(75) = 30\,000\pi$ cm^3.

key point
Radius $= \dfrac{1}{2}(40) = 20$ cm.

(ii)
key point
The mug is filled to exactly 2 cm below the rim
$\Rightarrow$ The height of the liquid
$= 14 - 2 = 12$ cm

Volume of cylindrical mug $= \pi r^2 h = \pi(5)^2(12) = 300\pi$ cm^3

(iii) Number of mugs that can be filled

$= \dfrac{\text{Volume of full cylinder of water}}{\text{Volume of water in mug}}$

$= \dfrac{30\,000\pi}{300\pi} = 100$

exam focus
In the above question, we were not given a value for π. In fact the question asks for the volume in terms of π. Notice in part (iii) the π's cancel each other. This often happens.

142 LESS STRESS MORE SUCCESS

A food production company has to decide between a closed cylindrical tin A or a rectangular carton B to hold a product they are marketing for the first time. Both containers have the same volume.

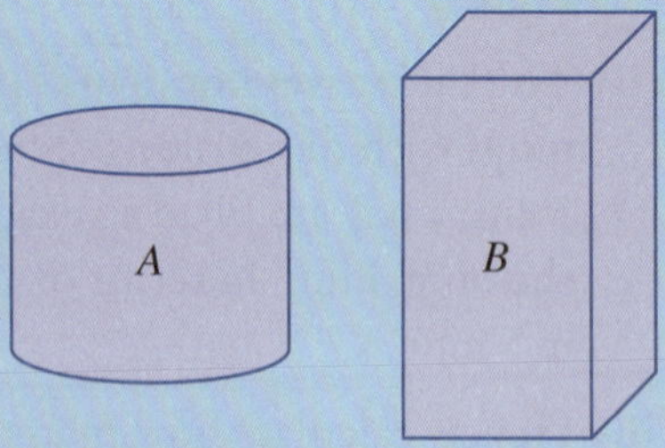

(a) Tin A has a radius of 3 cm and a height of 10 cm. Find the volume of tin A.

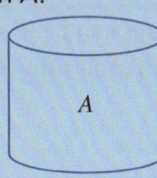

(b) Carton B has a square base of length 5 cm. Use the volume you got in (a) above to find the height of carton B. Give your answer correct to one decimal place.

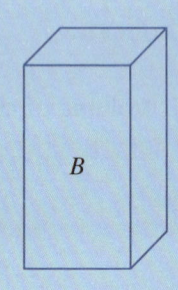

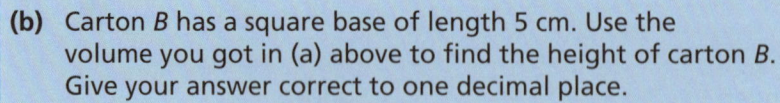

(c) Which one of the above containers do you think the company might choose? Give a reason for your answer.

Solution
(a) Volume of tin A = Volume of cylinder
$= \pi r^2 h = \pi(3)^2(10) = 90\pi$ cm^3

(b) Volume of carton B = Volume of cuboid
$= lbh = (5)(5)(h) = 25h$ cm^3

We are given volume of tin A = volume of carton B
$$90\pi = 25h$$
$$282 \cdot 7433388 = 25h$$
$$11 \cdot 30973355 = h \quad \text{(divide both sides by 25)}$$
$$11 \cdot 3 \text{ cm} = h \quad \text{(correct to one decimal place)}$$

(c) • Container A because a cylinder is the favourite shape of container for many food stuffs, e.g. beans, fish, soup.
   • Container B because a rectangular carton packs better in containers for transporting.

exam focus: Use the value of π on your calculator as we are not given a value for π.

exam focus: Either answer given for (c) may be used or one of your own. Remember to justify your answer.

PERIMETER, AREA, NETS AND VOLUME 143

(i) John's height is given as:
  (a) 167 cm (b) 1·67 m (c) 16·7 l (d) 1 670 mm
  One of the given answers is **incorrect**.
  Which one? Justify your answer.

(ii) Ray has a field with an area of:
  (a) 14·3 hectares (b) 1 430 m^3 (c) 143 000 m^2
  One of the given answers is **incorrect**. Which one? Justify your answer.

(iii) The volume of Erin's bedroom is given as:
  (a) 30 m (b) 30 m^2 (c) 30 m^3 (d) 3 000 cm^3
  Only one of the given answers is **correct**. Which one? Justify your answer.

Solution
(i) Height in mm; cm; m is allowed
  Height in litres is **not** allowed (c) Incorrect

(ii) Area in hectares or m^2 is allowed
  Area in m^3 is **not** allowed (b) Incorrect

(iii) Volume in m^3 or cm^3 is allowed; 3 000 cm^3 is far too small, it's the size of a shoe box!
  $\therefore$ (c) is correct

8 Fundamental Principles of Counting

aims
- ☐ To be able to list and calculate the number of outcomes of a situation
- ☐ To understand the two fundamental principles of counting

Outcomes

The result of an operation is called an outcome. For example, if we throw a die, one possible outcome is 2. If we throw a die there are six possible outcomes: 1, 2, 3, 4, 5 or 6.

Fundamental principle of counting 1

Suppose one operation has m possible outcomes and that a second operation has n possible outcomes. The number of possible outcomes when performing the first operation **followed by** the second operation is $m \times n$.

Performing one operation **and** another operation means we **multiply** the number of possible outcomes.

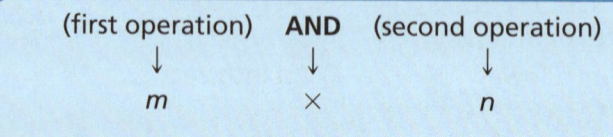

(first operation)   AND   (second operation)
         ↓   ↓   ↓
         m × n

'And' is understood to mean '**multiply**'.

Note: We assume that the outcome of one operation does not affect the number of possible outcomes of the other operation.

The fundamental principle of counting 1 can be extended to three or more operations.

Example

Sharon wants to buy a dress. The dress is available as follows:

Size	Small	Medium	Large
Colour	Blue	Red	

(i) How many possible outcomes are there for Sharon's purchase?
(ii) List these outcomes.

Solution

(i) Total number of outcomes = (number of sizes) AND (number of colours)
Total number of outcomes = (3) × (2)
Total number of outcomes = 6

(ii) The 6 possible outcomes are:

Small and Blue	Medium and Blue	Large and Blue
Small and Red	Medium and Red	Large and Red

> **exam focus**
>
> There are very few calculations involved with some of these questions. So, it is very important that you show the method you used to solve the problem. **In general, the answer alone, with no workings, may not be awarded full marks.**

Fundamental principle of counting 2

> Suppose one operation has m possible outcomes and that a second operation has n possible outcomes. Then the number of possible outcomes of the first operation **or** the second operation is given by $m + n$.

Performing one operation **or** another operation means we **add** the number of possible outcomes.

(first operation)   OR   (second operation)
↓   ↓   ↓
m + n

'Or' is understood to mean '**add**'.

Note: We assume it is not possible for both operations to occur. In other words, there is no overlap of the two operations.

The fundamental principle of counting 2 can be extended to three or more operations, as long as none of the operations overlap.

key point

- **'And'** is understood to mean **'multiply'**.
- **'Or'** is understood to mean **'add'**.

Example

Ciara goes to the shop to buy herself a snack. She plans to buy either a chocolate bar or a bag of crisps. The shop has 4 different types of chocolate bar. The shop has 5 different types of bags of crisps.
How many possible outcomes are there for the snack that Ciara buys?

Solution

Total number of outcomes = (no. of chocolate bars) OR (no. of bags of crisps)
Total number of outcomes = (4) + (5)
Total number of outcomes = 9

exam Q

A restaurant offers an early bird menu as follows:

Starters	Main courses	Dessert
Soup	Chicken and rice	Chocolate cake
Salad	Vegetarian curry	Apple tart
Spring rolls	Bangers and mash	Fruit salad
	Fish and chips	Ice cream
	Burger and chips	

How many different ways can you order a three-course meal?

Solution

Total number of ways = (starters) AND (main courses) AND (desserts)
Total number of ways = (3) × (5) × (4)
Total number of ways = 60

exam Q

Colin prints his holiday photographs in a camera shop. The shop can print photographs as follows:

Size	Colour	Finish
Small	Colour	Glossy
Medium	Black and White	Matt
Large		

(i) How many different ways are there for Colin to print a photograph?

(ii) Colin wants to print all his photos in medium size. How many ways are there for him to print his photos now?

Solution

(i) Total number of ways = (size) AND (colour) AND (finish)

Total number of ways = (3) × (2) × (2)

Total number of ways = 12

key point: In this question 'Black and white' counts as only one option.

(ii) Since Colin wants all his photos to be in medium size, then there is only one option for the size.

Total number of ways = (size) AND (colour) AND (finish)

Total number of ways = (1) × (2) × (2)

Total number of ways = 4

exam Q

Luke is going camping for the weekend. Each outfit he will wear consists of a pair of jeans, a shirt, a jumper and a pair of shoes. He has packed:

- 3 pairs of jeans (black, navy and blue)
- 4 shirts (white, green, yellow and red)
- 2 jumpers (black and brown)
- 2 pairs of shoes (boots and flip-flops)

(i) Write down two examples of different outfits Luke could wear.

(ii) How many different possible outfits can Luke wear over the weekend?

Solution

(i) Example 1: Black jeans, green shirt, brown jumper and flip-flops
 Example 2: Blue jeans, red shirt, black jumper and boots

(ii) Total number of outfits = (jeans) AND (shirts) AND (jumpers) AND (shoes)
$$= (3) \times (4) \times (2) \times (2)$$
$$= 48$$

Therefore, there are 48 different outfits Luke can wear.

---

exam Q

A restaurant advertises its lunch menu using the sign below:

> 3-course lunch for €15
> Choose from our range of
> starters, main courses and desserts
> 180 different lunches to choose from!

(i) The menu has a choice of five starters and nine main courses. How many items must appear on the dessert menu to justify the above claim of 180 different lunches?

(ii) On a particular day, one of the starters and one of the main courses is not available. How many different three-course lunches is it possible to have on that day?

Solution

(i) Total number of lunches = (starters) AND (main courses) AND (desserts)
$$180 = (5) \times (9) \times \text{(number of desserts)}$$
$$180 = 45 \times \text{(number of desserts)}$$
$$4 = \text{number of desserts}$$

(ii) There will now be four starters and eight main courses and four desserts
Total number of lunches = (starters) AND (main courses) AND (desserts)
$$= (4) \times (8) \times (4)$$
$$= 128$$

Therefore, there are 128 different three-course lunches possible on that day.

Sample space

A sample space is the set of all possible outcomes. A sample space can be very useful for seeing all possible outcomes and working out any appropriate probabilities.

A sample space can be represented as a list of outcomes, a two-way table or a tree diagram. These three methods are shown in the next example.

> **key point**
> All possible outcomes can be shown using a list, a two-way table or a tree diagram.

> **exam focus**
> You may be asked to represent all possible outcomes using a specific sample space, so it is vital that you are able to perform **all** three methods.

Example

A game consists of spinning a five-sided spinner, labelled P, Q, R, S and T, and tossing a coin.
An outcome is a letter and a head or a tail.

(i) How many outcomes of the game are possible?

(ii) List all the possible outcomes of the game.

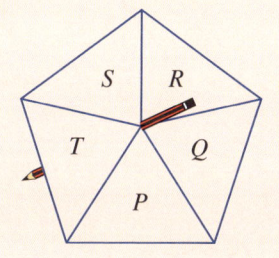

Solution

(i) Total number of outcome = (outcomes on spinner) AND (outcomes on coin)
$$= (5) \times (2)$$
$$= 10$$

(ii) There are three methods we can use to list the outcomes:

Method 1:
List of outcomes:

$(P, H), (Q, H), (R, H), (S, H), (T, H)$
$(P, T), (Q, T), (R, T), (S, T), (T, T)$

Method 2:
Using a two-way table (sample space):

		Spinner				
		P	Q	R	S	T
Coin	Head	•	•	•	•	•
	Tail	•	•	•	•	•

A dot indicates an outcome. There are 10 dots (5 × 2).

Method 3:
Tree diagram:

Outcomes

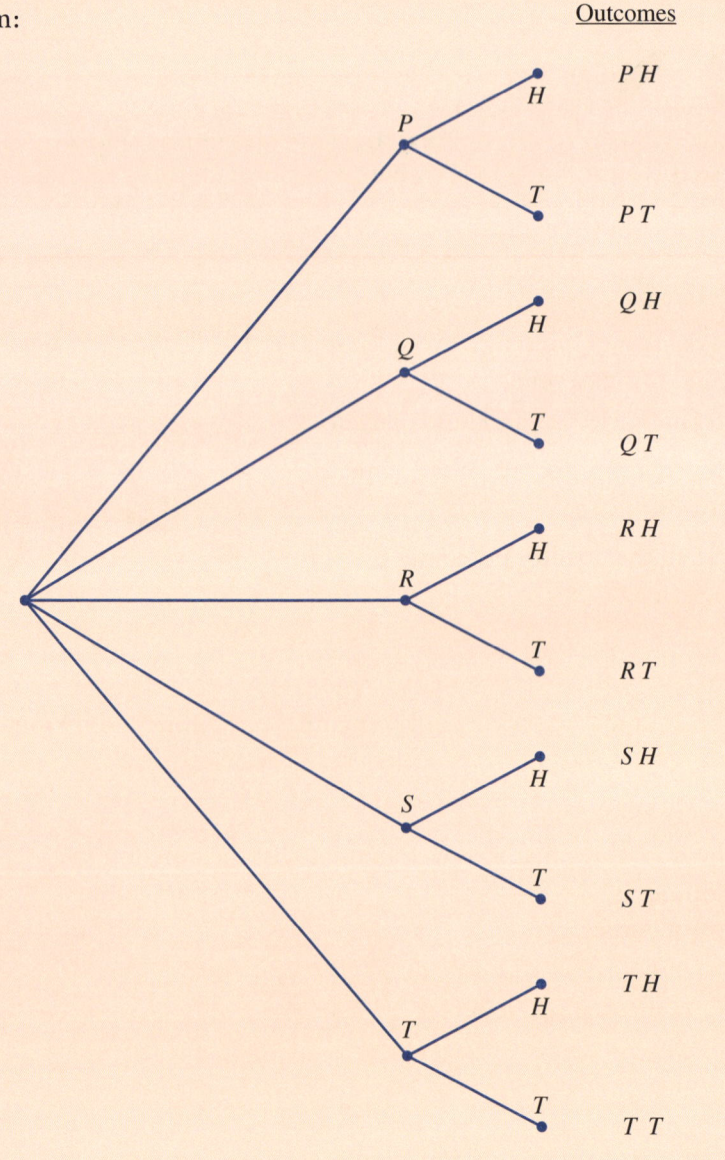

P H
P T
Q H
Q T
R H
R T
S H
S T
T H
T T

FUNDAMENTAL PRINCIPLES OF COUNTING

A cinema offers an €8 meal deal. Customers choose one snack and one drink from the following menu:

Snack	Drink
Popcorn	Juice
Nachos	Orange
Hot dog	Lemon
Sweets	Water
Crisps	

(i) How many different choices of a snack and drink are available in the cinema?

(ii) Complete the table below, showing all the possible choices for the meal deal:

	Popcorn (P)	Nachos (N)	Hot dog (H)	Sweets (S)	Crisps (C)
Juice (J)					
Orange (O)		(O, N)			
Lemon (L)					
Water (W)					(W, C)

(iii) How many of the choices include orange as the drink?

Solution

(i) Total number of choices = (Snack) AND (Drink)
$$= (5) \times (4)$$
$$= 20$$

(ii) Completing the table gives:

	Popcorn (P)	Nachos (N)	Hot dog (H)	Sweets (S)	Crisps (C)
Juice (J)	(J, P)	(J, N)	(J, H)	(J, S)	(J, C)
Orange (O)	(O, P)	(O, N)	(O, H)	(O, S)	(O, C)
Lemon (L)	(L, P)	(L, N)	(L, H)	(L, S)	(L, C)
Water (W)	(W, P)	(W, N)	(W, H)	(W, S)	(W, C)

(iii) From the table, we can see that five of the choices include orange as the drink: (O, P), (O, N), (O, H), (O, S), (O, C)

Die (dice for more than one):
A die is a cube with dots on each side.
The dots represent numbers from 1 to 6.
The numbers on the opposite sides of a die add up to 7.
A fair die is equally likely to land on any of the numbers from 1 to 6.

A game consists of spinning a spinner and rolling a die. The spinner has 4 segments coloured red, green, yellow and blue.

An outcome is a coloured segment and a number from the die.

(i) How many outcomes of the game are possible?
(ii) List all the possible outcomes of the game.
(iii) How many outcomes contain a prime number?

Solution
(i) Total number of outcomes = (outcomes on spinner) AND (outcomes on coin)
$$= (4) \times (6)$$
$$= 24$$

(ii) Using a two-way table (sample space):

		Die					
		1	2	3	4	5	6
Spinner	Red (R)	•	•	•	•	•	•
	Green (G)	•	•	•	•	•	•
	Yellow (Y)	•	•	•	•	•	•
	Blue (B)	•	•	•	•	•	•

A dot indicates an outcome.
There are 24 dots (4 × 6).

List of outcomes
(R, 1), (R, 2), (R, 3), (R, 4), (R, 5), (R, 6)
(G, 1), (G, 2), (G, 3), (G, 4), (G, 5), (G, 6)
(Y, 1), (Y, 2), (Y, 3), (Y, 4), (Y, 5), (Y, 6)
(B, 1), (B, 2), (B, 3), (B, 4), (B, 5), (B, 6)

(iii) Of the numbers on the die, 2, 3 and 5 are prime numbers.
Therefore, the 12 outcomes containing 2, 3 and 5 contain a prime number.

9 Probability

aims
- To understand that probabilities are measured on a scale from 0 to 1
- To be able to calculate the probability of an event occurring
- To understand the difference between theoretical and experimental probabilities
- To be able to use sample spaces, tree diagrams and Venn diagrams to calculate probabilities

Probability involves the study of the laws of chance. It is a measure of the chance, or likelihood, of something happening.

If you carry out an operation, or experiment, using coins, dice, spinners or cards, then each toss, throw, spin or draw is called a **trial**.

The possible things that can happen from a trial are called **outcomes**. The outcomes of interest are called an **event**. In other words, an event is the set of successful outcomes.

key point
You need to understand all words in bold print: **probability, trial, outcome, event**.

For example, if you throw a die and you are interested in the probability of throwing an even number, then the events 2, 4, 6 are the successful outcomes.

If E is an event, then $P(E)$ stands for the probability that the event occurs. $P(E)$ is read as 'the probability of E'.

The probability of an event is a number between 0 and 1, including 0 and 1.

$$0 \leq P(E) \leq 1$$

key point
Probability can **never** be a negative value or a value greater than 1.

The value of $P(E)$ can be given as a fraction, decimal or percentage.

Note: $P(E) = 0$ means that an event is **impossible**.
$P(E) = 1$ means that an event is **certain**.

The chance of an event happening can be shown on a **probability scale**:

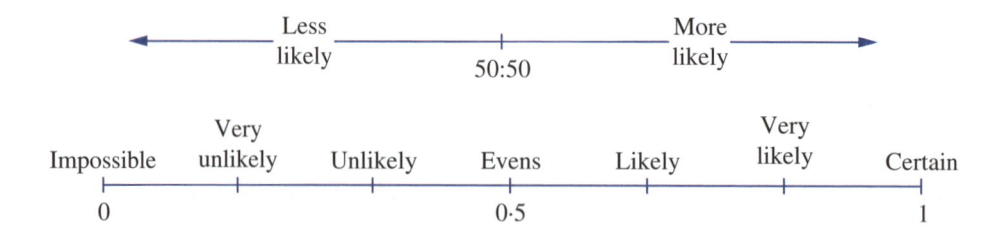

> The measure of the probability of an event, E, is given by:
>
> $$P(E) = \frac{\text{Number of successful outcomes}}{\text{Number of possible outcomes}}$$

Probability of an event not happening

If E is any event, then 'not E' is the event that E does not occur. Clearly, E and 'not E' cannot occur at the same time. Either E or 'not E' must occur. Thus, we have the following relationship between the probabilities of E and 'not E':

> $$P(E) + P(\text{not } E) = 1$$
> or
> $$P(\text{not } E) = 1 - P(E)$$

Example

A bag contains three red, three green and four blue marbles. A marble is selected at random from the bag.
  (i) What is the probability of selecting a blue marble?
 (ii) What is the probability of selecting a green marble?
(iii) What is the probability of selecting a marble which is not green?

Solution

(i) $P(\text{Blue marble}) = \dfrac{\text{Number of blue marbles}}{\text{Total number of marbles}}$

$P(\text{Blue marble}) = \dfrac{4}{10} = \dfrac{2}{5}$

key point
'Drawn at random' means that every item is equally likely to be drawn.

(ii) $P(\text{Green marble}) = \dfrac{\text{Number of green marbles}}{\text{Total number of marbles}}$

$P(\text{Green marble}) = \dfrac{3}{10}$

PROBABILITY

> **exam focus**
>
> When possible, give your answer for probabilities as a fraction and not a word. Giving answers such as 'likely' may not get full marks.

(iii) $P(\text{not green marble}) = \dfrac{\text{Number of marbles which are not green}}{\text{Total number of marbles}}$

$P(\text{not green marble}) = \dfrac{7}{10}$

Alternative method:
$P(\text{not green marble}) = 1 - P(\text{green marble})$

$P(\text{not green marble}) = 1 - \dfrac{3}{10}$

$P(\text{not green marble}) = \dfrac{7}{10}$

exam Q

(i) Let A be the set of months of the year. List the elements of A.
(ii) What is the probability that a month chosen at random from set A begins with the letter J?

Solution

(i) A = {January, February, March, April, May, June, July, August, September, October, November, December}

(ii) There are three months, in set A, which begin with the letter J:

$P(J) = \dfrac{\text{Number of elements beginning with } J}{\text{Total number of elements in } A}$

$= \dfrac{3}{12}$

$= \dfrac{1}{4}$

Therefore, $P(J) = \dfrac{1}{4}$

Example

The net of a cube is shown. This net is cut from cardboard and folded to make a cube. Each face of the cube has the letter A, B or C on it. The cube is then rolled and the side facing upwards is called the outcome.

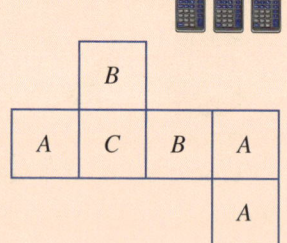

	B		
A	C	B	A
	A		

(i) What is the probability that the outcome will be A?
(ii) What is the probability that the outcome will be B?
(iii) What is the probability that the outcome will be C?

Solution

(i) $P(A) = \dfrac{\text{Number of faces with } A}{\text{Total number of faces}} = \dfrac{3}{6} = \dfrac{1}{2}$

(ii) $P(B) = \dfrac{\text{Number of faces with } B}{\text{Total number of faces}} = \dfrac{2}{6} = \dfrac{1}{3}$

(iii) $P(C) = \dfrac{\text{Number of faces with } C}{\text{Total number of faces}} = \dfrac{1}{6}$

exam focus: Notice the link here between probability and the topic of nets.

---

exam Q

(i) Let A = {1, 2, 3, 4, ..., 25}. Write out all the elements of A.
(ii) Write out all the elements of A that are divisible by 2.
(iii) Write out all the elements of A that are divisible by 3.
(iv) Write out all the elements of A that are divisible by 2 but **not** divisible by 3.
(v) What is the probability that a number chosen at random from the set A is divisible by 2 but not divisible by 3?

Solution

(i) All the elements of A are:

A = {1, 2, 3, 4, 5, 6, 7, 8, 9, 10, 11, 12, 13, 14, 15, 16, 17, 18, 19, 20, 21, 22, 23, 24, 25}

(ii) The elements of A which are divisible by 2:

{2, 4, 6, 8, 10, 12, 14, 16, 18, 20, 22, 24}

(iii) The elements of A which are divisible by 3: {3, 6, 9, 12, 15, 18, 21, 24}
(iv) The elements of A which are divisible by 2 but not divisible by 3:
{2, 4, 8, 10, 14, 16, 20, 22}
(v) The probability of choosing a number which is divisible by 2 but not divisible by 3:

$$= \frac{\text{Number of elements which are divisible by 2 but not divisible by 3}}{\text{Total number of elements in } A}$$

$$= \frac{8}{25}$$

Three athletes, Alan, Barry and Colm are equally likely to win a 3-man race.
(i) List all the ways in which the men can finish, assuming all finish the race and there is no dead-heat.
(ii) What is the probability that they finish in the order: Barry, Alan, Colm?
(iii) What is the probability that Colm wins?
(iv) What is the probability that Alan finishes last?

Solution

(i) Let A = Alan, B = Barry and C = Colm. The athletes can finish in the following orders:

$$ABC, ACB, BAC, BCA, CAB, CBA$$

(ii) $P(BAC) = \dfrac{\text{Number of arrangements with } BAC}{\text{Total number of arrangements}} = \dfrac{1}{6}$

(iii) $P(\text{Colm wins}) = \dfrac{\text{Number of arrangements with } C \text{ first}}{\text{Total number of arrangements}} = \dfrac{2}{6} = \dfrac{1}{3}$

(iv) $P(\text{Alan last}) = \dfrac{\text{Number of arrangements with } A \text{ at end}}{\text{Total number of arrangements}} = \dfrac{2}{6} = \dfrac{1}{3}$

Example

(i) One hundred and fifty students sitting an examination were grouped according to age (16, 17 or 18) and gender (female or male). The results are given in the following table:

	Age 16	Age 17	Age 18
Female	30	18	12
Male	60	27	3

One student is chosen at random. What is the probability that the student is:
(a) Male? (b) A 16-year-old female? (c) Younger than 18? (d) Older than 19?

(ii) Label the probability of each event with the letters A, B, C and D, respectively. Indicate the position of A, B, C and D on the probability scale.

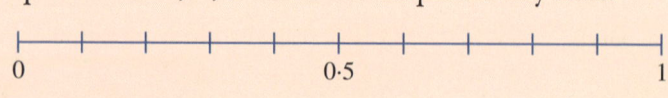

Solution

(i) (a) $P(\text{Male}) = \dfrac{\text{Number of males}}{\text{Total number of people}}$

$P(\text{Male}) = \dfrac{90}{150} = 0 \cdot 6$

(b) $P(\text{16 yr old female}) = \dfrac{\text{Number of 16 yr old females}}{\text{Total number of people}}$

$P(\text{16 yr old female}) = \dfrac{30}{150} = 0 \cdot 2$

(c) $P(\text{Younger than 18}) = \dfrac{\text{Number of people younger than 18}}{\text{Total number of people}}$

$P(\text{Younger than 18}) = \dfrac{135}{150} = 0 \cdot 9$

(d) $P(\text{Older than 19}) = \dfrac{\text{Number of people older than 19}}{\text{Total number of people}}$

$P(\text{Older than 19}) = \dfrac{0}{150} = 0$

key point

You must be able to calculate the probability of an event happening on the scale from 0 to 1.

(ii) Labelling the answers from (a), (b), (c) and (d) on the probability scale:

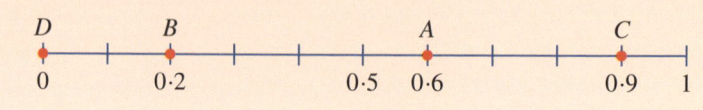

```
 D      B           A        C
 •──┼───•──┼───┼───•──┼───┼──•──┼
 0     0·2         0·5 0·6     0·9 1
```

PROBABILITY

In the coordinate diagram, 16 points are marked with a dot (•).

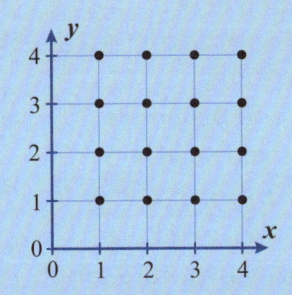

Louise picks 1 point at random from the 16 points marked with a dot in the diagram. She then finds the equation of the line that goes through this point and through (0, 0).
Find the probability that Louise's line has a slope that is greater than **1**.

Solution
A line will have a slope of 1 when the rise and the run are equal.
Starting at the origin (0, 0), a line will have a slope of 1 if it passes through any of the points (1, 1), (2, 2), (3, 3) or (4, 4). This line is shown in blue on the diagram.

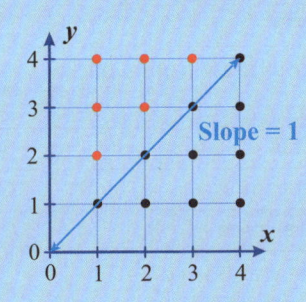

Starting at the origin, to have a slope greater than 1, the line Louise draws must pass through any of the 6 points above the blue line (coloured in red)

$$P(\text{slope} > 1) = \frac{6}{16} = \frac{3}{8}$$

exam focus

You must know the structure of a deck of playing cards.

There are **52 cards** in a deck of cards.

There are 4 suits: **Red: Hearts** and **Diamonds**
                   Black: Clubs and **Spades**

Each suit has 13 cards: Ace, 2, 3, 4, 5, 6, 7, 8, 9, 10, Jack, Queen and King.

Jack, Queen and King are known as 'picture cards'.

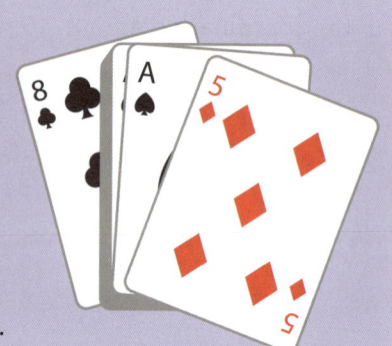

exam Q

A, B, C, D and E represent the probabilities of certain events occurring.

(i) Write the probability of each of the events listed into the table below.

Event		Probability
A club is selected in a random draw from a pack of playing cards	A	
A tossed fair coin shows a tail on landing	B	
The sun will rise in the east tomorrow	C	
May will follow directly after June	D	
A randomly selected person was born on a Thursday	E	

(ii) Place each of the letters A, B, C, D and E at its correct position on the probability scale below.

```
├─────────────────────────────────────┤
0                                     1
```

Solution

(i) A: $P(\text{Club}) = \dfrac{\text{Number of clubs}}{\text{Total number of cards}} = \dfrac{13}{52} = \dfrac{1}{4}$

B: $P(\text{Tail}) = \dfrac{\text{Number of tails}}{\text{Total number sides}} = \dfrac{1}{2}$

C: $P(\text{sun rising in the East})$ is a certainty, as the sun always rises in the East. Therefore, $P(\text{Sun rising in the East}) = 1$

D: $P(\text{May will follow directly after June})$ is an impossibility, as May comes before June.
Therefore, $P(\text{May will follow directly after June}) = 0$

E: $P(\text{Thursday}) = \dfrac{\text{Number of Thursdays}}{\text{Total number days in a week}} = \dfrac{1}{7}$

Completed table:

Event		Probability
A club is selected in a random draw from a pack of playing cards	A	$\dfrac{1}{4}$
A tossed fair coin shows a tail on landing	B	$\dfrac{1}{2}$ or **evens** or **50/50**
The sun will rise in the east tomorrow	C	1 or **certain**
May will follow directly after June	D	0 or **impossible**
A randomly selected person was born on a Thursday	E	$\dfrac{1}{7}$

exam focus

When possible, give answers for probabilities as a fraction and not a word. Giving answers such as 'likely' may not get full marks.

(ii) Entering A, B, C, D and E on the scale gives:

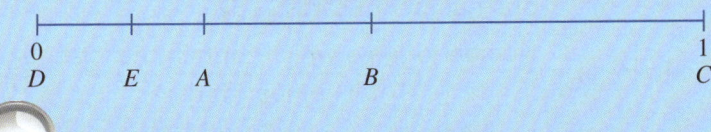

```
├──┼──┼───────┼─────────────────────────┤
0                                        1
   D  E  A    B                          C
```

exam focus

For this exam question, 15 marks were awarded for part (i). 10 out of the 15 marks were awarded for any one correct answer.

(i) Estimate the probability for each of the events *A, B, C, D* and *E* listed below.

   A name is picked at random from a list of 50 girls and 50 boys.

   A = A girl's name is picked

   A fair coin is tossed once.

   B = A head is the outcome.

   One card is drawn at random from a pack of playing cards.

   C = The card is a diamond

   A day is chosen at random from a list of the days of the week.

   D = The name of the day contains the letter *a*.

   One number is picked at random from the set {1, 2, 3, 4, 5, 7, 11, 13}

   E = The number chosen is a prime number.

(ii) Place the letter for each of the events at the most appropriate position on the probability scale below.

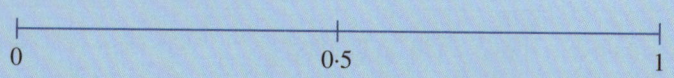

```
├─────────────────┼─────────────────┤
0                0·5                1
```

(iii) Write down another event that you think has a probability similar to that of *C* in the scale above.

(iv) Write down another event that you think has a probability similar to that of *D* in the scale above.

(v) In a multiple-choice quiz, three possible answers are given to a question. James does not know the answer and guesses which one is correct. Put an *X* on the scale above to show that probability that he has chosen the correct answer.

Solution

(i) **A:** $P(\text{Girl}) = \dfrac{\text{Number of girls' names}}{\text{Total number of names}} = \dfrac{50}{100} = 0\cdot 5$

B: $P(\text{Head}) = \dfrac{\text{Number of heads}}{\text{Total number of sides}} = \dfrac{1}{2} = 0\cdot 5$

C: $P(\text{Diamond}) = \dfrac{\text{Number of diamonds}}{\text{Total number of cards}} = \dfrac{13}{52} = 0\cdot 25$

D: $P(\text{Contains } a) = \dfrac{\text{Number of days which contain the letter } a}{\text{Total number of days}} = \dfrac{7}{7} = 1$

E: $P(\text{Prime}) = \dfrac{\text{Number of prime numbers}}{\text{Total number of numbers}} = \dfrac{6}{8} = 0\cdot 75$

PROBABILITY

> **key point**
>
> **Remember**
> A prime number is a number which has factors of one and itself. The number 1 is not a prime number.
> Primes: 2, 3, 5, 7, 11, 13, 17, . . .

(ii) Place the probabilities of events A, B, C, D and E on the scale:

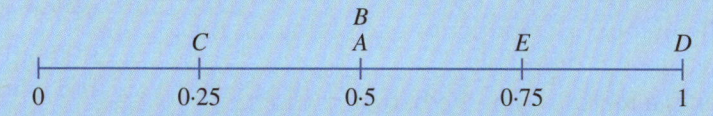

```
       C      B         E           D
              A
|------|------|---------|-----------|
0     0.25   0.5       0.75         1
```

(iii) $P(C) = 0.25 = \dfrac{1}{4}$

Given a bag containing 1 red, 1 blue, 1 green and 1 white marble, the probability of drawing a red marble is 0.25.

(iv) $P(D) = 1$

The probability that the sun will rise on any given day is a certainty. Therefore, it has a probability of 1.

(v) $P(\text{Correct answer}) = \dfrac{\text{Number of correct answers}}{\text{Total number of answers}} = \dfrac{1}{3}$

Marking this probability as X on the scale:

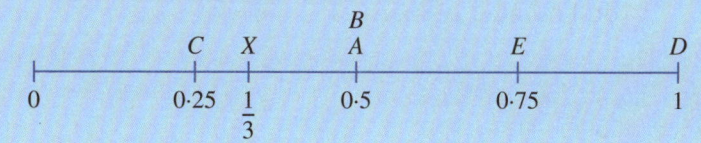

```
       C  X    B         E           D
               A
|------|--|----|---------|-----------|
0     0.25 1/3 0.5      0.75         1
```

exam Q

Mary has a bag of marbles.

The number of marbles of each colour is shown in the box.

Contents
7 yellow marbles
3 green marbles
4 red marbles
2 black marbles

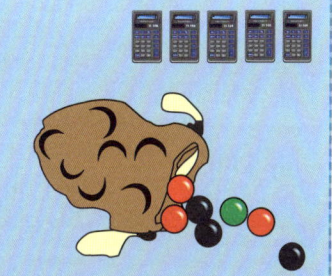

(i) How many marbles are in the bag?

(ii) Mary takes a marble from the bag at random. Complete the following sentence:

The probability that Mary will take a _____ marble from the bag is $\frac{1}{4}$.

(iii) 'The probability of taking a red marble is greater that the probability of taking a yellow marble.' Is this statement correct? Give a reason for your answer.

(iv) Mary found five more black marbles and added them to the bag.

Fill in the number of marbles of each colour in the bag after she has done this.

(v) Mary takes a marble from the bag at random. What is the probability that she will take a black marble from the bag?

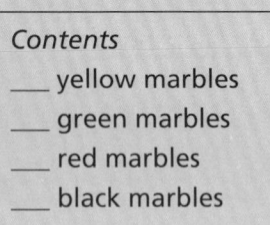

Contents
___ yellow marbles
___ green marbles
___ red marbles
___ black marbles

Solution

(i) Total number of marbles $= 7 + 3 + 4 + 2 = 16$

(ii) The probability that Mary will take a **red** marble from the bag is $\frac{1}{4}$.

This is because:

$$P(\text{Red}) = \frac{\text{Number of red marbles}}{\text{Total number of marbles}} = \frac{4}{16} = \frac{1}{4}$$

(iii) $P(\text{Red}) = \frac{1}{4}$

$$P(\text{Yellow}) = \frac{\text{Number of yellow marbles}}{\text{Total number of marbles}} = \frac{7}{16}$$

$$\frac{7}{16} > \frac{1}{4}$$

$0.4375 > 0.25$

Therefore, $P(\text{Yellow})$ is greater than $P(\text{Red})$ so the statement is incorrect.

(iv) After adding five more black marbles, the contents of the bag becomes:

Contents
_7_ yellow marbles
_3_ green marbles
_4_ red marbles
_7_ black marbles

(v) $P(\text{Black}) = \dfrac{\text{Number of black marbles}}{\text{Total number of marbles}} = \dfrac{7}{21} = \dfrac{1}{3}$

PROBABILITY

There are 80 members in a club. The table below shows the number of males and females who do or do not wear glasses:

	Male	Female	Total
Wearing glasses	4		12
Not wearing glasses		40	
Total	32		80

(i) Complete the table, by filling in the missing values.

(ii) A club member is selected at random. What is the probability that the club member is a:

(a) Male? (b) Person wearing glasses? (c) Female not wearing glasses?

(iii) A male from the club is selected at random.
What is the probability he wears glasses?

(iv) A member who wears glasses is selected at random.
What is the probability that the person is a female?

(v) All members who wear glasses resign from the club. What is the probability that a club member now selected at random is male?

Solution

(i)

	Male	Female	Total
Wearing glasses	4	8	12
Not wearing glasses	28	40	68
Total	32	48	80

(ii) (a) $P(\text{Male}) = \dfrac{\text{Number of males}}{\text{Total number of people}} = \dfrac{32}{80} = \dfrac{2}{5}$

(b) $P(\text{Wearing glasses}) = \dfrac{\text{Number of people wearing glasses}}{\text{Total number of people}} = \dfrac{12}{80} = \dfrac{3}{20}$

(c) $P(\text{Female and no glasses}) = \dfrac{\text{Number of females with no glasses}}{\text{Total number of people}} = \dfrac{40}{80} = \dfrac{1}{2}$

(iii) A male is selected, so we will only consider the males when working out the probabilities:

$P(\text{Wearing glasses}) = \dfrac{\text{Number of males wearing glasses}}{\text{Total number of males}} = \dfrac{4}{32} = \dfrac{1}{8}$

(iv) A person wearing glasses is selected, so we will only consider the people with glasses when working out the probabilities:

$$P(\text{Female}) = \frac{\text{Number of females wearing glasses}}{\text{Total number of people wearing glasses}} = \frac{8}{12} = \frac{2}{3}$$

(v) All members with glasses leave, so now there are only 28 males and 40 females, giving a total of 68 members.

$$P(\text{Male}) = \frac{\text{Number of males}}{\text{Total number of members}} = \frac{28}{68} = \frac{7}{17}$$

Sample space

A sample space is the set of all possible outcomes. A sample space can be very useful for seeing all possible outcomes and working out any appropriate probabilities.

A sample space can be represented by a list, a two-way table or a tree diagram. Sample spaces were covered in Chapter 8 on Fundamental Principles of Counting.

Example

A fair coin is tossed twice.
  (i) Find the probability that the coin lands on a tail, on the first toss.
 (ii) Draw a tree diagram to show all possible outcomes for the two tosses.
(iii) Use your tree diagram to find the probability that the coin lands on a head on both tosses.

Solution

(i) $P(\text{Tail}) = \dfrac{\text{Number of sides with a tail}}{\text{Total number of sides}} = \dfrac{1}{2} = 0.5$

(ii) Tree diagram:
   Mark the probabilities of each event along the stems of the tree.

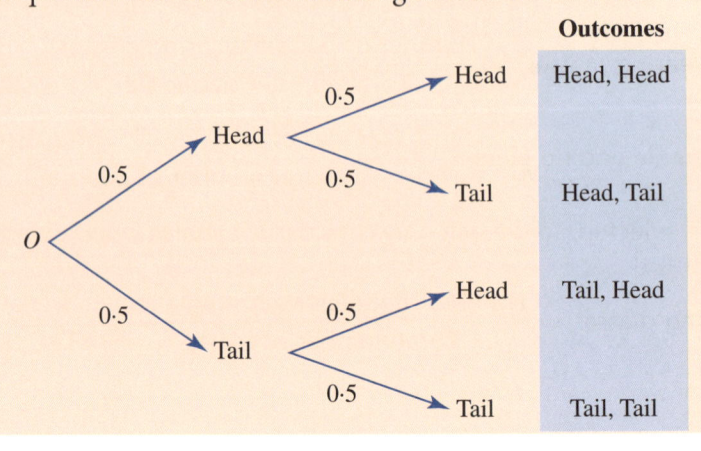

	Outcomes
Head, Head	
Head, Tail	
Tail, Head	
Tail, Tail	

Branches: O → Head (0.5) → Head (0.5) / Tail (0.5); O → Tail (0.5) → Head (0.5) / Tail (0.5)

(iii) $P(\text{Head, Head}) = 0.5 \times 0.5 = 0.25$

> **key point**
>
> To calculate the probability along a path, you multiply all probabilities along the branches on that path.

exam Q

Jack rolls a fair die and spins a fair spinner as shown.

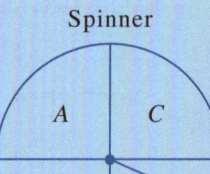

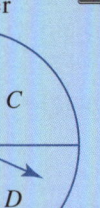

Die

Spinner

(i) Complete the table below showing all possible outcomes.

		Spinner			
		A	B	C	D
Die	1	(1, A)			
	2				
	3				
	4				
	5				
	6				(6, D)

(ii) How many possible outcomes are there?
(iii) How many outcomes consist of an odd number and B?
(iv) What is the probability that an outcome will contain an even number?

Solution

(i) Completed table:

		\multicolumn{4}{c}{Spinner}
		A	B	C	D
Die	1	(1, A)	(1, B)	(1, C)	(1, D)
	2	(2, A)	(2, B)	(2, C)	(2, D)
	3	(3, A)	(3, B)	(3, C)	(3, D)
	4	(4, A)	(4, B)	(4, C)	(4, D)
	5	(5, A)	(5, B)	(5, C)	(5, D)
	6	(6, A)	(6, B)	(6, C)	(6, D)

(ii) From the table, we can see there are: $6 \times 4 = 24$ outcomes

(iii) From the table, there are three outcomes which consist of an odd number and a B: (1, B), (3, B) and (5, B)

(iv) $P(\text{Even}) = \dfrac{\text{Number of outcomes which contain an even number}}{\text{Total number of outcomes}}$

$= \dfrac{12}{24}$

$= \dfrac{1}{2}$

Therefore, $P(\text{Even}) = \dfrac{1}{2}$

---

exam Q

Una rolls a die and flips a coin. One of the possible outcomes is (1, Head).

(i) Write out the remaining eleven possible outcomes.
(ii) How many outcomes consist of an odd number and a tail?
(iii) What is the probability that the outcome will contain a prime number?

Solution

(i) All outcomes:

(1, Head) (2, Head) (3, Head) (4, Head) (5, Head) (6, Head)
(1, Tail) (2, Tail) (3, Tail) (4, Tail) (5, Tail) (6, Tail)

(ii) Three outcomes contain an odd number and a Tail: (1, Tail), (3, Tail), (5, Tail)

PROBABILITY

(iii) The prime numbers on a die are: 2, 3, and 5.
Therefore, the outcomes containing a prime number are:
(2, Head), (2, Tail), (3, Head), (3, Tail), (5, Head), (5, Tail)

$$P(\text{Prime}) = \frac{\text{Number of outcomes containing a prime number}}{\text{Total number of outcomes}}$$

$$P(\text{Prime}) = \frac{6}{12}$$

$$P(\text{Prime}) = \frac{1}{2}$$

key point

Remember
A prime number is a number which has factors of one and itself. The number 1 is not a prime number.
Primes: 2, 3, 5, 7, 11, 13, 17, . . .

exam Q

A game consists of two spinners. One with four segments, numbered 1 to 4, and the second with five segments numbered 1 to 5. The spinners are spun.

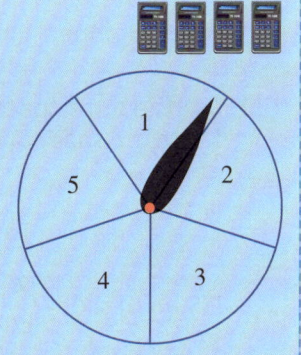

(i) Draw a sample space of all possible outcomes.
(ii) If the spinners are fair, what is the probability of getting two 4s?
(iii) If the spinners are fair, what is the probability the values on the spinners sum to 6?
(iv) Jason thinks that one of the spinners is biased. Describe an experiment that he could do to find out whether the spinner is biased.

key point

Biased means unfair. If a spinner or a die is biased it will land on some numbers more often than others.

Solution

(i) Sample space showing all possible outcomes:

		Spinner 1			
		1	2	3	4
Spinner 2	1	1, 1			1, 4
	2		2, 2		
	3				3, 4
	4	4, 1		4, 3	
	5				5, 4

key point

The numbers in the grid represent all the possible outcomes. A few have been filled in for you, to understand what the grid represents. Keep the order of the couples consistent.

(ii) There is only one outcome in which **both** spinners land on 4:

$$P(\text{Both spinners land on 4}) = \frac{\text{Number of favourable outcomes}}{\text{Total number of outcomes}} = \frac{1}{20}$$

(iii) Use the same space to determine which outcomes will give a sum of 6. These are shaded in the grid.

$$P(\text{Sum of six}) = \frac{\text{Number where sum is 6}}{\text{Total number of outcomes}}$$

$$P(\text{Sum of six}) = \frac{4}{20}$$

$$P(\text{Sum of six}) = \frac{1}{5}$$

		Spinner 1			
		1	2	3	4
Spinner 2	1				
	2				2, 4
	3			3, 3	
	4		4, 2		
	5	5, 1			

(iv) Jason should spin the spinner he thinks is biased many times and record the number it lands on. Consider spinner 1, if the spinner is fair, it should land on each number, from 1 to 4, approximately the same number of times. That is, it should land on each number approximately one-quarter of the time.

The arrows represent the different routes that a skier can take when skiing down a mountain. The circles on the diagram represent different points on the routes.

(i) When leaving any particular point on the mountain, a skier is **equally likely** to choose any of the available routes from the point.

Fill in the boxes in the diagram which represent the probability that the skier will take that route.

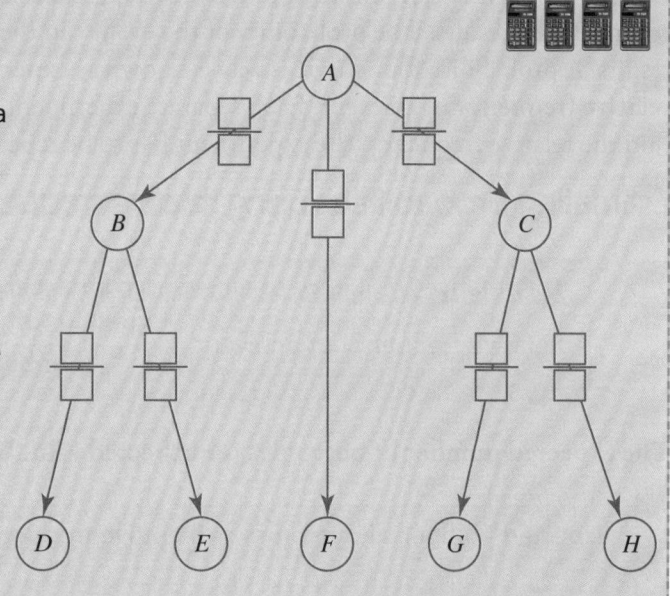

(ii) (a) If the skier starts at point A, find the probability that the skier will reach the point H.

(b) If the skier starts at point A, find the probability that the skier will reach the point E.

Solution

(i) The skier is equally likely to choose each path.

There are three paths leaving the point A. Therefore, the probability of each of these paths is $\frac{1}{3}$.

There are two paths leaving the points B and C. Therefore, the probability of each of these paths is $\frac{1}{2}$.

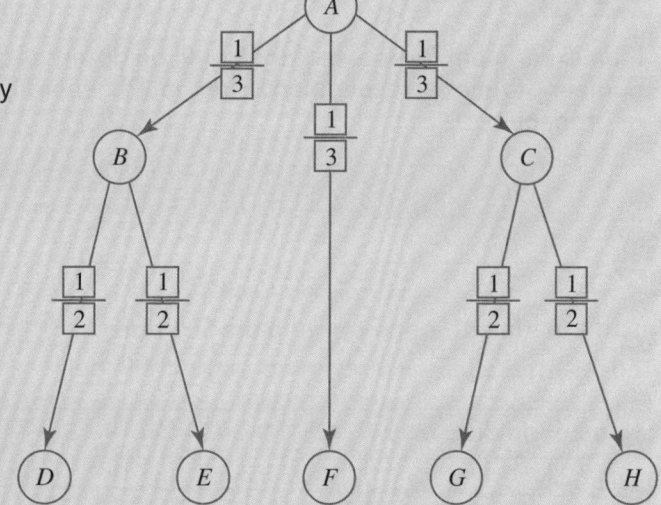

(ii) (a) To get to point H, the skier must go from A to C and then to H.

$$P(ACH) = \frac{1}{3} \times \frac{1}{2} = \frac{1}{6}$$

(b) To get to point E, the skier must go from A to B and then to E.

$$P(ABE) = \frac{1}{3} \times \frac{1}{2} = \frac{1}{6}$$

Experimental probability

Often a probability can only be found by carrying out a series of experiments and recording the results. The probability of the event can then be **estimated** from these results. A probability found in this way is known as **experimental probability** or the **relative frequency** of an event. Each separate experiment carried out is called a **trial**. To find the relative frequency, the experiment has to be repeated a number of times.

Estimating probabilities using relative frequency

> The relative frequency of an event in an experiment is given by:
>
> $$\text{Relative frequency of an event} = \frac{\text{Number of successful trials}}{\text{Number of trials}}$$

The expected number of outcomes (or expected value) is calculated as follows.

> Expected number of outcomes = (Relative frequency) × (Number of trials)
>
> or
>
> Expected number of outcomes = P(Event) × (Number of trials)

key point

If an experiment is repeated, there will be different outcomes. Increasing the number of times an experiment is repeated generally leads to better estimates of probability.

exam Q

In an experiment, Anne tossed a die 600 times.
The results are partially recorded in the table below.

Number on die	1	2	3	4	5	6
Frequency	92	101	115	98		105

(i) Calculate the number of times that a 5 appeared.
(ii) After looking at the results, Anne claims that the die is biased. Do you agree with her? Give a reason for your answer.
(iii) If this die is tossed 300 times, how many times would you expect to get an even number as a result? Give a reason for your answer.

Solution

(i) $600 = 92 + 101 + 115 + 98 + x + 105$
$600 = 511 + x$
$600 - 511 = x$
$89 = x$

Therefore, the number 5 was recorded 89 times.

(ii) No, I do not agree that the die is biased, I think the die is fair. If the die is fair, out of 600 throws you would expect each number to show 100 times. Since the frequency of each number is close to 100, I do not agree the die is biased.

OR

Yes, I do agree that the die is biased. If the die is fair, out of 600 throws you would expect each number to show 100 times. Since the number 3 was recorded 115 times and the number 5 was recorded only 89 times, then I would conclude the die is biased.

key point

You should notice that there were two possible answers for this question. As is often the case with questions involving opinion, sometimes more than one answer may be valid.

(iii) Answer: 150
Reason: Half of the numbers on the die are even, therefore you would expect an even number to be thrown half of the number of times that the die was tossed.

---

exam Q

(i) What is the probability of getting a 1 when a fair die is tossed?

(ii) A fair die is tossed 500 times. The results are recorded in the table below.

Number on die	1	2	3	4	5	6
Frequency	70	83	86	90	91	80
Relative frequency		$\frac{83}{500} = 0{\cdot}16$				

Calculate the relative frequency of each outcome and write it into the table above. Give your answer correct to 2 decimal places.

(iii) Give a possible reason for the difference in value between the relative frequency for 1 in the table and your answer to part (i).

Solution

(i) $P(1) = \dfrac{1}{6} = 0 \cdot 17$

(ii)

Number on die	1	2	3	4	5	6
Frequency	70	83	86	90	91	80
Relative frequency	$\dfrac{70}{500} = 0\cdot 14$	$\dfrac{83}{500} = 0\cdot 17$	$\dfrac{86}{500} = 0\cdot 17$	$\dfrac{90}{500} = 0\cdot 18$	$\dfrac{91}{500} = 0\cdot 18$	$\dfrac{80}{500} = 0\cdot 16$

(iii) Since the relative frequency (experimental probability) is less than the theoretical probability, the die may be biased towards the other numbers on the die.

key point

Relative frequency does not equal theoretical probability. Relative frequency is the fraction of times something actually happens. Hence, **relative frequency is an estimate of the theoretical probability.**

The value for relative frequency gets closer to the theoretical probability, as the number of trials (frequency) increases.

exam Q

In a survey, 1 500 people were asked which national radio station they listen to most often. The results of the survey are given in the table below.

	RTÉ 1	Today FM	Newstalk	Lyric FM	2FM	No national station
Frequency	375	195	120	45	165	
Relative frequency (as a fraction)	$\dfrac{375}{1\,500}$					
Relative frequency (as a decimal)			0·08			

(i) How many of the people surveyed do **not** listen to a national radio station?
(ii) Complete the table above.
(iii) Find the sum of the relative frequencies written as a fraction.
(iv) Find the sum of the relative frequencies written as decimals.

(v) Jackie wrote the relative frequencies as percentages. She found their sum to be 80%. Do you think her calculations are correct? Give a reason for your answer.

(vi) Denis looked at the data and said, 'I can find out how many people in the survey normally listen to local radio'. Do you agree or disagree with Denis? Explain your answer.

Solution

(i) People who do not listen to a national radio station are those who listen to 'no national station'.

No national station = 1 500 − (375 + 195 + 120 + 45 + 165)
= 1 500 − 900
= 600

(ii) Completing the table gives:

	RTÉ 1	Today FM	Newstalk	Lyric FM	2FM	No national station
Frequency	375	195	120	45	165	600
Relative frequency (as a fraction)	$\frac{375}{1\,500}$	$\frac{195}{1\,500}$	$\frac{120}{1\,500}$	$\frac{45}{1\,500}$	$\frac{165}{1\,500}$	$\frac{600}{1\,500}$
Relative frequency (as a decimal)	0·25	0·13	0·08	0·03	0·11	0·4

(iii) Sum of relative frequencies = $\frac{375}{1500} + \frac{195}{1500} + \frac{120}{1500} + \frac{45}{1500} + \frac{165}{1500} + \frac{600}{1500}$

Sum of relative frequencies = $\frac{1500}{1500} = 1$

(iv) Sum of relative frequencies = 0·25 + 0·13 + 0·08 + 0·03 + 0·11 + 0·4

Sum of relative frequencies = 1

(v) No, Jackie's calculations must be wrong because the percentages should add up to 100%.

(vi) I disagree with Denis. Although there are a lot of people in the survey who do not listen to a national radio station, we cannot conclude that they listen to local radio stations. They may not listen to the radio at all.

10 Statistics I: Statistical Investigations

aims
- To know the types of statistical data
- To be very familiar with the terms used in studying statistics. Referring to the glossary of statistical terms at the back of this book and when necessary be able to explain the terms in your own words
- To learn what is required when gathering and interpreting statistical data

Introduction to statistics

Statistics deals with the collection, presentation, analysis and interpretation of data. Social scientists, psychologists, pollsters, medical researchers, governments and many others use statistical methodology to study behaviours of **populations**.

A large part of any statistical investigation is the production of **data**.

In statistics, any collection of variables is called data and a population is the complete set of data under consideration.

> **key point**
> Statistics is a very important part of your course. You will use Statistical knowledge and skills to complete your CBA 2 during third year. See Chapter 13 for more on this.

Primary and secondary data

Primary data (first-hand data) are data that you collect yourself or are collected by someone under your direct supervision.

Secondary data (second-hand data) is data that have already been collected and made available from an external source such as newspapers, government departments, organisations or the internet.

Primary and secondary data have advantages and disadvantages.

Data	Advantages	Disadvantages	Sources
Primary	Know how it was obtained Accuracy is also known	Time consuming Can be expensive	Surveys Experiments
Secondary	Easy and cheap to obtain	Could be out of date May have mistakes and be biased Unknown source of collection	The internet Central Statistics Office

Steps in a statistical investigation

All statistical investigations begin with a question. The steps are:

1. Pose a question
2. Collect data
3. Present and analyse the information.
4. Interpret the results.

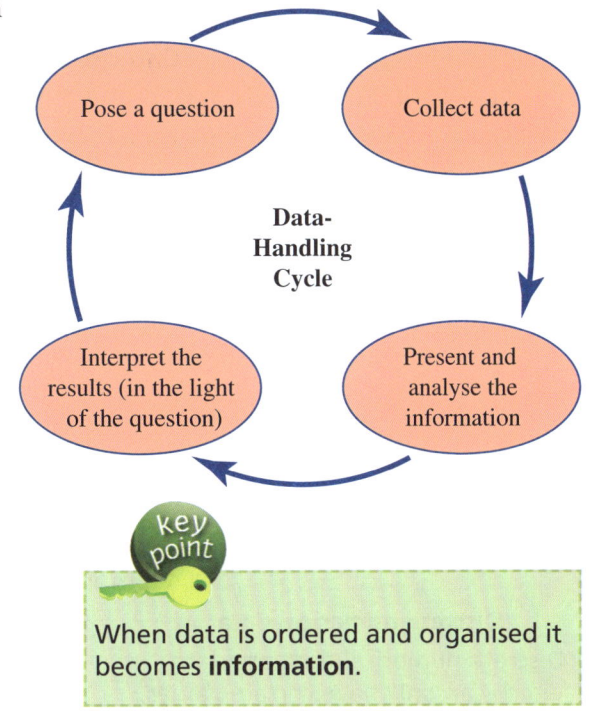

Data-Handling Cycle: Pose a question → Collect data → Present and analyse the information → Interpret the results (in the light of the question) → (back to Pose a question)

key point

When data is ordered and organised it becomes **information**.

There are many ways to collect data, e.g. surveys, observations, experiments, CensusAtSchool, reliable websites, etc.

It is vital when you are collecting data that your survey or source is **fair** and avoids **bias**.

Types of questions

Avoid using questions like: Do you agree the economy is in a very poor state?

This is a leading question and may lead to a biased response.

Avoid using sources that are not reliable, such as: The internet site that stated 75% of people believe the government of Fiji will destroy the moon on Friday. Many internet sites are not that crazy but are nontheless not reliable. Conclusions based on such sources will be unreliable.

Types of data

Data can be divided into two broad categories.

- Categorical data
- Numerical data.

These two categories are also subdivided in two as indicated.

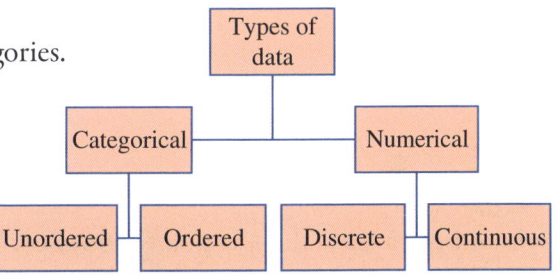

Types of data:
- Categorical: Unordered, Ordered
- Numerical: Discrete, Continuous

> **key point**
>
> ### Categorical data
>
> **Unordered categorical data**
>
> Unordered categorical data are data that can be *counted* but only described in words without any order or ranking.
>
> Examples are colours, names, type of car and gender (male or female).
>
> **Ordered categorical data**
>
> Ordered categorical data are data that can be counted but only described in words and have an order or ranking.
>
> Examples are examination grades, football divisions and income groups.

> **key point**
>
> ### Numerical data
>
> **Discrete numerical data**
>
> Discrete numerical data are data which can only have certain values, i.e. they can be *counted.*
>
> Examples are number of students in a school, number of goals scored in a match and shoe sizes (including half-sizes).
>
> **Continuous numerical data**
>
> Continuous data are data which can take any numerical value within a certain range.
>
> Examples are time, weight, height, temperature, pressure and area. (Accuracy depends on the measuring device used.)

> **key point**
>
> - Categorical data may also be referred to a qualitative data.
> - Numerical data may also be referred to as quantitative data.

> **exam focus**
>
> You need to learn the key points above off by heart.

exam Q

State whether the data in each of the situations A, B, C, D, E, F, and G is:
Numerical discrete, numerical continuous, unordered categorical data or ordered categorical data.

- A Breeds of dogs
- B The number of goals scored in a soccer match
- C Examination grades
- D The time it takes you to travel to school
- E The temperature of the air in a cinema
- F The months of the year in which students in the class were born
- G The number of people who voted for each act in a TV talent show

Solution

- A Unordered categorical data, e.g. collie, labrador, poodle
- B Numerical discrete, e.g. 0, 1, 2, …
- C Ordered categorical data, e.g. A, B, C, …
- D Numerical continuous
- E Numerical continuous
- F Ordered categorical data e.g. January, February, …
- G Numerical discrete, e.g. 4 807, 983,

Example

Sally wants to find out how often students in her school take an active part in sport. She goes to the school gym and gives a questionnaire to every student entering the gym. Does her method of carrying out her survey appear to be fair?

Solution

The survey method is not fair.

We expect the majority of students entering the gym would be working on their level of fitness. Hence, it seems reasonable to expect most of these students will take an active part in sport.

However, a significant number of students will seldom go to the school gym. Sally is automatically excluding these students from her survey. As a result, we conclude her survey is not fair. In statistics, we say her survey is biased.

Example

State whether or not the following surveys are biased. Justify your answer in each case.

(i) A fitness instructor interviewed 400 people in a shopping centre where he was planning to open a new gym. He discovered 12% of those people worked out in a gym at least twice a week.

(ii) While giving out prizes, an RTÉ radio presenter asked 60 listeners to name their favourite radio station. 92% of listeners replied 'RTÉ'.

Solution

(i) Not biased. 400 people in a shopping centre would appear to be a fair selection from the population who might use a gym.

(ii) Biased. The listeners were bribed with prizes. Also only listeners could take part in the survey.

Example

Complete the sentences from the list of words below:

Primary   Continuous   Discrete   Survey   Secondary

(i) We call data which can only have certain numerical values _____ data.
(ii) Data taken from a magazine is _____ data.
(iii) Data collected by the person who uses it is _____ data.
(iv) A _____ is a method of collecting data.
(v) We call data which can take any numerical value _____ data.

Solution

(i) Discrete
(ii) Secondary
(iii) Primary
(iv) Survey
(v) Continuous

exam focus: It could be worth learning this example off by heart.

Questions based on the results of a survey

The data in the table below is taken from CensusAtSchool.
The data gives information about how students recycle soft drink cans.

Student	Gender	Age	Year	Location	Cans bought	Cans recycled
A	Female	12	1st Year	Dublin	6	2
B	Male	13	1st Year	Tipperary	0	0
C	Male	14	2nd Year	Cork	1	1
D	Female	15	5th Year	Cavan	0	0
E	Male	15	4th Year	Cork	2	1
F	Male	13	1st Year	Offaly	5	2
G	Female	17	5th Year	Westmeath	1	1
H	Male	17	5th Year	Westmeath	2	0
I	Male	13	1st Year	Mayo	1	1
J	Male	13	2nd Year	Galway	2	2
K	Male	17	5th Year	Kilkenny	5	5
L	Female	12	1st Year	Dublin	3	1
M	Female	17	6th Year	Kerry	2	1
N	Female	17	5th Year	Dublin	3	1

(a) How many students are in the sample?
(b) Complete the table below to show the **junior** students (1st to 3rd year) in the sample and to show how many cans they each bought and recycled.

Student	A					L
Cans bought	6					3
Cans recycled	2					1

(c) How many soft drink cans were bought by the junior students?
(d) How many soft drink cans were recycled by the junior students?
(e) Based on the data, would you conclude that the junior students from this sample are better at recycling than the senior students (4th to 6th year)? Use calculations to justify your answer.

Solution

> **key point**
>
> It is worth remembering that this type of data taken from CensusAtSchool is secondary data.

(a) 14 students

(b)
Student	A	B	C	F	I	J	L
Cans bought	6	0	1	5	1	2	3
Cans recycled	2	0	1	2	1	2	1

(c) Junior students bought
$$6 + 0 + 1 + 5 + 1 + 2 + 3 = 18 \text{ Cans}$$

(d) Junior students recycled
$$2 + 0 + 1 + 2 + 1 + 2 + 1 = 9 \text{ Cans}$$

(e) Calculations could include:
Senior students bought
$$0 + 2 + 1 + 2 + 5 + 2 + 3 = 15 \text{ Cans}$$
Senior students recycled
$$0 + 1 + 1 + 0 + 5 + 1 + 1 = 9 \text{ Cans}$$

Junior students recycled	**Senior students recycled**
9 cans out of a total of 18 cans	9 cans out of a total of 15 cans
In percentages this is calculated by	In percentages this is calculated by
$\frac{9}{18} \times 100\% = 50\%$	$\frac{9}{15} \times 100\% = 60\%$

Hence, we conclude junior students are not better than senior students at recycling because from the given data we calculate junior students recycle 50% of their cans while senior students recycle 60% of their cans.

> **exam focus**
>
> Questions on the results of a given survey are frequently asked in our exam.

Tallying and frequency tables

One way data can be sorted easily is by using a **frequency table**.

A frequency table shows how frequently each piece of data occurs. It is good practice to include a tally row in your frequency table. Tallies are marks to help you keep track of counts. The marks are bunched together in groups of five.

When using tallies:

||| = 3 ||||| = 5 ||||| || = 7 ||||| ||||| || = 12, etc.

exam Q

Jack goes to an all-boys school. He decides to carry out a survey to determine the amount of time students spent on the internet per week. Jack chose 30 students at random from his own school register and asked each of these students the time, to the nearest hour, they spend on the internet. The raw data were recorded as follows.

8	15	0	9	22	11	8	17	17	23
1	7	10	15	16	20	22	19	4	2
12	15	18	18	18	4	9	20	21	0

Complete the following grouped frequency table.

Time spent on the internet	0–4	5–9	10–14	15–19	20–24
Tally					
Number of students					

(i) Is this primary or secondary data? Give a reason for your answer.
(ii) Is the data discrete or continuous? Explain your answer.
(iii) Jack's friend Jim says, 'A larger sample will always give a better estimate of what we are trying to measure for the population, regardless of how it is chosen.' Do you agree with Jim? Justify your opinion.
(iv) Can you identify two possible sources of bias in Jack's survey?
(v) Suggest two ways Jack could improve his sample to make it more representative nationally.

Solution

Time spent on the internet	0–4	5–9	10–14	15–19	20–24
Tally		|||| ||||	|||	|||| ||||	||||	
Number of students	6	5	3	10	6

(i) This is primary data, as Jack collected the data himself.

(ii) Times are rounded to the nearest hour. This is discrete data.

(iii) I disagree with Jim because a larger sample which is not representative of the underlying population will not give a better estimate of what we are trying to measure for the population. It must first be a random sample, where every item in the population has an equal probability of being selected in the sample.

(iv) Some examples of sources of bias:
- Only boys in the survey ⇒ gender bias
- Only one school surveyed ⇒ may not be representative of the population as a whole
- Survey may not have been answered honestly, e.g. students may understate internet time if they are embarrassed to admit the actual time spent on the internet.

(v) Some examples of how to improve his sample:
- Include an all-girls school
- Include a coeducation school
- Include schools from outside the area
- Ask better questions to eliminate over/underestimates from students
- Take account of how different age groups affect the result.

11 Statistics II: Central Tendency and Spread of Data

aims
- To know that mean, mode and median are all measures of average/central tendency
- To learn how to calculate mean, mode and median, both from lists of numbers and from frequency distribution tables
- To know how to calculate the range (spread) of data
- To learn how to handle questions linking statistics to other sections of our maths course or in-context questions

Averages

There are many types of averages. We will look at three: the mean, the mode and the median. They are also known as measures of central tendency.

Mean

The mean is the proper name for what most people call the average.

key point

The mean of a set of values is defined as the sum of all the values divided by the number of values. Remember, 'The sum of all the values' means add up.

That is:
$$\text{Mean} = \frac{\text{Sum of all the values}}{\text{Number of values}}$$

Mode

key point

The mode of a set of items is the item that occurs most often. If there are no repeated items, then the mode does not exist.

Median

> **key point**
>
> When the values are arranged in ascending or descending order of size, the median is the middle value. If the number of values is even, then the median is the average of the two middle values.

Note: Half the values lie below the median and half the values lie above the median. The median is also called the second quartile (Q_2).

Example

The ages of the seven dwarfs are as follows:

Name	Happy	Doc	Sleepy	Sneezy	Dopey	Grumpy	Bashful
Age	685	702	498	539	402	685	619

(i) Find the mean age.
(ii) Find the (mode) modal age.
(iii) Find the median age.

Solution

(i) Mean age = $\dfrac{\text{Sum of all their ages}}{\text{Number of dwarfs}}$

Mean = $\dfrac{685 + 702 + 498 + 539 + 402 + 685 + 619}{7}$

μ = Mean = $\dfrac{4\,130}{7}$ = 590

(ii) Mode = 685   The number that occurs most often
(Happy and Grumpy are twins!)

(iii) Median = middle value in ascending or descending order
= 702, 685, 685, **619**, 539, 498, 402
= 619

> **key point**
>
> The mean and the median need not necessarily be members of the original set of values, while the mode, if it exists, is always a member of the original set of values.

STATISTICS II: CENTRAL TENDENCY AND SPREAD OF DATA

A note on averages

Average	Advantages	Disadvantages
Mean	• Useful for further analysis • Uses all the data • Easy to calculate	• Distorted by extreme results • Mean is not always a given data value
Mode	• Easy to find • Not influenced by extreme values • Is the only measure suitable for qualitative nominal data	• Not very useful for further analysis • May not exist
Median	• Useful for further analysis • Unaffected by extremes • Easy to calculate if data are ordered	• Not always a given data value • Can be difficult to calculate

Example

Lily visits her aunt Carol who owns three dogs. The mean age of the three dogs is 6 years and the mode is 7 years. Calculate the age of each dog.

Solution

The mean age of the three dogs is 6 years
$\Rightarrow$ Total age of the three dogs = 6 × 3 = 18
The mode (most common age is 7) $\Rightarrow$ two of the dogs are age 7.
Ages of the three dogs are 7, 7 and x.
But $7 + 7 + x = 18$
$\Rightarrow \quad 14 + x = 18$
$\quad\quad\quad x = 18 - 14$
$\quad\quad\quad x = 4$
Answer 7, 7 and 4 are the ages of each dog.

key point
All three dogs are not aged 7 years because 3 × 7 = 21 ≠ 18.

---

exam Q

27 students in a class each recorded the amount they spent in the school shop during the Monday morning break. The total amount spent was €57·24.
  (i) Find the mean amount spent per student during the Monday morning break.
 (ii) One extra student joined the class and reported she spent €5·20 during the Monday morning break. Calculate the new mean including the extra student.

Solution

(i) Mean = $\dfrac{\text{Total amount spent}}{\text{Total number of students}} = \dfrac{57 \cdot 24}{27} = €2 \cdot 12$

(ii) Total for 28 students = €57·24 + €5·20 = €62·44

New mean = $\dfrac{62 \cdot 44}{28} = €2 \cdot 23$

Example

Write down a set of five positive integers with:

(i) Mean of 8
(ii) Mean of 8 and mode of 3
(iii) Mean of 8, mode of 3 and median of 9

Solution

To have a mean of 8 the five numbers must sum to 40.

(i) {5, 6, 7, 8, 14} or {1, 2, 3, 4, 30} or lots of other choices
(ii) {3, 3, 3, 14, 17} or {3, 3, 7, 10, 17} or {1, 2, 3, 3, 31} or lots of other choices
(iii) {3, 3, 9, 10, 15} fewer choices here

Example

A survey of a housing estate with 36 houses is undertaken by a city council.
The survey recorded the number of occupants per house as follows:

```
 0  7  5  5  6  6  2  4  5  6  7  4
 4  6  5  6  5  5  4  3  2  7  6  5
 0  6  5  6  6  6  4  6  6  5  4  2
```

(i) Complete the following frequency distribution table:

Number of occupants per house	0	1	2	3	4	5	6	7
Tally								
Number of houses								

(ii) Calculate (a) The total number of occupants in the housing estate
(b) The mean number of occupants per house.
(iii) What is the mode?

(iv) Suggest a reason why two houses recorded no occupants.
(v) What insights can you draw from yours answers (i) to (iv) as to the number of people, age distribution and social conditions in the estate?

Solution

(i) Complete the following frequency distribution table.

Number of occupants per house	0	1	2	3	4	5	6	7
Tally	||		|||	|	⊬⊬⊬ |	⊬⊬⊬ ||||	⊬⊬⊬ ⊬⊬⊬ ||	|||
Number of houses	2	0	3	1	6	9	12	3

(ii) (a) The total number of occupants in the estate is given by

$$(2)(0) + (0)(1) + (3)(2) + (1)(3) + (6)(4) + (9)(5) + (12)(6) + (3)(7)$$
$$= 0 + 0 + 6 + 3 + 24 + 45 + 72 + 21$$
$$= 171$$

(b) Mean = $\dfrac{\text{The sum of the values}}{\text{The number of values}}$

$$= \dfrac{(2)(0) + (0)(1) + (3)(2) + (1)(3) + (6)(4) + (9)(5) + (12)(6) + (3)(7)}{2 + 0 + 3 + 1 + 6 + 9 + 12 + 3}$$

$$= \dfrac{0 + 0 + 6 + 3 + 24 + 45 + 72 + 21}{36} = \dfrac{171}{36} = 4 \cdot 75$$

(iii) Mode = most common number = 6, which is recorded 12 times.

(iv) Two houses recorded no occupants because:
- The houses were unoccupied for some reason (fire, vandalism, holidays)
- No one answered when the surveyors called
- Houses were for sale.

(v)
- 171 people with a mean house occupancy of almost five (4·75) could indicate large young families (or extended families).
- Two unoccupied houses might indicate a somewhat derelict neighbourhood if boarded up.

exam focus: In (iv) and (v), choose **one** of these answers **or** construct your own.

Given the mean

Often we are given the mean and we need to find one of the values or frequencies. Basically, we are given an equation in disguise. We use this equation to find the missing value or frequency.

Example

The following frequency table shows the ages of the seven dwarfs and Snow White:

Name	Snow White	Happy	Doc	Sleepy	Sneezy	Dopey	Grumpy	Bashful
Age	x	685	702	498	539	402	685	619

If their mean age was 518·5, find the value of x.

Solution

Equation in disguise:

$$\text{Mean} = \frac{\text{The sum of the values}}{\text{The number of values}}$$

Mean = 518·5

By comparison

$$\frac{x + 685 + 702 + 498 + 539 + 402 + 685 + 619}{1 + 1 + 1 + 1 + 1 + 1 + 1 + 1} = 518\cdot5$$

$$\frac{x + 4\,130}{8} = 518\cdot5$$

$$x + 4\,130 = 8(518\cdot5)$$

$$x + 4\,130 = 4\,148$$

$$x = 4\,148 - 4\,130$$

$$x = 18$$

A measure of spread

The range

The range is the difference between the highest data value and the lowest data value.

key point
Range = Highest value − Lowest value

Example

Write down the age range for:

(i) The seven dwarfs

Name	Happy	Doc	Sleepy	Sneezy	Dopey	Grumpy	Bashful
Age	685	702	498	539	402	685	619

(ii) Snow White and the seven dwarfs.

Name	Snow White	Happy	Doc	Sleepy	Sneezy	Dopey	Grumpy	Bashful
Age	18	685	702	498	539	402	685	619

Solution

(i) Range = Highest age − Lowest age
$\phantom{\text{Range }}$ = 702 − 402
$\phantom{\text{Range }}$ = 300

(ii) Range = 702 − 18 = 684

Example

Find the mean and the range of the following sets of numbers:

(i) 4, 4, 4, 4, 4

(ii) $1, 3, 3\frac{1}{2}, 4 \cdot 2, 8 \cdot 3$

(iii) −196, −49, 25, 66, 174

(iv) Hence, interpret what your answers imply.

Solution

(i) Mean = $\dfrac{\text{The sum of the values}}{\text{The number of values}} = \dfrac{4+4+4+4+4}{1+1+1+1+1} = \dfrac{20}{5} = 4$

Range = Highest value − Lowest value
$\phantom{(i) \text{Range }}$ = 4 − 4
$\phantom{(i) \text{Range }}$ = 0

(ii) Mean = $\dfrac{\text{The sum of the values}}{\text{The number of values}} = \dfrac{1 + 3 + 3\frac{1}{2} + 4\cdot2 + 8\cdot3}{1+1+1+1+1} = \dfrac{20}{5} = 4$

Range = Highest value − Lowest value
$\phantom{(ii) \text{Range }}$ = 8·3 − 1
$\phantom{(ii) \text{Range }}$ = 7·3

(iii) Mean = $\dfrac{\text{The sum of the values}}{\text{The number of values}} = \dfrac{-196 - 49 + 25 + 66 + 174}{1+1+1+1+1} = \dfrac{20}{5} = 4$

> Range = Highest value − Lowest value
> = 174 − (−196)
> = 174 + 196 = 370
>
> **(iv)** Interpretation
> Each set has a mean = 4, and while set (i) has data that is not spread out at all, set (iii) has a much higher range than set (ii), confirming that set (iii) is much more spread out than set (ii).

exam Q

Maryam writes down the following 6 numbers, where $A \in \mathbb{N}$ and $A \geq 20$:   11, 11, 12, 18, 19, A

(a) Work out the median of Maryam's 6 numbers.

(b) Maryam works out the mean of the 6 numbers. She then increases the value of A by 60.
What will this increase do to the mean of the 6 numbers?

Solution

(a) Since $A \geq 20$, the numbers are in ascending order.
Median is the middle value, so it will be halfway between 12 and 18:

$$\text{Media} = \frac{12 + 18}{2} = \frac{30}{2} = 15$$

11, 11, 12, 18, 19, A
              ↑
           Median

(b) If the last number is increased by 60, then the sum of all of the numbers is increased by 60.
When we find the mean, by dividing the sum by 6, the mean will be 10 more than it was before.
So, the mean will have increased by 10.

STATISTICS II: CENTRAL TENDENCY AND SPREAD OF DATA

exam Q

A test consisted of seven questions. One mark was awarded per question for a correct solution and no marks for an incorrect solution. The following distribution table shows how a class of students scored in the test:

Mark	0	1	2	3	4	5	6	7
Number of students	1	7	6	5	2	6	3	0

(i) How many students are in the class?
(ii) Find the total number of marks awarded to all the students in the class.
(iii) Show that the mean mark of the class was 3.
(iv) Five new students joined the class. The new students took the same test and achieved marks of 0, 1, 1, 3 and 7.
In each of the following questions, determine the correct answer.
When the results of the five students were included with the original results.
  (a) The mean mark for the class was:
     X − unchanged   Y − decreased   Z − increased
  (b) The range for the class was:
     X − unchanged   Y − decreased   Z − increased
Justify your answer in each case.

Solution

(i) Total number of students in the class
$= 1 + 7 + 6 + 5 + 2 + 6 + 3 + 0$
$= 30$

(ii) The total marks awarded to all the students in the class is given by:
$(1)(0) + (7)(1) + (6)(2) + (5)(3) + (2)(4) + (6)(5) + (3)(6) + (0)(7)$
$= 0 + 7 + 12 + 15 + 8 + 30 + 18 + 0$
$= 90$ marks

(iii) The mean mark of the class $= \dfrac{\text{The sum of the marks awarded}}{\text{The number of students in the class}}$
$= \dfrac{90}{30}$
$= 3$

(iv) (a) Answer Y because the mean mark of the five new

students $= \dfrac{0 + 1 + 1 + 3 + 7}{5} = \dfrac{12}{5} = 2.4$

Since $2.4 < 3$, which was the original mean, we conclude that the addition of five new students decreased the mean.

> **key point**
>
> An alternative method is to find the mean for the new set of 35 students to find
>
> Mean $= \dfrac{\text{The sum of the marks}}{35} = \dfrac{90 + 0 + 1 + 1 + 3 + 7}{35}$
>
> Mean $= \dfrac{102}{35} = 2.91 < 3$
>
> Hence, the mean is decreased.

(b) Answer Z because one of the new students achieved a score of seven. This new student increased the range from $6 - 0 = 6$ to $7 - 0 = 7$, thus the results were more spread out, which means the range was increased.

exam Q

The size, mean and range of four sets of data, A, B, C and D, are given in this table:

	A	B	C	D
Size (n)	12	50	50	500
Mean (μ)	15	15	55	5
Range	40	50	22	15

Complete the sentences below by inserting the relevant letter in each space.

(i) On average, the data in set _____ are the biggest numbers and the data in set _____ are the smallest numbers.

(ii) The set that contains more numbers than any other is _____ and the set that contains fewer numbers than any other is _____.

(iii) The data in set _____ has the greatest difference between its highest and lowest values.

STATISTICS II: CENTRAL TENDENCY AND SPREAD OF DATA

Solution

(i) On average, the data in set __C__ are the biggest numbers and the data in set __D__ are the smallest numbers.

> **key point**
> C has a mean = 55 which is by far the biggest mean.

(ii) The set that contains more numbers than any other is __D__ and the set that contains fewer numbers than any other is __A__.

> **key point**
> D has 500 numbers; A has only 12 numbers.

(iii) The data in set __B__ (with a range of 50) has the greatest difference between its highest and lowest values.

---

exam Q

The average weekly earnings of people working for manufacturing industries in Ireland from 1998 to 2006 are given in the table below. The earnings are given to the nearest euro.

Year	1998	1999	2000	2001	2002	2003	2004	2005	2006
Male	429	453	478	512	538	565	589	610	624
Female	285	298	325	347	365	394	407	430	451
All persons	375	397	423	457	483	512	534	558	575

Source: Central Statistics Office

(a) Find the difference between the average male earnings and the average female earnings in the years 1998 and 2006.

1998 Male   =
      Female   =
      Difference =

2006 Male   =
      Female   =
      Difference =

(b) Write the average female earnings as a percentage of the average male earnings for the years 1998 and 2006. Give your answers correct to two significant figures.

Solution
(a)

1998	2006
Male = 429	Male = 624
Female = 285	Female = 451
Difference = 144	Difference = 173

(b)

1998:
$$\frac{\text{Female earnings}}{\text{Male earnings}} \times \frac{100}{1} = \frac{285 \times 100\%}{429}$$
$$= 66 \cdot 43\%$$
$$= 66\%$$

2006:
$$\frac{\text{Female earnings}}{\text{Male earnings}} = \frac{451}{624} \times \frac{100}{1}$$
$$= 72 \cdot 27\%$$
$$= 72\%$$

> **key point**
>
> Some examples of correct to two significant figures
>
> $17 \cdot 143 \to 17$ $0 \cdot 6333 \to 0 \cdot 63$
>
> $9 \cdot 58 \to 9 \cdot 6$ $49\ 274 \to 49\ 000$
>
> $273 \cdot 9 \to 270$ $4 \cdot 2225 \to 4 \cdot 2$

> **exam focus**
>
> In the above exam question:
> - Part (a) was awarded 10 marks with a minimum of 6 marks for any one correct step. This is lots of marks for very little work.
> - Part (b) was awarded 5 marks.
>
> You can observe how important it is to make an attempt at every part of the question. Candidates who do so are well rewarded.

12 Statistics III: Representing Data

aims
- To know how to construct and answer questions on:
  - Bar charts
  - Line plots
  - Histograms
  - Stem and leaf plots
  - Pie charts
- To be able to tackle exam questions incorporating statistical information and displays

Diagrams

Many people find numerical data easier to understand if it is presented in a diagram. On this course, there are five ways of representing data in a diagram.

1. Bar charts
2. Line plots
3. Histogram
4. Stem and leaf plots
5. Pie charts

key point

When drawing a statistical diagram, the following is important:
- Label both axes (where appropriate) and include a title.
- Use scales that are easy to read and give a clear overall impression.
- Use a ruler to draw the bars.

Bar charts

Bar charts are a simple and effective way of displaying categorical, ordinal and discrete data. The bars can be drawn vertically or horizontally. The height, or length, of each bar represents the frequency. Each bar must be the same width and leave the same space between the bars. The bar with the greatest height, or longest length, represents the mode.

key point

A bar chart **cannot** be used to represent continuous data. This is the reason a gap is left between the bars.

exam Q

Michelle and Jerry visit their local shop each day. The amount each of them spent in the shop during one week is given in the table below.

	Monday	Tuesday	Wednesday	Thursday	Friday	Saturday	Sunday
Michelle	€16	€12	€20	€5	€24	€8	€27
Jerry	€10	€18	€25	€19	€26		

(a) On which day of the week did Michelle spend the most?

(b) Find the difference between the most and the least amount that Michelle spent in a day.

(c) Draw a bar chart to illustrate the amount Michelle spent each day.

(d) Jerry spent a total of €140 during the week. He spent equal amounts on Saturday and Sunday. How much did he spend on Saturday?

(e) Who spent most money in the week, Michelle or Jerry? Justify your answer.

Solution

(a) Michelle spent most on Sunday (€27).

(b) €5 is the least amount that Michelle spent in a day.

∴ The difference between the most and the least amount spent by Michelle = 27 − 5 = €22

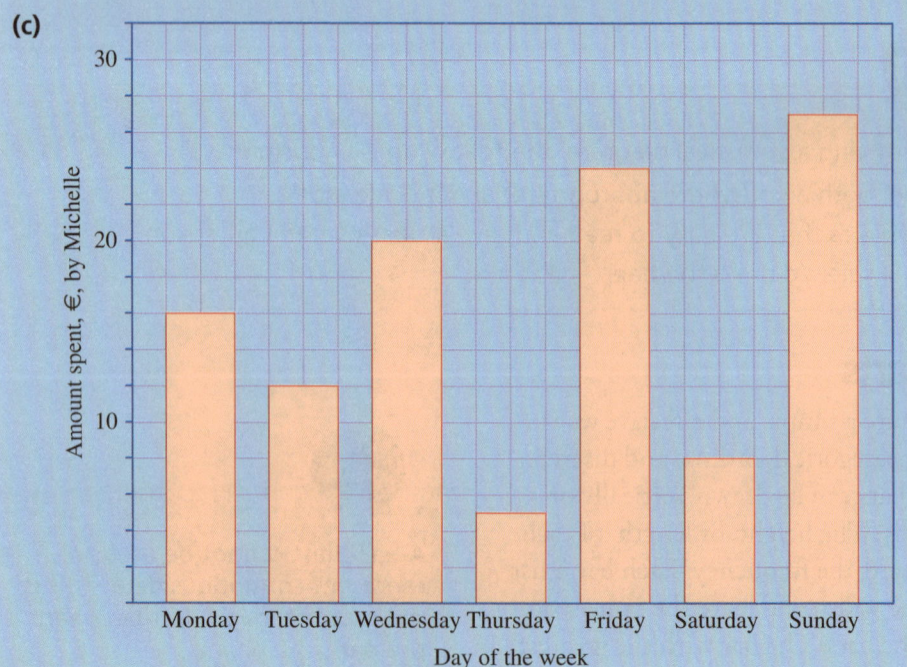

(c)

(d) Let x = amount spent by Jerry on Saturday
x = amount spent by Jerry on Sunday
Equation in disguise.
$$\text{Total spent by Jerry} = 140$$
$$10 + 18 + 25 + 19 + 26 + x + x = 140$$
$$98 + 2x = 140$$
$$2x = 140 - 98$$
$$2x = 42$$
$$x = €21$$

(e) Total spent by Michelle = $16 + 12 + 20 + 5 + 24 + 8 + 27$
$$= €112$$

Since part (d) told us Jerry spent € 140, we state that Jerry spent most. The above work is my justification.

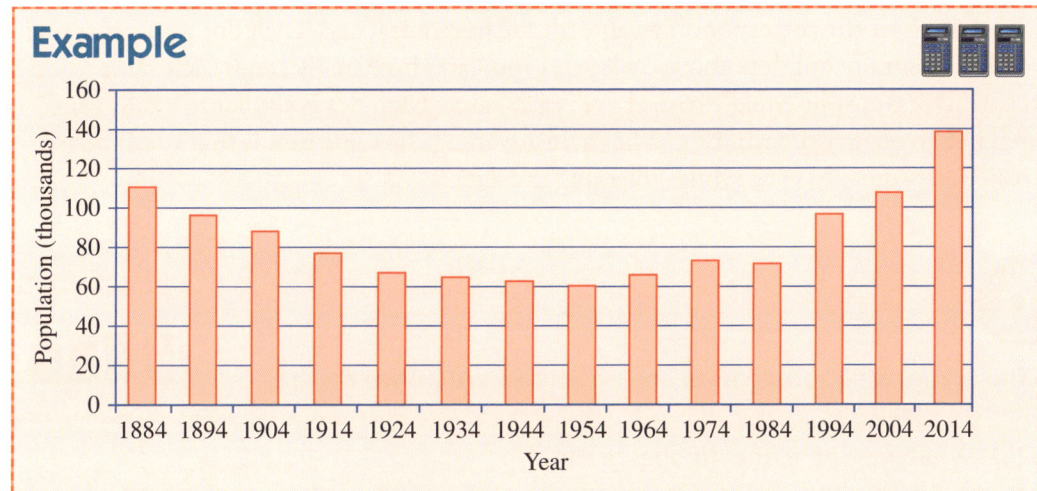

Example

The bar chart shows the population of an area from 1884 to 2014. Answer the following questions based on the data above.

(a) In which year was the population at its lowest?

(b) In which years was the population of the area higher than the population in 2004?

(c) Greg was asked to comment on the graph. In his answer, Greg said the population in the area had been rising steadily over the 130-year time frame. Greg's teacher said that this answer was incorrect. Using the information in the bar chart above, explain why Greg is incorrect.

(d) Write down your estimate for the population of the area in the year 2024. Comment on your answer.

Solution

(a) 1954 was the year of lowest population.

(b) 1884 and 2014 had higher populations than 2004.

(c) From 1884 to 1954 the population decreased $\Rightarrow$ Greg's answer is incorrect.

(d) The trend since 1984 was one of population increase. From 2004 to 2014, the increase was the highest ever recorded. If the pattern continues then 160 000 or more people in 2024 is a reasonable estimate.

Line plots

Line plots are used for categorical, ordinal and discrete data. A line plot is similar to a bar chart, with the bars replaced with dots. A line plot is often called a **dot plot**. It is used for small sets of data, usually fewer than 50 values. It consists of a horizontal axis on which the values (or categories) are evenly marked, from the smallest value to the largest value, including any value in between that does not occur. Each value is indicated with a dot over the corresponding value on the horizontal axis. Each dot represents **one** value. The number of dots above each value indicates how many times each value occurs. Dots must be equally spaced over each value. Each dot is similar to a tally mark used in a frequency distribution. The main advantage of a line plot is that it can be created very quickly, even while collecting the data.

exam Q

The grades for 25 students in an English test are shown on the line plot below:

(a) What was the modal (mode) grade?

(b) Calculate the percentage of students who got a grade C or higher.

(c) A student is selected at random from the class. Find the probability that the student achieved a grade E.

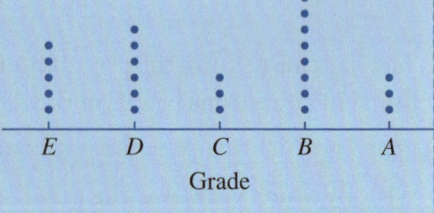

(d) Louise scored a grade C in the test. She claimed it was a very difficult English test. Comment on Louise's claim.

(e) State whether the data in the line plot are:
  (i) Numerical discrete
  (ii) Numerical continuous
  (iii) Unordered categorical
  (iv) Ordered categorical.

STATISTICS III: REPRESENTING DATA

Solution

(a) Modal class = Most common grade achieved = B

(b) Number of students with grade C or higher = 3 + 8 + 3 = 14

Percentage of students with grade C or higher

$= \dfrac{\text{Number of student with grade C or higher}}{\text{Total number of students who did the test}} \times \dfrac{100}{1} \%$

$= \dfrac{14}{25} \times \dfrac{100}{1} = \dfrac{1\,400}{25} = 56\%$

(c) 5 students scored an E grade

∴ Probability of a student selected at random scored an E grade

$= P$ (a student with an E grade)

$= \dfrac{5}{25}$

$= \dfrac{1}{5}$

(d) • Since 11 students scored a grade D or lower then Louise is correct.

• Grades very spread out so it is difficult to say if Louise is correct.

• Since 11 students scored a grade B or higher then Louise is not correct.

> **key point**
> You choose one of these answers.

(e) (iv) is correct, because exam grades are categories and A, B, C, D, E are ordered.

---

exam Q

Karen went on holidays for two weeks in August 2011. Below is a record of the daily temperature for the two weeks in August 2011.

Day	Temperature	Day	Temperature
Monday 15th	17°	Monday 22nd	19°
Tuesday 16th	18°	Tuesday 23rd	17°
Wednesday 17th	16°	Wednesday 24th	15°
Thursday 18th	17°	Thursday 25th	15°
Friday 19th	16°	Friday 26th	15°
Saturday 20th	18°	Saturday 27th	14°
Sunday 21st	17°	Sunday 28th	17°

(a) What was the temperature on Thursday 18th of August?
(b) Use a line plot to show the number of times each temperature was recorded.

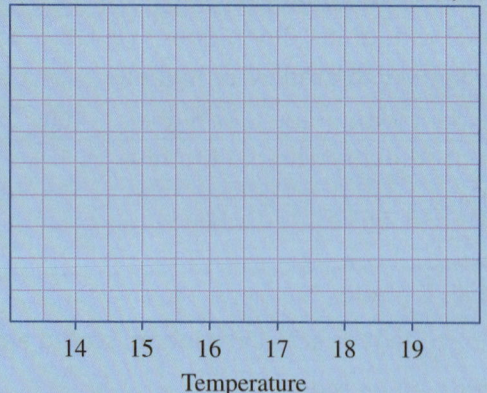

```
                14  15  16  17  18  19
                       Temperature
```

(c) What is the range of the data?
(d) What is the mode of the data?
(e) Karen says, 'On average it was warmer during the first week than the second week of my holiday.' Do you agree with Karen? Explain your answer.

Solution

(a) Temperature on Thursday 18th was 17°.

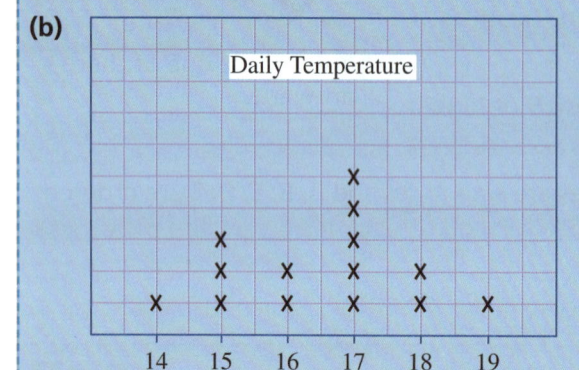

(b)

Daily Temperature

```
                    X
                    X
            X       X
            X   X   X
        X   X   X   X   X
    X   X   X   X   X   X
    14  15  16  17  18  19
           Temperature
```

exam focus
A • or an x or other suitable symbols may be used on a line plot.

(c) Range = Highest value – Lowest value
= 19 – 14
= 5°

(d) The mode = The most common temperature = 17°

(e) Total for the first week
= 17 + 18 + 16 + 17
+ 16 + 18 + 17
= 119°

Mean for the first week
= $\frac{119}{7}$ = 17°

Total for the second week
= 19 + 17 + 15 + 15
+ 15 + 14 + 17
= 112°

Mean for the second week
= $\frac{112}{7}$ = 16°

Since the mean temperature for the first week (17°) is greater than the mean temperature for the second week (16°), we agree with Karen.

STATISTICS III: REPRESENTING DATA

exam focus

The question on the previous page was awarded a total of 20 marks as follows:
- Part (a) 5 marks, great marks for a very simple question.
- Part (b) 5 marks, straightforward but you must be careful – any error and you lose 2 marks.
- Part (c) and (d) together 5 marks, a tough, fair question. You must learn off the meaning of many words in statistics, in this case range and mode.
- Part (e) 5 marks, be sure to give an answer **and** an explanation.

Histogram

A histogram is often used to display information contained in a frequency distribution. The essential characteristic of a histogram is that the area of each rectangle represents the frequency, and the sum of the areas of the rectangles is equal to the sum of the frequencies.

Example

The histogram below shows the time spent by a group of women in a boutique.

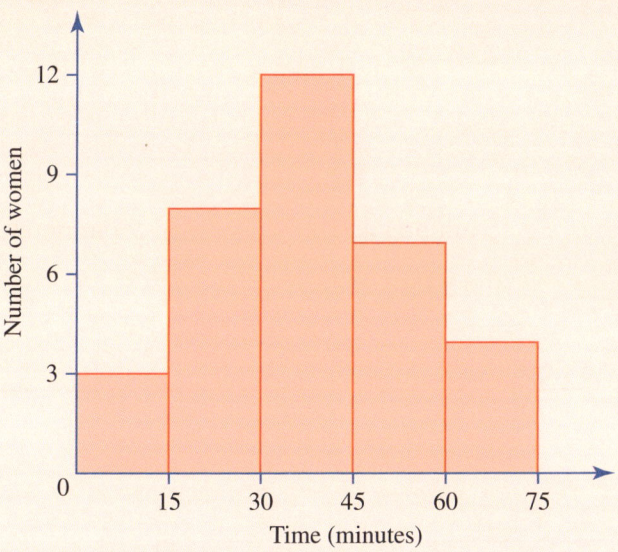

(i) Complete the following table.

Time (minutes)	0–15	15–30	30–45	45–60	60–75
Number of women					

(**Note:** 0–15 means 0 or more but less than 15, etc.)

(ii) How many women are in the group?

(iii) What is the least possible number of women who spent more than 50 minutes in the boutique?

(iv) The sentences below describe the time spent in the boutique.
Delete the incorrect word in each pair of brackets.
This is a set of [Qualitative/Quantitative] data.
The data are [Discrete/Continuous].

Solution

(i)

Time (minutes)	0–15	15–30	30–45	45–60	60–75
Number of women	3	8	12	7	4

(ii) 3 + 8 + 12 + 7 + 4 = 34 women in the group

(iii) The seven women in the class interval 45–60 minutes could all have spent less than 50 minutes in the boutique.
∴ Least possible number of women who spent more than 50 minutes in the boutique is four, i.e. all those in the class interval 60–75 minutes.

(iv) This is a set of [~~Qualitative~~/Quantitative] data.
The data are [~~Discrete~~/Continuous].

key point

Time is a quantity.

key point

Time is continuous, e.g. 15 minutes and 43 seconds; 58·99 minutes; $20\frac{1}{9}$ minutes, etc.

exam focus

It is useful to remember that:
- Bar charts have equal gaps between the bars.
- Histograms have no gaps between the bars.
- Bar charts can only represent discrete data.
- Histograms can represent discrete or continuous data.

Stem and leaf diagrams

A stem and leaf diagram is a useful way of presenting data.

It is similar to a horizontal histogram, with the numbers themselves forming the rectangles. Since stem and leaf plots show the original data, they can be more useful than histograms in calculations.

Stem and leaf diagrams are suitable only for small amounts of data.

The ages of a group of 12 people are given as:

$$6, 8, 12, 15, 17, 23, 23, 28, 30, 32, 37, 44$$

This can be represented on an ordered stem and leaf plot as shown below:

0	6 8
1	2 5 7
2	3 3 ⑧
3	0 2 7
4	4

This represents 28: stem = 2, leaf = 8.

Key: 1|7 = 17

You must always add a key to show how the stem and leaf combine.

exam focus

Many candidates do not include the key in stem and leaf plots. It is a mistake you can easily avoid.

exam Q

The ordered stem and leaf plot shows the age, in years, of each patient who visited the accident department in a hospital over a two-hour period.

0	6	8	8	9		
1	0	4	5	6	8	
2	4	4	7			
3	1	2	6	6	6	9
4	3	6				
5	0	0	5	8		
6	2	2	7	9		
7	1	4	5	5	6	8
8	2	3	7			

Key: 4|3 = 43

(a) How many patients visited the accident department during the two-hour period?

(b) What was the age of the oldest patient who visited the accident department?

(c) Calculate the age range of the patients who visited the accident department.

(d) What was the modal age of the patients who visited the accident department.

(e) Find the median age of the patients who visited the accident department.

key point

Each leaf in the plot represents a patient. Simply count them.

Solution

(a) 37 patients in total

(b) Age of oldest patient is 87 years.

(c) Age range = Highest age − Lowest age
$$= 87 - 6 = 81$$

(d) Modal age = most common age
= 36   (in blue colour below)

(e)

0	6	8	8	9		
1	0	4	5	6	8	
2	4	4	7			
3	1	2	6	6	6	9
4	3	6				
5	0	0	5	8		
6	2	2	7	9		
7	1	4	5	5	6	8
8	2	3	7			

The median is associated with the middle. With a total of 37 patients, the median (middle) patient is the 19th patient in the given ordered stem and leaf plot.

∴ 43 is the median age (in red colour)

exam Q

A group of students was asked how many text messages each had sent the previous day. The results were:

14   32   6   17   19   15   3   35   42   25
9   28   34   18   40   11   16   28   31   7

STATISTICS III: REPRESENTING DATA

(a) How many students were in the group?
(b) Represent the data on a stem and leaf diagram.

0									
1									
2									
3									
4					Key:				

(c) Find the mode of the data.
(d) Find the mean of the data.
(e) What percentage of students sent more than 30 texts?

Solution

(a) 20 students.
(b) First we construct an unordered stem-and-leaf plot.

0	6	3	9	7					
1	4	7	9	5	8	1	6		
2	5	8	8						
3	2	5	4	1					
4	2	0				Key: 2|5 = 25 texts			

Then we construct an ordered stem and leaf plot

0	3	6	7	9					
1	1	4	5	6	7	8	9		
2	5	8	8						
3	1	2	4	5					
4	0	2				Key: 2|5 = 25 texts			

> **exam focus**
>
> It there is not enough space provided in the exam booklet for both stem and leaf plots, you could draw the first (unordered) stem and leaf plot on a loose page (provided by the supervisor in the exam) and then fill the second (ordered) stem and leaf plot in the exam booklet.

(c) Mode = most common number of texts sent
        = 28   (see blue colour in ordered stem and leaf plot)

(d) Mean = $\dfrac{\text{Total number of texts}}{\text{Total number of students}}$

$= \dfrac{14 + 32 + 6 + 17 + 19 + 15 + \cdots + 16 + 28 + 31 + 7}{20}$

$= \dfrac{430}{20}$

$= 21\cdot 5$

exam focus

Good concentration is required here to add up the twenty given numbers.

(e) From the ordered stem and leaf plot, we observe six students sent more than 30 texts.

$\dfrac{\text{Number of students who sent more than 30 texts}}{\text{Total number of students}} \times \dfrac{100}{1}\%$

$= \dfrac{6}{20} \times 100 = 30\% =$ Answer

exam Q

Jim's third year maths class did a test on algebra. The result in percentages of each student is shown on the unordered stem and leaf plot below:

4	6
5	7
6	8 9 8
7	8 5 5 2 2 3 4 2 7 6 4 2 5 2 2 2 5 9
8	1 0 2 0 4 2 3

Key: 7|8 = 78%

(a) Construct an ordered stem-and-leaf plot.
(b) How many students are in the class?
(c) Write down the median percentage mark for the class.
(d) Calculate the range of marks in percentages for the class.
(e) Do you think the range is a true reflection of the spread of this data? Comment on your answer.
(f) Jim achieved a score of 68% in the test. How does this compare to the rest of the class?

(g) Complete the following frequency distribution:

Percentage mark	45–54	55–64	65–74	75–84
Tally				
Frequency				

Solution

(a) Ordered stem and leaf plot:

```
4 | 6
5 | 7
6 | 8 8 9
7 | 2 2 2 2 2 2 3 4 4 5 5 5 5 6 7 8 9
8 | 0 0 1 2 2 3 4
```

(b) 30 students in the class

(c) Median $= \dfrac{74 + 75}{2} = \dfrac{149}{2} = 74.5$

key point
Median is associated with the middle result, see ↓ above.

(d) Range = Highest value − Lowest value
       = 84 − 46
       = 38

(e) The range is not a true reflection of the spread in this case. The majority of the students scored between 72 and 80, which gives a range of 8.

(f) At 68%, Jim is in the bottom section of the class in this test. 26 students scored higher then Jim. We could write the much-used phrase 'Jim could do better'.

(g)

Percentage Mark	45–54	55–64	65–74	75–84
Tally	|	|	𝍱 𝍱 |||	𝍱 𝍱 𝍱
Frequency	1	1	13	15

Pie charts

A pie chart is a circle divided into sectors in proportion to the frequency of the information. It displays the proportions as angles, measured from the centre of the circle.

To draw a pie chart:

1. Add up all the frequencies.
2. Divide this total into 360°.
3. Multiply the answer in step 2 by each individual frequency.
   (This gives the size of the angle for each sector.)
4. Draw the pie chart, label each sector, and give it a title.
   (It is a good idea to write the size of each angle on the pie chart.)

key point

It is good practice to check that all your angles add up to 360° before drawing the pie chart.

Example

In a survey, 72 transition year students were asked to choose from an option of 4 activities. The results are in the table below:

Watch TV	Play computer games	Go on Facebook	Take a walk
15	24	21	12

(i) Illustrate the data with a pie chart.
(ii) The survey activities can be classified as **one** of the following. Tick the correct answer and give a reason.

Ordered categorical ☐
Unordered categorical ☐
Discrete numerical ☐
Continuous numerical ☐

Solution

(i) 72 transition year students are to be represented by 360°

Thus 72 students = 360°

$\therefore$ 1 student = $\dfrac{360}{72}$ (divide both sides by 72)

1 student = 5°

In other words, one student will take up 5° on the pie chart. We make up a table to work out the angles for each sector.

key point

Keep degrees on the right because we want our answers in degrees.

Sector	Number of students	Angle
Watch TV	15	15 × 5 = 75°
Play computer games	24	24 × 5 = 120°
Go on Facebook	21	21 × 5 = 105°
Take a walk	12	12 × 5 = 60°
Total	72	360°

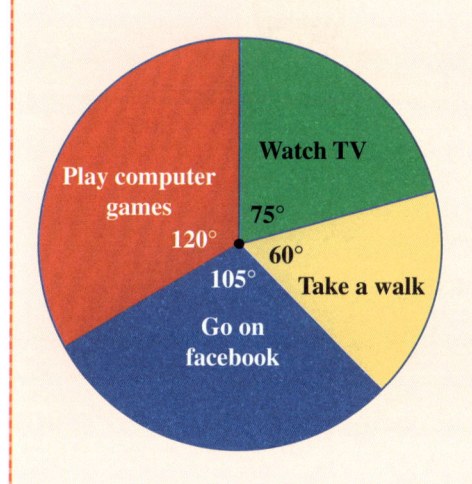

(ii) The activities are categories. The categories can appear in any order.

Unordered categorical ✓

exam Q

The pie chart represents the ages of three children Siobhán, Seán and Sue.

At eleven years old Siobhán is the eldest child.

Calculate:

(i) Sue's age
(ii) Seán's age.

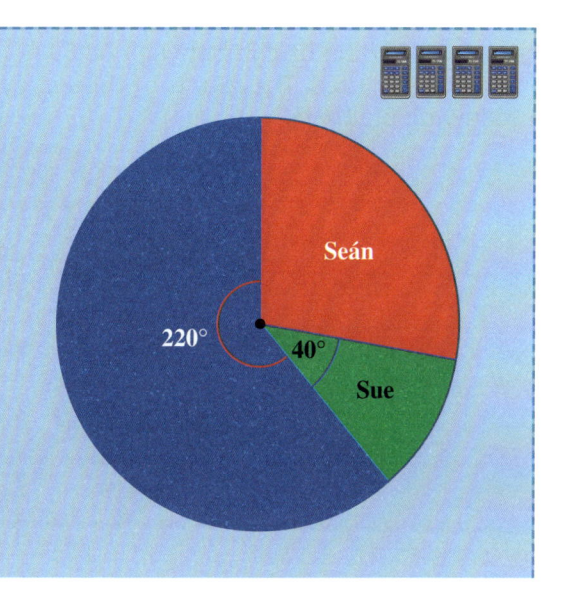

Solution

(i) 220° represents 11 years

1° represents $\dfrac{11}{220}$ years

40° represents $\left(\dfrac{11}{220} \times 40\right)$ years = Sue's age

40° represents $\dfrac{440}{220}$ years = Sue's age

40° represents 2 years = Sue's age

> **key point**
> 220° represents Siobhán's age.

(ii) 220° + 40° + Seán's angle = 360°

260° + Seán's angle = 360°

Seán's angle = 360° − 260°

Seán's angle = 100°

From part (i), 1° represents $\dfrac{11}{220}$ years

100° represents $\left(\dfrac{11}{220} \times 100\right)$ years = Seán's age

100° represents $\dfrac{1\,100}{220}$ years = Seán's age

100° represents 5 years = Seán's age

> **key point**
> In the pie chart the sum of the angles = 360°

---

exam Q

In a survey, the number of people travelling in each car which crossed a certain bridge between 08:00 hours and 08:15 hours on a particular day was recorded. The results of the survey of sixty cars are contained in the following pie chart.

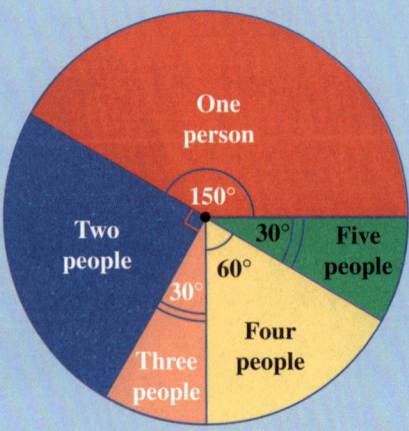

STATISTICS III: REPRESENTING DATA

(i) Complete the following table:

Number of people per car	1	2	3	4	5
Number of cars					

(ii) Calculate the total number of people in the sixty cars surveyed.
(iii) Calculate the mean number of cars which crossed the bridge per minute while the survey was taking place.
(iv) Calculate the mean number of people per car.

Solution

(i) 360° represents 60 cars

1° represents $\frac{60}{360}$ cars

1° represents $\frac{1}{6}$ of a car

key point: Keep cars on the right because we want our answer in cars.

In other words, 1° on the pie chart represents $\frac{1}{6}$ of a car.

We make up a table to work out the number of cars in each sector:

Sector	Angle	Number of cars
Car with 1 person	150°	$150 \times \frac{1}{6} = 25$
Car with 2 people	90°	$90 \times \frac{1}{6} = 15$
Car with 3 people	30°	$30 \times \frac{1}{6} = 5$
Car with 4 people	60°	$60 \times \frac{1}{6} = 10$
Car with 5 people	30°	$30 \times \frac{1}{6} = 5$

Finally we complete the table:

Number of people per car	1	2	3	4	5
Number of cars	25	15	5	10	5

(ii) To find the total number of people in the cars:
25 × 1 = 25
15 × 2 = 30
5 × 3 = 15
10 × 4 = 40
5 × 5 = 25
Total = 135 people in the sixty cars

> **key point**
> The time of the survey was (08:00 to 08:15). given in the question.

(iii) $\dfrac{\text{Mean number of cars which}}{\text{crossed the bridge per minute}} = \dfrac{\text{Total number of cars}}{\text{Number of minutes}} = \dfrac{60}{15} = 4$

(iv) $\dfrac{\text{Mean number of}}{\text{people per car}} = \dfrac{\text{Total number of people}}{\text{Total number of cars}} = \dfrac{135}{60} = 2\cdot 25$

exam Q

The table below shows the level and type of internet connection in households in Ireland in 2005 and 2011.

Year	Internet connection		
	Broadband	Other	None
2005	20%	30%	50%
2011	65%	10%	25%

(i) What was the total percentage of households in Ireland that had an internet connection
   (a) In 2005?   (b) In 2011?

> **exam focus**
> In this question, the solution is done part by part.

Solution

(i) (a) In 2005, the total percentage of households with internet connections
= 20% + 30% = 50%

(b) In 2011, the total percentage of households with internet connections
= 65% + 10% = 75%

(ii) Construct a pie chart for each of the years 2005 and 2011:

Solution

100% represents 360°

1% represents $\dfrac{360°}{100} = 3.6°$

> **key point**
> Keep degrees on the right because we want our answers in degrees.

Year 2005

Sector	Percentage	Angle
Broadband	20%	3·6 × 20 = 72°
Other	30%	3·6 × 30 = 108°
None	50%	3·6 × 50 = 180°

2005

Other 108°, Broadband 72°, None 180°

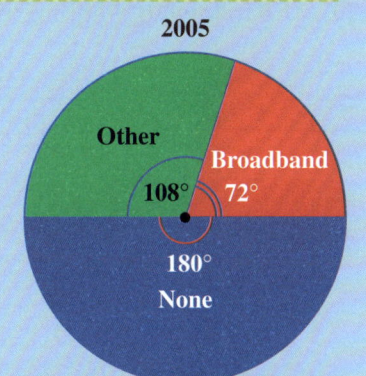

Year 2011

Sector	Percentage	Angle
Broadband	65%	3·6 × 65 = 234°
Other	10%	3·6 × 10 = 36°
None	25%	3·6 × 25 = 90°

2011

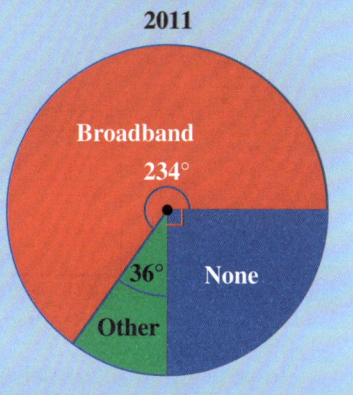

Broadband 234°, None, Other 36°

(iii) Hence or otherwise, describe one change in the type of internet connection that has taken place in Ireland between 2005 and 2011.

Solution

The percentage of households with no internet connection decreased from 50% to 25%.

Or the percentage of households with internet connection increased from 50% to 75%.

(iv) 1 467 440 households completed the survey on Internet connection type in 2011. How many of those households were recorded as having broad band connection to the internet?

Solution

$$100\% = 1\ 467\ 440$$

$$1\% = \frac{1\ 467\ 440}{100}$$

With broadband $= 65\% = \frac{1\ 467\ 440}{100} \times 65 = 953\ 836$ households

(v) The following diagram shows the information using a bar chart:

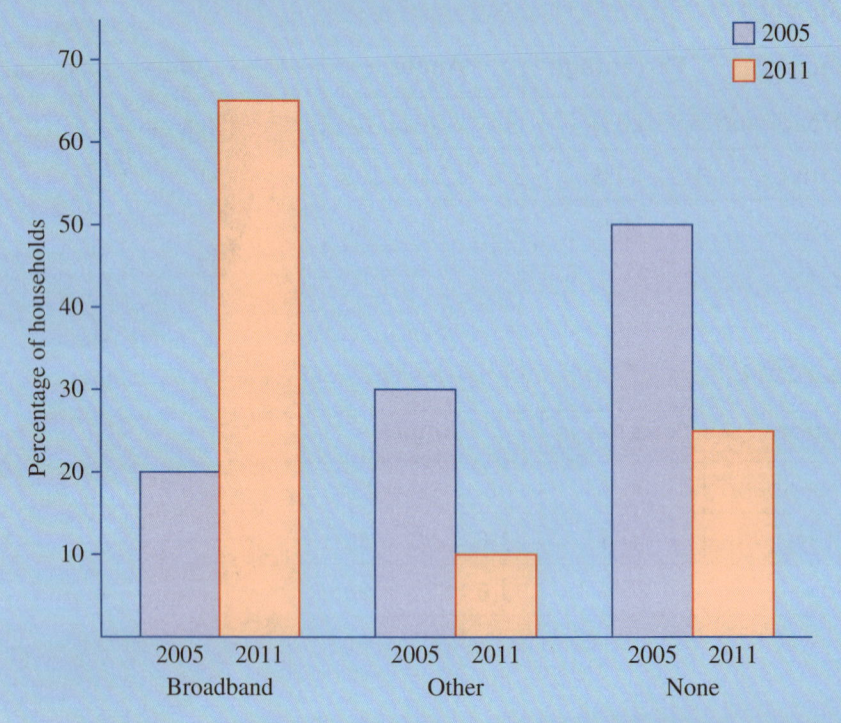

In your opinion, which diagram **(a)** the pie charts or **(b)** the bar charts are more suitable to illustrate the changes that have taken place. Give a reason for your choice.

Solution

In my opinion (b) the bar charts are more suitable because:

- they are simpler to construct
- they give a more direct comparison.

You might decide (a) the pie charts are more suitable because:

- they clearly show the ratios of the connection types for each year
- or you may have some other reason.

exam focus: Remember in part (v) give your opinion and back it up with a fact from the question.

Example

(i) From the methods of representing data that you have studied state which method you would use to represent the following three data sets:

(a) The number of people in each car as it crossed a toll bridge was recorded as follows:

1	2	1	2	4	1	9	1	3	2	1	2	4	3
9	3	7	2	3	5	4	1	2	5	1	1	3	1
1	1	3	4	2	5	2	3	2	8	2	1	3	1

(b) The grades awarded in a class of students was as follows:

B	A	C	D	C	C	C	B	D	C
A	D	C	B	B	C	B	C	B	D
C	B	B	C	A	C	B	C	B	C

(c) The number of students studying in a certain university was as follows:

Year	First year	Second year	Third year	Fourth year
Number of students	690	540	480	470

(ii) Hence, use your choice to represent each data set.

(iii) For each of the three data sets, name a method of representing data that would not be suitable and justify your choice.

Solution

(i) (a) A line (dot) plot
    (b) A pie chart
    (c) A bar chart

(ii) (a)

key point

A line plot is an excellent way to represent this data because it gives a very clear picture and it could be carried out as the cars passed the toll bridge.

Number of cars passing toll bridge

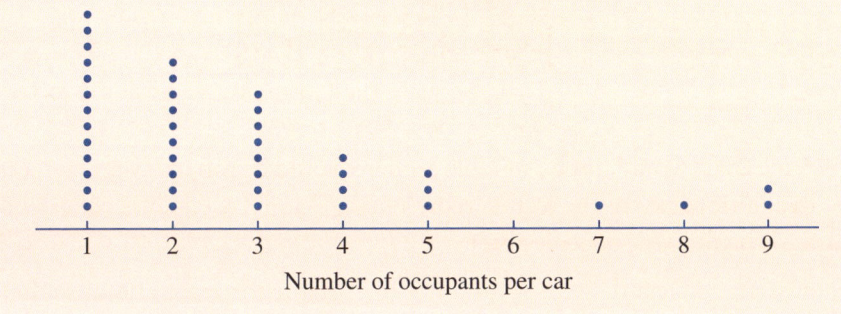

Number of occupants per car

(b)

> **key point**
>
> 3 grade A; 10 grade B; 13 grade C; 4 grade D 30 students with only four different grades are very clearly represented on a pie chart.

30 students = 360°

$$1 \text{ student} = \frac{360}{30} = 12°$$

3 grade A students = 12 × 3 = 36°
10 grade B students = 12 × 10 = 120°
13 grade C students = 12 × 13 = 156°
4 grade D students = 12 × 4 = 48°

exam focus

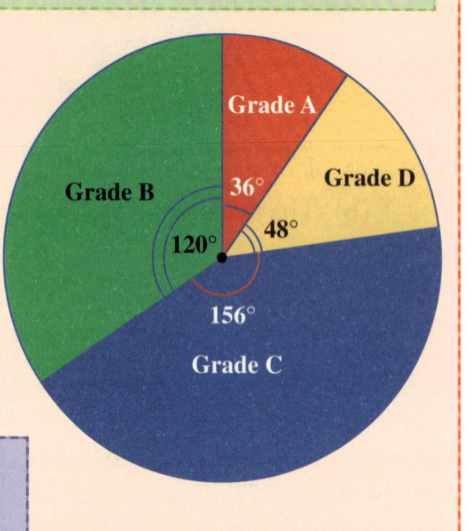

Check that 36° + 120° + 156° + 48° = 360°

(c) A bar chart (or histogram) is very suitable here.

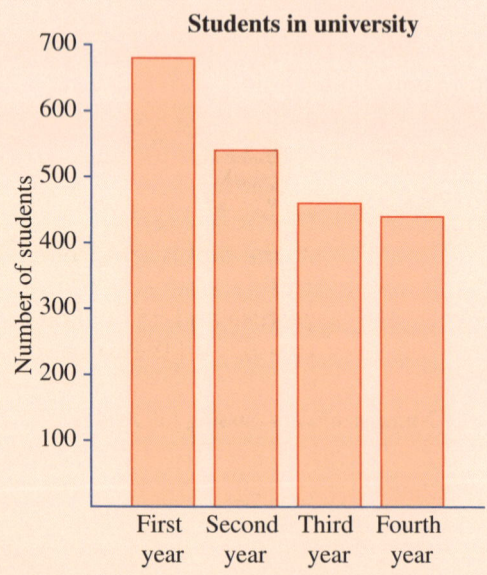

Students in university

(iii) (a) A pie chart would not be suitable as there would be too many (eight) sectors. In addition, two of the sectors representing 7 and 8 occupants per car would be difficult to see on a pie chart.

(b) A stem and leaf diagram would not be suitable for grades because the letters A, B, C and D have no stems.

(c) In this case, a line plot is not suitable because it is not practical to represent 690 first year students with 690 dots.

> **exam focus**
>
> Remember the answers given to the above question are not the only acceptable answers. In the exam when asked for your ideas, you must express them.

Misuses of statistics
Misleading graphs and diagrams

Many advertisements frequently use graphs and diagrams to present information. In most cases, the graphs and diagrams are well presented and give an honest and fair representation of the facts. However, some are deliberately drawn to mislead. The most common method to present correct information in misleading graphs and diagrams is to use a false origin, insert no scale or a non-uniform scale on the vertical axis or drawing graphs with unequal widths and dimensions. Other misleading methods to watch out for are using a biased sample or a sample that is too small; deliberate omissions, errors and exaggerations; misleading comparisons; and using unreliable sources.

Consumers should try to spot misleading graphs and diagrams, errors, omissions and exaggerations when presented with information (statistics).

Example

The pie chart displays data on the percentages of Leaving Certificate students taking mathematics at different levels in an exam.

Find two aspects of the pie chart which are incorrect.

Solution

- $28·7\% + 13·3\% + 67\% = 109\%$. This should total 100%.
- 67% at Ordinary Level should occupy more than half the pie.

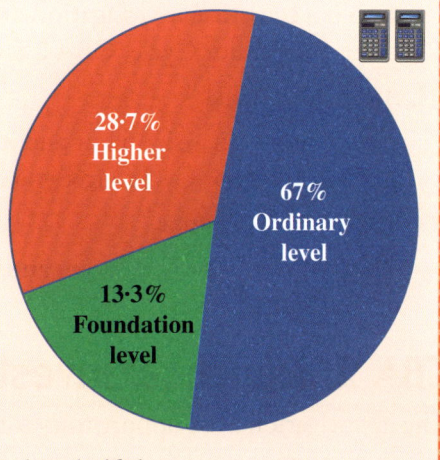

13 Classroom-Based Assessments (CBAs)

aims
- ☐ To become familiar with the four elements of assessment for Junior Cycle Mathematics
- ☐ To be familiar with the details of the Classroom-Based Assessment 2
- ☐ To be able to understand and apply the Statistical-Enquiry Cycle
- ☐ To be familiar with the criteria of quality for assessment
- ☐ To understand the four descriptors for the CBA and the criteria associated with each descriptor
- ☐ To understand the steps involved in starting your investigation and examining a menu of suggestions for investigation
- ☐ To be familiar with the procedure involved with how to carry out a statistical investigation
- ☐ To be able to use the checklist provided to ensure that you haven't missed any key elements in your investigation

Introduction

As mentioned in the Introduction chapter of this book, your assessment in Junior Cycle Mathematics consists of four elements.

1. **Classroom-Based Assessment 1 (CBA 1)**

   This is a mathematical investigation and it is carried out during your second year of the three-year Junior Cycle. **CBA 1 is covered in *Less Stress More Success Maths Book 1*.**

2. **Classroom-Based Assessment 2 (CBA 2)**

   This is a statistical investigation and it is carried out during your third year of the three-year Junior Cycle. **CBA 2 is covered in this chapter.**

3. **Assessment Task**

   This is a written assignment and it is carried out during your third year of the three-year Junior Cycle, after you have completed CBA 2.

4. **Written exam paper**

   This is a 2-hour written exam and it take place at the end of third year, with the rest of your written exams.

CBA 2: Statistical Investigation

The investigation is an opportunity for you to show that you can apply statistics to an area that interests you. Your teacher will give you a timetable and deadline for submitting your investigation.

CLASSROOM-BASED ASSESSMENTS (CBAs)

The details of the investigation are as follows:

Format: A report may be presented in a wide range of formats.
Preparation: A student will, over a three-week period in third year, follow the Statistical-Enquiry Cycle to investigate a mathematical problem.

The Statistical-Enquiry Cycle is as follows:
1. Formulate a question
2. Plan and collect unbiased, representative data
3. Organise and manage the data
4. Explore and analyse the data, using appropriate displays and numerical summaries
5. Answer the original question, giving reasons based on the analysis section

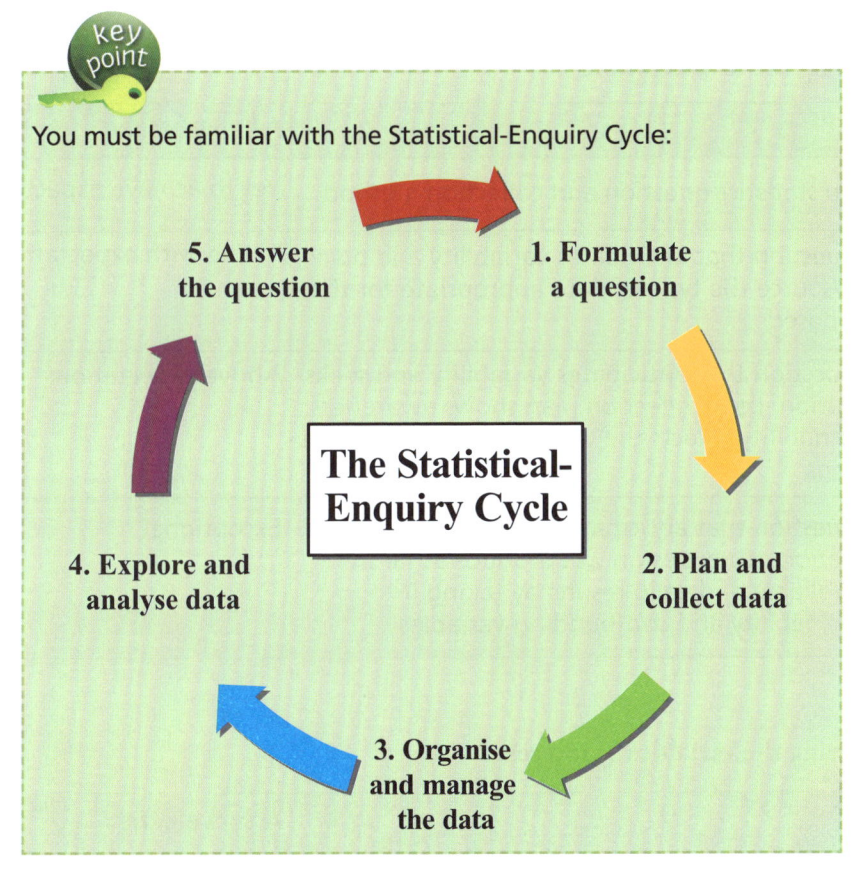

key point

You must be familiar with the Statistical-Enquiry Cycle:

The Statistical-Enquiry Cycle
1. Formulate a question
2. Plan and collect data
3. Organise and manage the data
4. Explore and analyse data
5. Answer the question

CBA 2: Assessment criteria and four descriptors

The investigation is assessed by the class teacher. A student will be awarded one of the following categories of achievement:
- Yet to meet expectations
- In line with expectations
- Above expectations
- Exceptional

Assessment criteria

A good investigation should be clear and easily understood by one of your fellow classmates (peers) and self-explanatory all of the way through.

The criteria are split into four areas A, B, C and D:

A. Designing the investigation

B. Identifying the variables of interest

C. Organising and managing the data

D. Analysing and interpreting data summaries

Linking the criteria with the four categories of achievement (descriptors)

A. Designing the investigation

Criteria	Achievement
Uses given statistics question and collection method	Yet to achieve expectations
Poses a question that anticipates variability and plans to collect/source the type of data appropriate for the question posed	In line with expectations
Poses a question that anticipates variability and seeks generalisation; data collection plan shows awareness of how variability affects the validity and reliability of the findings	Above expectations
Poses a question that anticipates variability and seeks generalisation, study design will produce as far as practical reliable and valid results by taking into account variability and confounding variables	Exceptional

B. Identifying the variables of interest

Criteria	Achievement
Gathers and displays data	Yet to achieve expectations
Identifies variable and develops a measuring strategy for measuring the dependent and independent variable	In line with expectations
Chosen measuring strategy provides valid and reliable data	Above expectations
Describes relationship between the variables and describes considerations related to reliability and fairness	Exceptional

C. Organising and managing the data

Criteria	Achievement
Makes statements about the data displayed	Yet to achieve expectations
Displays data in a way that allows patterns to be identified; identifies patterns and describes the data in terms of those patterns	In line with expectations
Uses appropriate data displays and describes the data in terms of measures of centre and spread	Above expectations
Uses distributions to analyse the data and justifies measures of centre used to describe the data	Exceptional

D. Analysing and interpreting data summaries

Criteria	Achievement
No concrete connection back to the original question	Yet to achieve expectations
Makes a concrete connection to the original question of the investigation but does not look beyond the data	In line with expectations
Reports the findings and the conclusion refers to the original question and attempts to look beyond the data	Above expectations
Interprets the data in relation to the original question; conclusion displays understanding of the limitations of generalising to the population and considers the need to reformulate the original question in light of the findings	Exceptional

Academic honesty

Academic honesty means that your work is based on your own original ideas and not copied from other people. However, you may draw on the work and ideas of others, but this must be acknowledged. This would be put into a reference list at the end of your investigation, known as a bibliography. In addition, you should use your own language and expression.

Record-keeping

Throughout the investigation, keep a journal, either on paper or online. This journal will also help you to demonstrate academic honesty. The journal will be of great assistance in focusing your efforts when writing your CBA 2 investigation.

- Make notes of any websites or books you use
- You are encouraged to use a variety of support materials and present your work in a variety of formats
- Keep a record of your actions so you can show your teacher how much time you are spending on your investigation
- Remember to follow your teacher's advice and meet your CBA 2 timetable
- The teacher is there to facilitate you, so do not be afraid to ask for guidance. The more focused your questions are, the better guidance your teacher can give you.

Evidence of learning

The following evidence is required

- A report
- Student research records

You must report your research and findings in a format of your choice. The report can be completed at the end of the investigation. If a typed or hand-written report is the format of choice, the total length of the report would typically be in the 650–800 words range (excluding tables, graphs, reference list and research records), but this should not be regarded as a rigid requirement.

A statistical investigation may be presented in other formats, quite effectively (e.g. posters, podcasts or multimedia). However, you must take care that all the research can be judged on the final product alone. For example, a poster presentation may allow you to select and present highlights of your research, but it is also necessary to include a written report of approximately 400 words to show the deeper research carried out.

Vital tools for the Statistical Investigation

The following tools should prove very useful to you when carrying out your Statistical Investigation:

- The three chapters in this book
    - Statistics I: Statistical Investigations
    - Statistics II: Central Tendency and Spread of Data
    - Statistics III: Representing Data
- Two pages on 'Glossary of Statistical Terms' at the end of this chapter
- *Census at schools* website, which has a large store of recorded data. This could help you to prove or disprove your assertions
- Be familiar with appropriate use of technology to sort and display data (e.g. spreadsheets)
- Highlight the data points that belong to you in your displays (if appropriate)

Choosing a topic

You should choose a topic that you are interested in, because then you will be inclined to put more effort into the project. In addition, you will enjoy working on your project and this will shine through. You should discuss the topic with your teacher before you put too much time and effort into it, in case your idea is not in line with what a Statistical Investigations should be.

If you cannot think of a topic yourself, then you can ask your teacher for help in coming up with a topic to investigate. Below are some ideas that might help you to come up with an investigation of your own.

Suggestions for investigation, with ideas to consider:

- Investigate eating trends of today's youths.
    - Sample group
    - Survey on eating habits
    - Vegetarians?
    - Fruit or vegetable intake
    - Sugar intake

- Investigate if there is a connection between the time it takes to get to school and the distance a student lives from school.
    - Sample group
    - Distance from school and time taken to travel daily
    - Compare
- Investigate the usage of social media among teenagers.
    - Sample group
    - How often does a teenager open a social media app in a day?
    - Time spent on an app
    - Number of apps
    - Logging screen time and activity?
- Investigate the real-world relationships that a teenager has with their 'friends' on social media.
    - Select a sample
    - How many of your social media friends have you met in person?
    - How many do you: See every day? See every week? Ever met?
    - How many could you call on, if you had a problem?
- Investigate the average increase in height of a first year student, over a period of time.
    - Select a sample
    - Decide a time frame
    - Make measurements
    - Perform calculations
- Investigate musical interests.
    - Sample group
    - Favourite type of music
    - Attend live concerts? How often?
    - Buy CDs or use streaming apps?
    - Subscription to app?
- Investigate whether boys or girls are more likely to be left-handed.
    - Select a sample
    - Research recorded data (e.g. census at school)
    - Perform calculations
- Investigate ideas for an app for a smartphone.
    - Come up with a concept
    - Target audience?
    - Questionnaire to gather data
    - Charge for the app?
    - Costs involved in development

- Investigate demographic of social media apps.
    - Data available online?
    - Most popular apps
    - Breakdown of users: gender/age group/country
- Investigate transport to school.
    - Select a sample
    - Type of transportation (most popular? Least popular?)
    - Duration of journey
    - Expand investigation to other types of schools (co-ed or single sex)
    - Expand investigation to other geographical areas (urban or rural school)
    - Expand investigation to other age groups (primary or secondary school)
- Investigate traffic system at a junction.
    - Observe a junction
    - Volume of traffic (cars/motorbikes/vans)
    - Peak times for traffic
    - Pedestrian traffic at the junction
    - Should traffic lights be put in place?
    - What cycle should be on the lights?

Getting started

One approach to deciding on an investigation topic might be to have a brain-storming session in a class group. The steps outlined in this are as follows:

Perhaps you plan to write an **investigation comparing teenagers in different countries.** You wish to find out everything you can about habits, interests, education, etc.

1. Individually brainstorm at least six ideas for survey topics that could be used for research.
   Write each idea on a sticky note and display it on a board.
2. As a class group, discuss the ideas that you all came up with and join ideas together to make better ones.
3. As a class group select the five best ideas.
4. Present the ideas to the class and improve the ideas, if possible. Attempt to answer any questions the class might have about the ideas.
5. Use one of the selected ideas in the Statistical-Enquiry Cycle.

Once you have chosen your investigation, the next step is to do some research. The purpose of this research is to determine the suitability of your investigation. Do not limit your research to the internet. Your local or school library will have books on mathematics that are interesting and may be useful.

The following questions may help you decide if your chosen investigation is suitable:
- What area of Statistics are contained in your investigation?
- Can you understand and use the mathematics required?
- Are you totally familiar with the Statistical-Enquiry Cycle?
- Have you the question clearly defined?
- How can you show the work you did, as part of your investigation?
- Can you limit your work to the 650–800 word range report (excluding tables, graphs, reference list, bibliography and research records) if you choose this investigation?

If your original investigation is not suitable, has your research suggested another, better investigation? Otherwise, could you either narrow down or widen out your investigation to make it suitable?

Once you think you have a workable investigation, then you must start into the Statistical-Enquiry Cycle by carrying out the following steps:

1. Formulate a question
2. Plan and collect unbiased, representative data
3. Organise and manage the data
4. Explore and analyse the data, using appropriate displays and numerical summaries
5. Answer the original question, giving reasons based on the analysis section

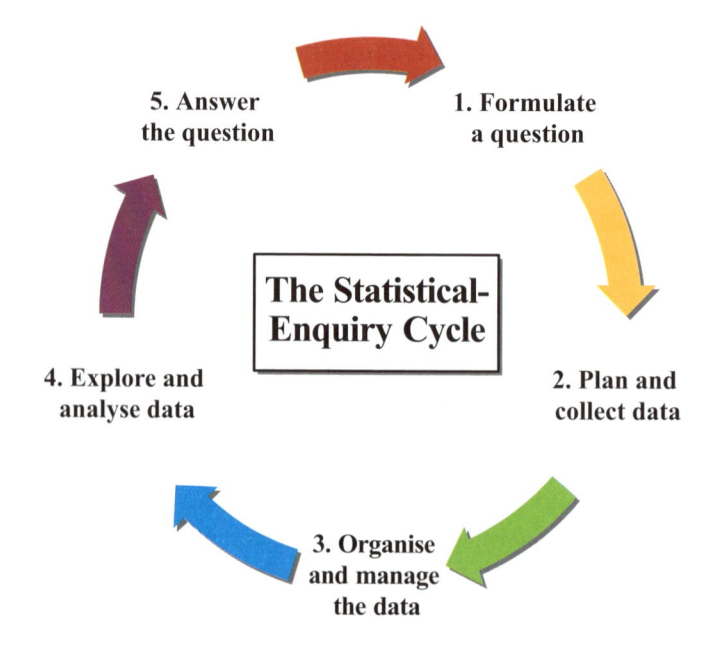

The Statistical-Enquiry Cycle

1. Formulate a question
2. Plan and collect data
3. Organise and manage the data
4. Explore and analyse data
5. Answer the question

Now you are ready to start writing your investigation in detail.
Remember that your peers (fellow students) should be able to read and understand your investigation.
The following table, designed to support teachers in giving feedback to their students, will help you when carrying out each step of your investigation.

Area of activity	Questions to focus on during formative feedback	Vocabulary to build
Formulating a statistics question	Does the question anticipate an answer that varies? Might different people answer the question differently? Does your question look to generalise to beyond your sample?	Variability Statistics question
Formulating a statistics question	Does the question specify the population you will be gathering the data from? Does the question specify the measurements you will be making?	Populations Measurements
Gathering unbiased representative data	Is the sample big enough to capture variability? Have you controlled for confounding variables?	Sampling Sample size
Gathering unbiased representative data	How do you know that the sample is representative of the full population? How do you know that the data you will gather is not biased?	Sampling techniques
Identifying the variables	What quantities are important? Which ones change and which ones stay the same?	Variables
Identifying the variables	How will you gather data on each variable? Will the methods you'll use give valid data? Will the data be reliable?	Measurements Valid, reliable
Organising and managing data	What pictures, diagrams or graphs might help people understand your information? Do the pictures, diagrams or graphs adequately show the variability in the data?	Diagrams, graphs, tables
Organising and managing data	Can you describe your data using numbers? Have you identified which summary measure is most appropriate (mean/mode/median)? Have you quantified the variability in the data?	Data Summaries

Area of activity	Questions to focus on during formative feedback	Vocabulary to build
Interpreting the data	When does your conclusion hold up? When do you need to be careful about what you can conclude?	Limitations
Interpreting the solution	Could you do anything to make your statistical investigation better or more accurate?	Improvement, iteration
Communicating /Reporting results	How did each of your teammates help?	Collaboration
Communicating /Reporting results	What are the most important things for your audience to understand about your statistical investigation?	Audience

Source: www.ncca.ie

Mind map for CBA

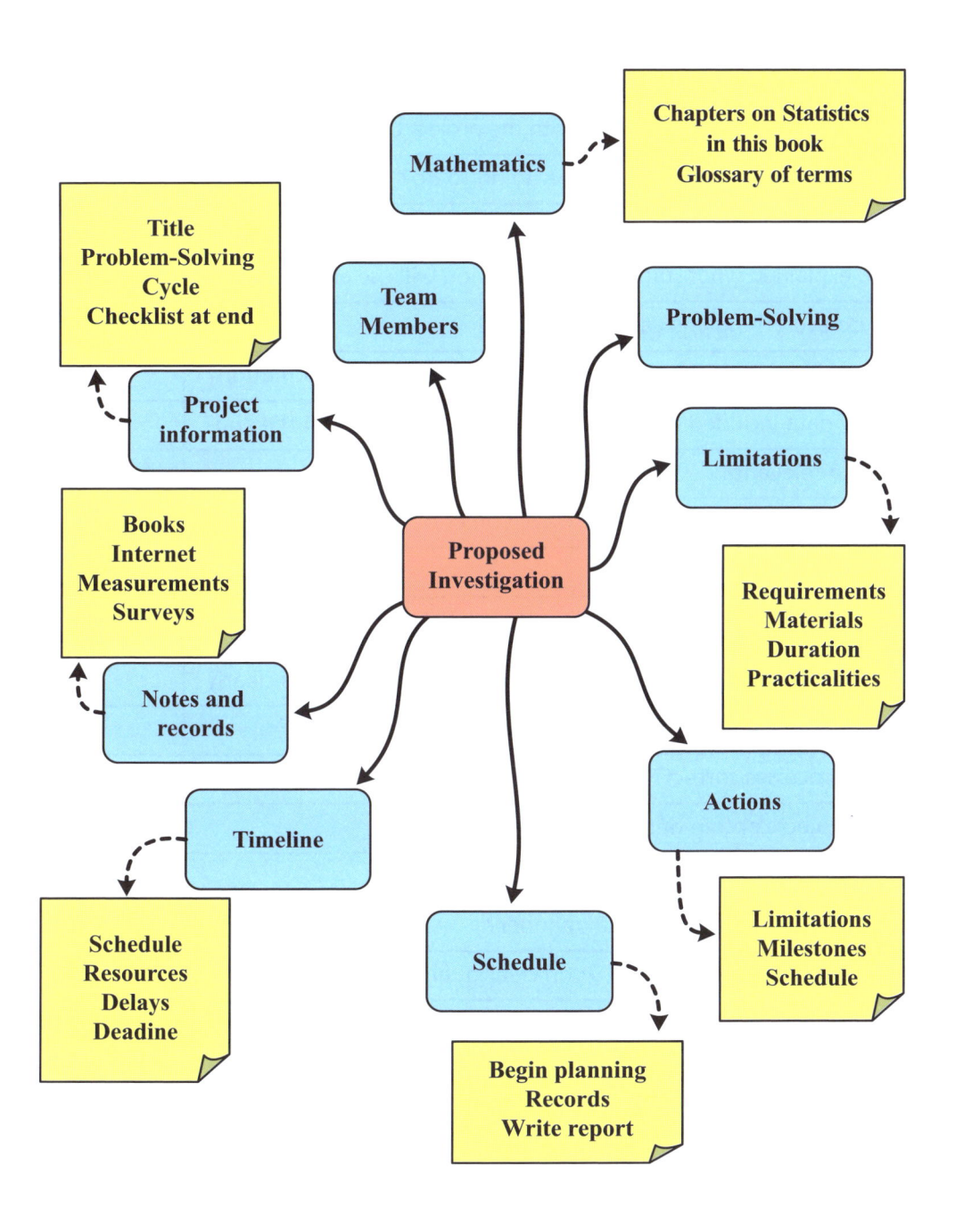

Proposed Investigation

- **Mathematics** → Chapters on Statistics in this book / Glossary of terms
- **Team Members**
- **Problem-Solving**
- **Limitations** → Requirements / Materials / Duration / Practicalities
- **Actions** → Limitations / Milestones / Schedule
- **Schedule** → Begin planning / Records / Write report
- **Timeline** → Schedule / Resources / Delays / Deadine
- **Notes and records** → Books / Internet / Measurements / Surveys
- **Project information** → Title / Problem-Solving Cycle / Checklist at end

Classroom-Based Assessment Investigation Checklist

Before completing your CBA, go through the following checklist and make sure that you have completed each task.

Activity	Completed?
Does your project have a front cover with the project title and your name?	
Have you started clearly what you are going to do?	
Have you explained how you are going to do it?	
Have you explained what statistical methods you will use and why?	
Did you do everything you said you would do?	
Have you collected data or generated measurements or information?	
Is your raw data included in the project or in the appendix, at the end?	
Is your data relevant?	
Is your data sufficient in quantity? Have you enough data?	
Do you have quality data?	
Is your data ready to use immediately, or do you need to do some work on it first?	
If you used a sample, have you described the sampling process clearly?	
Have you performed relevant mathematical processes?	
Are these processes correct?	
Does the project contain only correct notation?	
Does the project contain only correct terminology?	
Is your project laid out in a logical manner?	
Are your diagrams and tables of good clear quality?	
Have you commented on your results?	
Are your comments consistent with your analysis?	
Have you commented thoroughly on everything that you have done?	
Have you commented on validity?	
Do you have an appendix, if one is needed?	
Do you have a bibliography?	

Glossary of Statistical Terms

> **key point**
>
> This glossary is to help your understanding of statistical terms. You are not required to learn these terms off by heart. However, you may be asked to explain them in your own words.

Arithmetic mean A measure of central tendency that sums all the scores in the data sets and divides by the number of scores.

Bar chart A diagram consisting of a sequence of vertical or horizontal bar or rectangles, all of equal width. The height of each bar is proportional to the quantities in each class/interval.

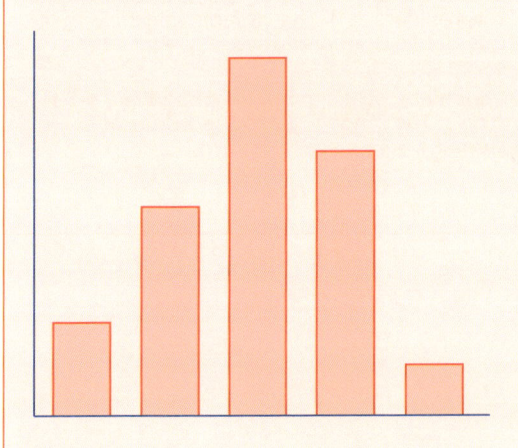

Bias Systematic errors in the way a survey was carried out. It can be caused by many things, e.g. poorly worded questions, non-response, under coverage, etc.

Categorical data Non-numerical data that can be counted but only described in words. Such data may be ordered or unordered.

Continuous numerical data Data which can take any numerical value within a certain range.

Data Any collection of variables.

Data point An observation.

Data set A set of data points.

Discrete numerical data Data which can only have certain values.

Frequency distribution A method for illustrating the distribution of scores within class intervals. Often given in tabular form (frequency distribution table).

Histogram A graphical representation of data. Similar to a bar chart but with no spaces between the bars.

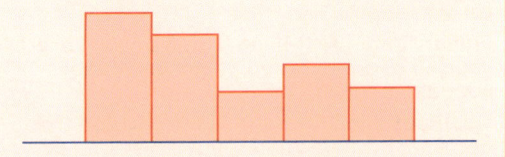

Line plot (dot plot) A simple display. It places a dot along an axis for each case in the data.

Mean The value where scores are summed and divided by the number of observations.

Measures of central tendency The mean, median and mode.

Median The point at which 50% of the cases in a distribution fall below and 50% fall above.

Mode The most frequently occurring score in a distribution.

Nominal data Categorical data that has no order.

Numerical data Data that can be counted or measured.

Observed score The score that is recorded or observed.

Obtained value The value that results from the application of a statistical test.

Ordinal data Categorical data that has order.

Outlier A point in a sample widely separated from the main cluster of points in the sample.

Pie chart A circular diagram divided into sectors of which the areas are proportional to the magnitudes of the quantities represented, as shown.

Population The complete set of data under consideration.

Primary data First-hand data that you collect yourself or are collected by someone under your direct supervision.

Qualitative data A type of information that describes or characterises, but does not measure, data. Often referred to as categorical data.

Quantitative data A type of information that can be counted or expressed numerically. Often referred to as numerical data.

Questionnaire A set of questions used to obtain data from a population.

Random Chosen without regard to any characteristics of the individual members of the population so that each has an equal chance of being selected.

Random sample A sample selected so that its distribution can be taken to be representative of the whole population.

Range The highest value minus the lowest value.

Sample A subset of a population, that is, a set of individuals or events selected in a survey of a population.

Secondary data Data that have already been collected and made available from an external source such as newspapers, government departments or the internet.

Statistics A set of tools and techniques used to collect, organise, represent and interpret information.

Univariate data A survey that looks at only one variable (data set). The variable may be either qualitative or quantitative, e.g. ages of the seven dwarfs.

Variability The amount of spread in a set of scores. The range is a good indicator of spread.

Calculator Instructions

Casio Natural Display calculator

Before starting any procedures on the calculator, you should clear the memory:

To clear the memory:
>Shift *then* 9 : CLR
>3 : All
>= : Yes
>[AC]

To perform a statistical calculation, you must create a frequency table.

To enter a frequency table, you must switch Frequency on:
>Shift *then* Mode
>Down Arrow
>3 : STAT
>1 : ON

To enter a table of data:
>Mode
>2 : STAT
>1 : 1-VAR

Enter the data into the table, followed by the = sign each time. Once you have finished entering the data, press the AC button.

To analyse the data in the table:
>Shift *then* 1 : STAT
>4 : Var

Options are as follows:
>2 : $\bar{x}$ (the mean of the terms, also known as μ)

> **key point**
> For simplicity, to find the mean of a **single list of data,** create a frequency table and set all the frequencies to 1.

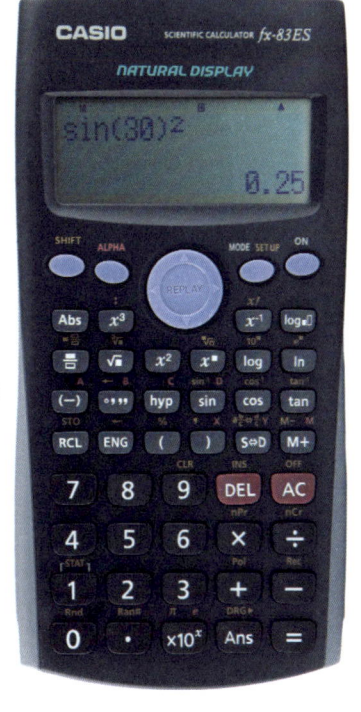

Practice exercise

Use your calculator to find the mean of the following table of data:

Value	2	4	6	8	10
Frequency	13	6	9	2	6

The answer is:
>Mean $\mu = \bar{x} = 5$

Sharp WriteView calculator

Before starting any procedures on the calculator, you should clear the memory:
To clear the memory:

2nd F *then* ALPHA : M-CLR
1 : Memory
0 : Clear

To put the calculator into Statistics mode:

Mode
1 : STAT

To enter the data:

Take each value and frequency as a pair of data.
Enter each pair, separated by a comma.
Then press the DATA button
(e.g. enter: 2, 13 DATA).

Once all the pairs of data have been entered, press:

ON / C

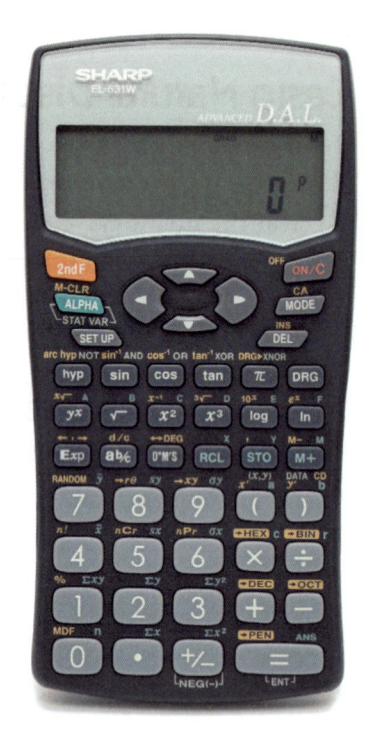

> **key point**
>
> To find the mean of a **single list of data** press the DATA button after each value. Leave out the comma and frequency value.

To analyse the data entered:
ALPHA *then* 4 *then* = : $\bar{x}$ (the mean of the terms, also known as μ)

Practice exercise

Use your calculator to find the mean of the following table of data:

Value	2	4	6	8	10
Frequency	13	6	9	2	6

The answer is:

Mean $\mu = \bar{x} = 5$